LETTERS FROM AN AMERICAN FARMER

LETTERS

FROM AN

AMERICAN FARMER

By

J. HECTOR ST. JOHN DE CRÈVECŒUR

A Dutton  *Paperback*

NEW YORK
E. P. DUTTON & CO., INC.

MICHEL-GUILLAUME JEAN DE CRÈVECŒUR, commonly known as J. Hector St. John de Crèvecœur was born in 1735 near Caen in Normandy. He spent some time in England and then emigrated to America. After traveling in the Great Lakes region and the Ohio valley and working as a surveyor in Pennsylvania, he became a naturalized citizen in 1764 and settled on a farm in Orange County, N. Y. In 1783 he became French Consul in New York and returned to France to live in 1790. He died in 1813.

LETTERS FROM AN AMERICAN FARMER was first published in 1782.

INTRODUCTION

MORE than eighty years ago Hazlitt wrote that of the three notable writers whom the eighteenth century had produced, in the North American colonies, one was "the author (whoever he was) of the *American Farmer's Letters.*" Crèvecœur was that unknown author; and Hazlitt said further of him that he rendered, in his own vividly characteristic manner, "not only the objects, but the feelings, of a new country." Great is the essayist's relish for passages descriptive of "a battle between two snakes," of "the dazzling, almost invisible flutter of the humming-bird's wing," of the manners of "the Nantucket people, their frank simplicity, and festive rejoicings after the perils and hardships of the whale-fishing." "The power to sympathize with nature, without thinking of ourselves or others, if it is not a definition of genius, comes very near to it," writes Hazlitt of our author. And his references to Crèvecœur are closed with the remark: "We have said enough of this ILLUSTRIOUS OBSCURE; for it is the rule of criticism to praise none but the over-praised, and to offer fresh incense to the idol of the day."

Others, at least, have followed that "rule of criticism," and the American Farmer has long enjoyed undisturbed seclusion. Only once since the eighteenth century has there been a new edition of his *Letters,* that were first published at London in 1782, and reissued, with a few corrections, in the next year. The original American edition of this book about America was that published at Philadelphia in 1793, and there was no reprint till 1904,[1] when careless editing did all it could to destroy

[1] References may be found to American editions of 1794 and 1798, but no copies of such editions are preserved in any library to which the editor has had access.

vii

the value of the work, the name of whose very author was misstated. Yet the facts which we have concerning him are few enough to merit truthful presentation.

I

Except by naturalization, the author of *Letters from an American Farmer* was not an American; and he was no ordinary farmer. Yet why quarrel with him for the naming of his book, or for his signing it "J. Hector Saint-John," when the "Hector" of his title-pages and American biographers was only a *prénom de faintaisie?* We owe some concessions to the author of so charming a book, to the eighteenth-century Thoreau. His life is certainly more interesting than the real Thoreau's—and would be, even if it did not present many contradictions. Our records of that life are in the highest degree inexact; he himself is wanting in accuracy as to the date of more than one event. The records, however, agree that Crèvecœur belonged to the *petite noblesse* of Normandy. The date of his birth was January 31, 1735, the place was Caen, and his full name (his great-grandson and biographer vouches for it) was Michel-Guillaume Jean de Crèvecœur. The boy was well enough brought up, but without more than the attention that his birth gave him the right to expect; he divided the years of his boyhood between Caen, where his father's town-house stood, and the Collège du Mont, where the Jesuits gave him his education. A letter dated 1785 and addressed to his children tells us all that we know of his school-days; though it is said, too, that he distinguished himself in mathematics. "If you only knew," the reminiscent father of a family exclaims in this letter, "in what shabby lodging, in what a dark and chilly closet, I was mewed up at your age; with what severity I was treated; how I was fed and dressed!" Already his powers of observation, that were so to distinguish him, were quickened by his old-world milieu.

"From my earliest youth," he wrote in 1803, "I had a passion for taking in all the antiques that I met with: moth-eaten furniture, tapestries, family portraits, Gothic manuscripts (that I had learned how to decipher), had for me an indefinable charm. A little later on, I loved to walk in the solitude of cemeteries; to examine the tombs and to trace out their mossy epitaphs. I knew most of the churches of the canton, the date of their foundation, and what they contained of interest in the way of pictures and sculptures."

The boy's gift of accurate and keen observation was to be tested soon by a very different class of objects: there were to be no crumbling saints and canvases of Bed-Chamber Grooms for him to study in the forests of America; no reminders of the greatness of his country's past, and the honor of his family.

From school, the future woodsman passed over into England. A distant relative was living near Salisbury; for one reason or another the boy was sent thither to finish his schooling. From England, with what motives we know not, he set out for the New World, where he was to spend his busiest and happiest days. In the *Bibliotheca Americana Nova* Rich makes the statement that Crèvecœur was but sixteen when he made the plunge, and others have followed Rich in this error. The lad's age was really not less than nineteen or twenty. According to the family legend, his ship touched at Lisbon on the way out; one cannot decide whether this was just before or immediately after the great earthquake. Then to New France, where he joined Montcalm. Entering the service as cadet, he advanced to the rank of lieutenant; was mentioned in the *Gazette;* shared in the French successes; drew maps of the forests and

block-houses that found their way to the king's cabinet;
served with Montcalm in the attack upon Fort William
Henry. With that the record is broken off: we can less
definitely associate his name with the humiliation of the
French in America than with their brief triumphs. Yet
it is quite certain, says Robert de Crèvecœur, his descendant, that he did not return to France with the
rag-tag of the defeated army. Quebec fell before Wolfe's
attack in September 1759; at some time in the course
of the year 1760 we may suppose the young officer to
have entered the British colonies; to have adopted his
family name of "Saint John" (Saint-Jean), and to have
gradually worked his way south, probably by the Hudson.
The reader of the *Letters* hardly supposes him to have
enjoyed his frontier life; nor is there any means of
knowing how much of that life it was his fortune to
lead. In time, he found himself as far south as Pennsylvania. He visited Shippensburg and Lancaster and
Carlisle; perhaps he resided at or near one of these
towns. Many years later, when his son Louis purchased
a farm of two hundred acres from Chancellor Living-
stone, at Navesink, near the Blue Mountains, Crèvecœur
the elder was still remembered; and it may have been
at this epoch that he visited the place. During the term
of his military service under Montcalm, Crèvecœur saw
something of the Great Lakes and the outlying country;
prior to his experience as a cultivator, and, indeed, after
he had settled down as such he "traveled like Plato,"
even visited Bermuda, by his own account. Not until
1764, however, have we any positive evidence of his
whereabouts; it was in April of that year that he took
out naturalization papers at New York. Some months
later, he installed himself on the farm variously called
Greycourt and Pine Hill, in the same state; he drained a
great marsh there, and seems to have practiced agriculture upon a generous scale. The certificate of the mar-

riage of Crèvecœur to Mehitable Tippet, of Yonkers, is dated September 20, 1769; and of this union three children were the issue. And more than children: for with the marriage ceremony once performed by the worthy Têtard, a clergyman of New York, formerly settled over a French Reformed Church at Charleston, South Carolina, Crèvecœur is more definitely than ever the "American Farmer"; he has thrown in his lot with that new country; his children are to be called after their parent's adopted name, Saint-John; the responsibilities of the adventurer are multiplied; his life in America has become a matter more easy to trace and richer, perhaps, in meaning.

II

One of the historians of American literature has written that these *Letters* furnish "a greater number of delightful pages than any other book written in America during the eighteenth century, save only Franklin's *Autobiography*." A safe compliment, this; and yet does not the very emptiness of American annals during the eighteenth century make for our cherishing all that they offer of the vivid and the significant? Professor Moses Coit Tyler long ago suggested what was the literary influence of the American Farmer, whose "idealized treatment of rural life in America wrought quite traceable effects upon the imaginations of Campbell, Byron, Southey, Coleridge, and furnished not a few materials for such captivating and airy schemes of literary colonization in America as that of 'Pantisocracy.'" Hazlitt praised the book to his friends and, as we have seen, commended it to readers of the *Edinburgh Review*. Lamb mentions it in one of his letters—which is already some distinction. Yet when was a book more completely lost to popular view—even among the books that have deserved oblivion? The *Letters* were published, all the

same, at Belfast and Dublin and Philadelphia, as well
as at London; they were recast in French by the author,
translated into German and Dutch by pirating penny-a-
liners, and given a "sequel" by a publisher at Paris.[1]

The American Farmer made his first public appearance eleven years before Chateaubriand found a publisher for his *Essai sur les Révolutions,* wherein the great
innovator first used the American materials that he
worked over more effectively in his travels, tales, and
memoirs. In Saint-John de Crèvecœur, we have a contemporary—a correspondent, even—of Franklin; but if
our author shared many of poor Richard's interests, one
may travel far without finding a more complete anti-
thesis to that common-sense philosopher.

Crèvecœur expresses mild wonderment that, while so
many travelers visit Italy and "the town of Pompey
under ground," few come to the new continent, where
may be studied, not what is found in books, but "the
humble rudiments and embryos of society spreading
everywhere, the recent foundations of our towns, and the
settlements of so many rural districts." In the course of
his sixteen or seventeen years' experience as an American
farmer he himself studied all these matters; and he gives
us a charming picture of them. Though his book has
very little obvious system, its author describes for us
frontier and farm; the ways of the Nantucket fishermen
and their intrepid wives; life in the Middle Colonies;
the refinements and atrocities of Charleston. Crèvecœur's account of the South (that he knew but super-
ficially and—who knows?—more, it may be, by Têtard's
anecdotes than through personal knowledge) is the least
satisfactory part of his performance. One feels it to be

[1] *Ouvrage pour servir de suite aux Lettres d'un cultivateur Américain,* Paris, 1785. The work so offered seems to have been a translation of John Filson's *History of Kentucky* (Wilmington, Del.,
1784).

the most "literary" portion of a book whose beauty is *naïveté*. But whether we accept or reject the story of the negro malefactor hung in a cage from a tree, and pecked at by crows, it is certain that the traveler justly regarded slavery as the one conspicuous blot on the new country's shield. Crèvecœur was not an active abolitionist, like that other naturalized Frenchman, Benezet of Philadelphia; he had his own slaves to work his northern farms; he was, however, a man of humane feelings—one who "had his doubts." [1] And his narrative description of life in the American colonies in the years immediately preceding the Revolution is one that social historians cannot ignore.

Though our Farmer emphasizes his plainness, and promises the readers of his *Letters* only a matter-of-fact account of his pursuits, he has his full share of eighteenth-century "sensibility." Since he is, however, at many removes from the sophistications of London and Paris, he is moved, not by the fond behavior of a lap-dog, or the "little arrangements" carters make with the bridles of their faithful asses (that they have driven to death, belike), but by such matters as he finds at home. "When I contemplate my wife, by my fire-side, while she either spins, knits, darns, or suckles our child, I cannot describe the various emotions of love, of gratitude, or conscious pride which thrill in my heart, and often overflow in voluntary tears . . ." He is like that old class-mate of Fitzgerald's, buried deep "in one of the most out-of-the-way villages in all England," for if he goes abroad, "it is always involuntary. I never return home without feeling some pleasant emotion, which I often suppress as useless and foolish." He has his reveries;

[1] In his *Voyage dans la Haute Pensylvanie* (sic) *et dans l'Etat de New York* (Paris, 1801) slavery is severely attacked by Crèvecœur. His descendant, Robert de Crèvecœur, refers to him as "a friend of Wilberforce."

but they are pure and generous; their subject is the future of his children. In midwinter, instead of trapping and "murthering" the quail, "often in the angles of the fences where the motion of the wind prevents the snow from settling, I carry them both chaff and grain: the one to feed them, the other to prevent their tender feet from freezing fast to the earth as I have frequently observed them to do." His love of birds is marked: this in those provinces of which a German traveler wrote: "In the thrush kind America is poor; there is only the red-breasted robin. . . . There are no sparrows. Very few birds nest in the woods; a solemn stillness prevails through them, interrupted only by the screaming of the crows." It is good, after such a passage as this has been quoted, to set down what Crèvecœur says of the bird kingdom. "In the spring," he writes, "I generally rise from bed about that indistinct interval which, properly speaking, is neither night nor day:" for then it is that he enjoys "the universal vocal choir." He continues—more and more lyrically: "Who can listen unmoved, to the sweet love-tales of our robins, told from tree to tree? Or to the shrill cat birds? The sublime accents of the thrush from on high, always retard my steps, that I may listen to the delicious music." And the Farmer is no less interested in "the astonishing art which all birds display in the construction of their nests, ill provided as we may suppose them with proper tools; their neatness, their convenience." At some time during his American residence he gathered the materials for an unpublished study of ants; and his bees proved an unfailing source of entertainment. "Their government, their industry, their quarrels, their passions, always present me with something new," he writes; adding that he is most often to be found, in hours of rest, under the locust tree where his beehive stands. "By their movements," says he, "I can predict the weather, and can tell the day of their swarming." When other men go hunting game, he goes bee-hunting. Such are the matters he tells of in his *Letters*.

One difference from the stereotyped "sensibility" of the old world one may discover in the openness of Crèvecœur's heart; and that is the completeness of his interest in all the humbler sorts of natural phenomena. Nature is, for him, no mere bundle of poetic stage-properties, soiled by much handling, but something fresh and inviting and full of interest to a man alive. He takes more pleasure in hunting bees than in expeditions with his dogs and gun; the kingbirds destroy his bees —but, he adds, they drive the crows away. Ordinarily he could not persuade himself to shoot them. On one occasion, however, he fired at a more than commonly impertinent specimen, "and immediately opened his maw, from which I took 171 bees; I laid them all on a blanket in the sun, and to my great surprise fifty-four returned to life, licked themselves clean, and joyfully went back to the hive, where they probably informed their companions of such an adventure and escape, as I believe had never happened before to American bees." Must one regard this as a fable? It is by no means as remarkable a yarn as one may find told by other naturalists of the same century. There is, for example, that undated letter of John Bartram's, in which he makes inquiries of his brother William concerning "Ye Wonderful Flower;"[1] there is, too, Kalm's report of Bartram's bear: "When a bear catches a cow, he kills her in the following manner: he bites a hole into the hide and blows with all his power into it, till the animal swells excessively and dies; for the air expands greatly between the flesh and the hide." After these fine fancies, where is the improbability of Crèvecœur's modest adaptation of the

[1] See "A Botanical Marvel," in *The Nation* (New York), August 5, 1909, and Note viii in this book.

Jonah-allegory that he applies to the king-bird and his bees? The episode suggests, for that matter, a chapter in Mitchell's *My Farm at Edgewood.* Mitchell, a later American farmer, describes the same king-birds, the same bees; has, too, the same supremely gentle spirit. "I have not the heart to shoot at the king-birds; nor do I enter very actively into the battle of the bees. . . . I give them fair play, good lodging, limitless flowers, willows bending (as Virgil advises) into the quiet water of a near pool; I have even read up the stories of a poor blind Huber, who so dearly loved the bees, and the poem of Giovanni Rucellai, for their benefit." Can the reader state, without stopping to consider, which author it was that wrote thus—Mitchell or Crèvecœur? Certainly it is the essential modernity of the earlier writer's style that most impresses one, after the charm of his pictures. His was the age of William Livingston—later Governor of the State of New Jersey; and in the very year when a London publisher was bringing out the first edition of the Farmer's *Letters,* Livingston, described on his title-page as a "young gentleman educated at Yale College," brought out his *Philosophic Solitude* at Trenton, in his native state. It is worth quoting *Philosophic Solitude* for the sake of the comparison to be drawn between Crèvecœur's prose and contemporary American verse:

> Let ardent heroes seek renown in arms,
> Pant after fame, and rush to war's alarms . . .
> Mine be the pleasures of a *rural* life.

The thought is, after all, the same as that which we have found less directly phrased in Crèvecœur. But let us quote the lines that follow the exordium—now we should find the poet unconstrained and fancy-free:

> Me to sequestred scenes, ye muses, guide,
> Where nature wantons in her virgin-pride;
> To mossy banks edg'd round with op'ning flow'rs,
> Elysian fields, and amaranthin bow'rs. . . .

Welcome, ye shades! all hail, ye vernal blooms!
Ye bow'ry thickets, and prophetic glooms!
Ye forests hail! ye solitary woods. . . .

and the "solitary woods" (rhyming with "floods") are a
good place to leave the "young gentleman educated at
Yale College." Livingston was, plainly enough, a poet
of his time and place. He had a fine eye for Nature—
seen through library windows. He echoed Goldsmith and
a whole line of British poets—echoed them atrociously.

That one finds no "echoes" in Crèvecœur is one of
our reasons for praising his spontaneity and vigor. He
did not import nightingales into his America, as some
of the poets did. He blazed away, rather, toward our
present day appreciation of surrounding nature—which
was not banal then. Crèvecœur's honest and unconven-
tionalized love of his rural environment is great enough
to bridge the difference between the years 1782 and the
present. It is as easy for us to pass a happy evening with
him as it was for Thomas Campbell, figuring to himself
a realization of Cowley's dreams and of Rousseau's poetic
seclusion; "till at last," in Southey's words, "comes an
ill-looking Indian with a tomahawk, and scalps me—a
most melancholy proof that society is very bad." It is
the freshness, the youthfulness, of these *Letters,* after
their century and more of dust-gathering, that is least
likely to escape us. And this "Farmer in Pennsylvania"
is almost as unmistakably of kin with good Gilbert
White of Selborne as he is the American Thoreau's
eighteenth-century forerunner.

III

It is time, indeed, that we made the discovery that
Crèvecœur was a modern. He was, too, a dweller in the
young republic—even before it *was* a republic. Twice a
year he had "the pleasure of catching pigeons, whose
numbers are sometimes so astonishing as to obscure the

sun in their flight." There is, then, no poetic license about Longfellow's description, in *Evangeline,* of how—

A pestilence fell on the city
Presaged by wondrous signs, and mostly by flocks of wild pigeons,
Darkening the sun in their flight, with naught in their craws but
    an acorn.

Longfellow could have cited as his authority for this flight of pigeons Mathew Carey's *Record of the Malignant Fever lately Prevalent,* published at Philadelphia, which, to be sure, discusses a different epidemic, but tells us that "amongst the country people, large quantities of wild pigeons in the spring are regarded as certain indications of an unhealthy summer. Whether or not this prognostic has ever been verified, I cannot tell. But it is very certain that during the last spring the numbers of these birds brought to market were immense. Never, perhaps, were there so many before."

Carey wrote in 1793, the year, as has been noted, of the first American reprint of the *Letters,* that had first been published at London. Carey was himself Crève-cœur's American publisher; and he may well have thought as he wrote the lines quoted of Crèvecœur's earlier pigeons "obscuring the sun in their flight." Crève-cœur had by this time returned to France, and was never more to ply the avocations of the American farmer. In the interval, much had happened to this victim of both the revolutions. Though the *Letters* are distinguished by an idyllic temper, over them is thrown the shadow of impending civil war. The Farmer was a man of peace, for all his experience under Montcalm in Canada (and even there his part was rather an engineer's than a combatant's); he long hoped, therefore, that peaceful counsels would prevail, and that England and the colonies would somehow come to an understanding without hostilities. Then, after the Americans had boldly broken with the home government, he lent them all his sympathy but not his arms. He had his family to watch over; likewise his two farms, one in Orange County, New York, one in New Jersey. As it was, the Indians in the royal service burned his New Jersey estate; and after his first return to France (he was called thither by his father, we are told, though we know nothing of the motives of this recall) he entered upon a new phase of his career. "After his first return to France," I have said, as if that had been an entirely simple matter. One cannot here describe all its alleged difficulties; his arrest at New York as a suspected spy (though after having secured a pass from the American commander, General MacDougal, he had secured a second pass from General Clinton, and permission to embark for France); his detention in the provost's prison in New York; the final embarkation with his oldest son—this on September 1, 1780; the shipwreck which he described as occurring off the Irish coast; his residence for some months in Great Britain, and during a part of that time in London, where he sold the manuscript of the *Letters* for thirty guineas. One would like to know Crèvecœur's emotions on finally reaching France and joining his father and relatives at Caen. One would like to describe his romantic succor of five American seamen, who had escaped from an English prison and crossed the Channel in a sloop to Normandy. A cousin of one of these seamen, a Captain Fellowes of Boston, was later to befriend Crèvecœur's daughter and younger son in the new country; that was after the Loyalists and their Indian allies had destroyed the Farmer's house at Pine Hill, after his wife had fled to Westchester with her two children, and had died there soon after, leaving them unprotected. But all this must, in nautical phrase, "go by the board," including the novel founded upon the episode. Nor can we linger over Crèvecœur's entry into polite society, both in the Norman capital and at

Paris. Fancy the returned prodigal—if one may so describe him—in the salon of Madame d'Houdetot, Rousseau's former mistress! He was fairly launched, this American Farmer, in the society of the *lettrés*.

"Twice a week," he wrote, some years after, "I went with M. de Turgot to see the Duchesse de Beauvilliers, his sister; and another twice-a-week I went with him to the Comte de Buffon's. . . . It was at the table of M. de Buffon, it was in his salon, during long winter evenings, that I was awakened once more to the graces, the beauties, the timid purity of our tongue, which, during my long sojourn in North America, had become foreign to me, and of which I had almost lost command—though not the memory."

Madame d'Houdetot presented Crèvecœur to the families of La Rochefoucauld, Liancourt, d'Estissac, Bréteuil, Rohan-Chabot, Beauvau, Necker; to the academicians d'Alembert, La Harpe, Grimm, Suard, Rulbrière; to the poet-academician Delille. We have in the *Mémoires* of Brissot an allusion to his entrance into this society, under the wing of his elderly protectress:

> Proud of possessing an American savage, she wished to form him, and to launch him in society. He had the good sense to refuse and to confine himself to the picked society of men of letters.

It was at a later period that Brissot and Crèvecœur were to meet; their quarrel, naturally, came later still.

Madame d'Houdetot did more than entertain the Farmer, whose father had been one of her oldest friends. She secured his nomination as Consul-General to the United States, now recognized by France; it was at New York that he took up residence. Through the influence of Madame d'Houdetot and her friends, he retained the appointment through the stormy years that followed, though in the end he was obliged to make way for a successor more in sympathy with the violent republicanism of the age. Throughout the years of the French

Revolution, the ex-farmer lived a life of retirement, and, if never of conspicuous danger, of embarrassment enough, and of humiliation. We need not discuss those years spent at Paris; or the visits paid, after the close of the Revolution, to his son-in-law and daughter, for his daughter Frances-America was married to a French Secretary of Legation, who became a Count of the Empire. Now he was in Paris or the suburbs; now in London, or Munich. Five years of the Farmer's later life were spent at the Bavarian capital; Maximilian entertained him there, and told him that he had read his book with the keenest pleasure and great profit too. He busied himself in preparing his three-volume *Voyage dans la Haute Pensylvanie* (sic) *et dans l'Etat de New York,* and in adding to his paper on potato culture,[1] a second on the false acacia; but his best work was done and he knew it. Crèvecœur lived on until 1813, dying in the same year with Madame d'Houdetot, who was so much his elder. He paid a worthy tribute to that lady's character; perhaps we do her an injustice in knowing her only for the *liaison* with Jean-Jacques. He died on November 12, 1813: member of agricultural societies and of the Academy (section of moral and political science), and of Franklin's Philosophical Society at Philadelphia. A town in Vermont had been named St. Johnsbury in his honor; he had the freedom of more than one New England city. It is, nonetheless, as the author of the *Letters from an American Farmer,* published in 1782, and written, for the most part, years before that date, that we remember him—so far as we do remember.

IV

Much remains unsaid—much, even, of the essential. Some of the facts are still unknown; others may be looked for in the biography written by his great-grand-

---

[1] *Traité de la Culture des Pommes de Terre,* 1782.

son, Robert de Crèvecœur, and published at Paris in 1883. There is hardly occasion to discuss here what Crèvecœur did, as consul at New York, to encourage the exchange of French manufactures and American exports; or to tell of his packet-line—the first established between New York and a French port; or to set down the story of his children; or to describe those last sad years, at home and abroad, after the close of his consular career. There is no room at all for the words of praise that were spoken of the *Letters* by Franklin and Washington, who recommended them to intending immigrants as a faithful, albeit "highly colored" picture. We must let the writings of the American Farmer speak for themselves: they belong, after all, to literature.

It was a modest man—a modest life; a life filled, nonetheless, with romantic incident. All this throws into relief the beauty of its best fruits. Crèvecœur made no claim to artistry when he wrote his simple, heartfelt *Letters;* and yet his style, in spite of occasional defects and extra flourishes, seems to us worthy of his theme. These *Letters from an American Farmer* have been an inspiration to poets—and they "smell of the woods."

In a prose age, Crèvecœur lived a kind of pastoral poetry; in an age largely blind, he saw the beauties of nature, less through readings in the *Nouvelle Héloïse* and Bernardin's *Etudes* than with his own keen eyes; he was a true idealist, besides, and as such kindles one's enthusiasm. The man's optimism, his grateful personality, his saneness, too—for here is a dreamer neither idle nor morbid—are qualities no less enduring, or endearing, than his fame as "poet-naturalist." The American Farmer might have used Cotton's *Retirement* for an epigraph on his title-page:

> Farewell, thou busy world, and may
>   We never meet again,
> Here I can eat and sleep and pray. . . .

but for the fact that he found time to turn the clods, withal, and eyes to watch the earth blackening behind the plough. "Our necessities," wrote Poe, who contended, in a halfhearted way, that the Americans of his generation were as poetical a people as any other, "have been mistaken for our propensities. Having been forced to make railroads, it has been deemed impossible that we should make verse." But here was Saint-John de Crève-cœur writing, in the eighteenth century, his idyllic *Letters,* while, if he did not build railways, he interested himself in the experiments of Fitch and Rumsey and Parmentier, and organized a packet-line between New York and Lorient, in Brittany. This Crèvecœur should from the first have appealed to the imagination—especially to the American imagination—combining as he did the faculty of the ideal and the achievement of the actual. It is not too late for him to appeal today; in spite of all his quaintness, Crèvecœur is a contemporary of our own.

WARREN BARTON BLAKE

CONTENTS

LETTERS

FROM AN

AMERICAN FARMER;

DESCRIBING
CERTAIN PROVINCIAL SITUATIONS, MANNERS, AND CUSTOMS,

NOT GENERALLY KNOWN;

AND CONVEYING

SOME IDEA OF THE LATE AND PRESENT INTERIOR CIRCUMSTANCES

OF THE

BRITISH COLONIES

IN

NORTH AMERICA.

WRITTEN FOR THE INFORMATION OF A FRIEND
IN ENGLAND,

By J. HECTOR ST. JOHN,

A FARMER IN PENNSYLVANIA

LONDON,
PRINTED FOR THOMAS DAVIES IN RUSSELL STREET COVENT-
GARDEN, AND LOCKYER DAVIS IN HOLBORN.
M DCC LXXXII.

ADVERTISEMENT

[To the First Edition, 1782.]

The following Letters are the genuine production of the American Farmer whose name they bear. They were privately written to gratify the curiosity of a friend; and are made public, because they contain much authentic information, little known on this side the Atlantic: they cannot therefore fail of being highly interesting to the people of England, at a time when everybody's attention is directed toward the affairs of America.

That these letters are the actual result of a private correspondence may fairly be inferred (exclusive of other evidence) from the style and manner in which they are conceived; for though plain and familiar, and sometimes animated, they are by no means exempt from such inaccuracies as must unavoidably occur in the rapid effusions of a confessedly inexperienced writer.

Our Farmer had long been an eye-witness of transactions that have deformed the face of America: he is one of those who dreaded, and has severely felt, the desolating consequences of a rupture between the parent state and her colonies: for he has been driven from a situation, the enjoyment of which the reader will find pathetically described in the early letters of this volume. The unhappy contest is at length, however, drawing toward a period; and it is now only left us to hope, that the obvious interests and mutual wants of both countries, may in due time, and in spite of all obstacles, happily re-unite them.

Should our Farmer's letters be found to afford matter of useful entertainment to an intelligent and candid pub-

lic, a second volume, equally interesting with those now published, may soon be expected.

ADVERTISEMENT

[To the Second Edition, 1783.]

Since the publication of this volume, we hear that Mr. St. John has accepted a public employment at New York. It is therefore, perhaps, doubtful whether he will soon be at leisure to revise his papers, and give the world a second collection of the American Farmer Letters.

ABBÉ RAYNAL, F.R.S.

BEHOLD, Sir, an humble American Planter, a simple cultivator of the earth, addressing you from the farther side
of the Atlantic; and presuming to fix your name at the
head of his trifling lucubrations. I wish they were worthy of so great an honour. Yet why should not I be
permitted to disclose those sentiments which I have so
often felt from my heart? A few years since, I met acci-
dentally with your *Political and Philosophical History,*
and perused it with infinite pleasure. For the first time
in my life I reflected on the relative state of nations; I
traced the extended ramifications of a commerce which
ought to unite but now convulses the world; I admired
that universal benevolence, that diffusive goodwill, which
is not confined to the narrow limits of your own country; but, on the contrary, extends to the whole human
race. As an eloquent and powerful advocate you have
pleaded the cause of humanity in espousing that of the
poor Africans: you viewed these provinces of North
America in their true light, as the asylum of freedom;
as the cradle of future nations, and the refuge of distressed Europeans. Why then should I refrain from loving and respecting a man whose writings I so much
admire? These two sentiments are inseparable, at least
in my breast. I conceived your genius to be present at
the head of my study: under its invisible but powerful
guidance, I prosecuted my small labours: and now, permit me to sanctify them under the auspices of your name.
Let the sincerity of the motives which urge me, prevent
you from thinking that this well meant address contains
aught but the purest tribute of reverence and affection.
There is, no doubt, a secret communion among good

men throughout the world; a mental affinity connecting them by a similitude of sentiments: then, why, though an American, should not I be permitted to share in that extensive intellectual consanguinity? Yes, I do: and though the name of a man who possesses neither titles nor places, who never rose above the humble rank of a farmer, may appear insignificant; yet, as the sentiments I have expressed are also the echo of those of my countrymen; on their behalf, as well as on my own, give me leave to subscribe myself,

Sir,

Your very sincere admirer,

J. HECTOR ST. JOHN

CARLISLE IN PENNSYLVANIA

LETTERS FROM AN AMERICAN FARMER

LETTER I

WHO would have thought that because I received you with hospitality and kindness, you should imagine me capable of writing with propriety and perspicuity? Your gratitude misleads your judgment. The knowledge which I acquired from your conversation has amply repaid me for your five weeks' entertainment. I gave you nothing more than what common hospitality dictated; but could any other guest have instructed me as you did? You conducted me, on the map, from one European country to another; told me many extraordinary things of our famed mother-country, of which I knew very little; of its internal navigation, agriculture, arts, manufactures, and trade: you guided me through an extensive maze, and I abundantly profited by the journey; the contrast therefore proves the debt of gratitude to be on my side. The treatment you received at my house proceeded from the warmth of my heart, and from the corresponding sensibility of my wife; what you now desire must flow from a very limited power of mind: the task requires recollection, and a variety of talents which I do not possess. It is true I can describe our American modes of farming, our manners, and peculiar customs, with some degree of propriety, because I have ever attentively studied them; but my knowledge extends no farther. And is this local and unadorned information sufficient to answer all your expectations, and to satisfy your curiosity? I am surprised that in the course of your American travels you should not have found out persons more enlightened and better educated than I am; your predilection excites my wonder much more than my vanity; my share of the latter being

3

confined merely to the neatness of my rural operations.

My father left me a few musty books, which *his* father brought from England with him; but what help can I draw from a library consisting mostly of Scotch Divinity, the *Navigation of Sir Francis Drake,* the *History of Queen Elizabeth,* and a few miscellaneous volumes? Our minister often comes to see me, though he lives upwards of twenty miles distant. I have shown him your letter, asked his advice, and solicited his assistance; he tells me that he hath no time to spare, for that like the rest of us must till his farm, and is moreover to study what he is to say on the sabbath. My wife (and I never do anything without consulting her) laughs, and tells me that you cannot be in earnest. What! says she, James, wouldst thee pretend to send epistles to a great European man, who hath lived abundance of time in that big house called Cambridge; where, they say, that worldly learning is so abundant, that people gets it only by breathing the air of the place? Wouldst not thee be ashamed to write unto a man who has never in his life done a single day's work, no, not even felled a tree; who hath expended the Lord knows how many years in studying stars, geometry, stones, and flies, and in reading folio books? Who hath travelled, as he told us, to the city of Rome itself! Only think of a London man going to Rome! Where is it that these English folks won't go? One who hath seen the factory of brimstone at Suvius, and town of Pompey under ground! wouldst thou pretend to letter it with a person who hath been to Paris, to the Alps, to Petersburg, and who hath seen so many fine things up and down the old countries; who hath come over the great sea unto us, and hath journeyed from our New Hampshire in the East to our Charles Town in the South; who hath visited all our great cities, knows most of our famous lawyers and cunning folks; who hath conversed with very many king's men, governors, and counsellors, and yet pitches upon thee for his correspondent, as thee calls it? surely he means to jeer thee! I am sure he does, he cannot be in a real fair earnest. James, thee must read this letter over again, paragraph by paragraph, and warily observe whether thee can'st perceive some words of jesting; something that hath more than one meaning: and now I think on it, husband, I wish thee wouldst let me see his letter; though I am but a woman, as thee mayest say, yet I understand the purport of words in good measure, for when I was a girl, father sent us to the very best master in the precinct.—She then read it herself very attentively: our minister was present, we listened to, and weighed every syllable: we all unanimously concluded that you must have been in a sober earnest intention, as my wife calls it; and your request appeared to be candid and sincere. Then again, on recollecting the difference between your sphere of life and mine, a new fit of astonishment seized us all!

Our minister took the letter from my wife, and read it to himself; he made us observe the two last phrases, and we weighed the contents to the best of our abilities. The conclusion we all drew made me resolve at last to write.——You say you want nothing of me but what lies within the reach of my experience and knowledge; this I understand very well; the difficulty is, how to collect, digest, and arrange what I know? Next you assert, that writing letters is nothing more than talking on paper; which, I must confess, appeared to me quite a new thought.—Well then, observed our minister, neighbour James, as you can talk well, I am sure you must write tolerably well also; imagine, then, that Mr. F. B. is still here, and simply write down what you would say to him. Suppose the questions he will put to you in his future letters to be asked by his *viva voce*, as we used to call it at the college; then let your answers be conceived and expressed exactly in the same language as if he was present. This is all that he requires from you, and I am sure the task is not difficult. He is your friend: who would be ashamed to write to such a person? Although he is a man of learning and taste, yet I am sure he will read your letters with pleasure: if they be not elegant, they will smell of the woods, and be a little wild; I know your turn, they will contain some matters which he never knew before. Some people are so fond of novelty, that they will overlook many errors of language for the sake of information. We are all apt to love and admire exotics, tho' they may be often inferior to what we possess; and that is the reason I imagine why so many persons are continually going to visit Italy.— That country is the daily resort of modern travellers.

James. I should like to know what is there to be seen so goodly and profitable, that so many should wish to visit no other country?

Minister. I do not very well know. I fancy their object is to trace the vestiges of a once flourishing people now extinct. There they amuse themselves in viewing the ruins of temples and other buildings which have very little affinity with those of the present age, and must therefore impart a knowledge which appears useless and trifling. I have often wondered that no skilful botanists or learned men should come over here; methinks there would be much more real satisfaction in observing among us the humble rudiments and embryos of societies spreading everywhere, the recent foundation of our towns, and the settlements of so many rural districts. I am sure that the rapidity of their growth would be more pleasing to behold, than the ruins of old towers, useless aqueducts, or impending battlements.

James. What you say, minister, seems very true: do go on: I always love to hear you talk.

Minister. Don't you think, neighbour James, that the mind of a good and enlightened Englishman would be more improved in remarking throughout these provinces the causes which render so many people happy? In delineating the unnoticed means by which we daily increase the extent of our settlements? How we convert huge forests into pleasing fields, and exhibit through these thirteen provinces so singular a display of easy subsistence and political felicity.

In Italy all the objects of contemplation, all the reveries of the traveller, must have a reference to ancient generations, and to very distant periods, clouded with the mist of ages.—Here, on the contrary, everything is modern, peaceful, and benign. Here we have had no war to desolate our fields:[1] our religion does not oppress the cultivators: we are strangers to those feudal institutions which have enslaved so many. Here nature opens her broad lap to receive the perpetual accession of new comers, and to supply them with food. I am sure I cannot be called a partial American when I say that the spectacle afforded by these pleasing scenes must be more entertaining and more philosophical than that which arises from beholding the musty ruins of Rome. Here everything would inspire the reflecting traveller with the most philanthropic ideas; his imagination, instead of submitting to the painful and useless retrospect of revolutions, desolations, and plagues, would, on the contrary, wisely spring forward to the anticipated fields of future cultivation and improvement, to the future extent of those generations which are to replenish and embellish this boundless continent. There the half-ruined amphitheatres, and the putrid fevers of the Campania, must fill the mind with the most melancholy reflections, whilst he is seeking for the origin and the intention of those structures with which he is surrounded,

[1] The troubles that now convulse the American colonies had not broke out when this and some of the following letters were written.

and for the cause of so great a decay. Here he might contemplate the very beginnings and outlines of human society, which can be traced nowhere now but in this part of the world. The rest of the earth, I am told, is in some places too full, in others half depopulated. Misguided religion, tyranny, and absurd laws everywhere depress and afflict mankind. Here we have in some measure regained the ancient dignity of our species; our laws are simple and just, we are a race of cultivators, our cultivation is unrestrained, and therefore everything is prosperous and flourishing. For my part I had rather admire the ample barn of one of our opulent farmers, who himself felled the first tree in his plantation, and was the first founder of his settlement, than study the dimensions of the temple of Ceres. I had rather record the progressive steps of this industrious farmer, throughout all the stages of his labours and other operations, than examine how modern Italian convents can be supported without doing anything but singing and praying.

However confined the field of speculation might be here, the time of English travellers would not be wholly lost. The new and unexpected aspect of our extensive settlements; of our fine rivers; that great field of action everywhere visible; that ease, that peace with which so many people live together, would greatly interest the observer: for whatever difficulties there might happen in the object of their researches, that hospitality which prevails from one end of the continent to the other would in all parts facilitate their excursions. As it is from the surface of the ground which we till that we have gathered the wealth we possess, the surface of that ground is therefore the only thing that has hitherto been known. It will require the industry of subsequent ages, the energy of future generations, ere mankind here will have leisure and abilities to penetrate deep, and, in the bowels of this continent, search for the subterranean riches it no doubt contains.—Neighbour James, we want much the assistance of men of leisure and knowledge, we want eminent chemists to inform our iron masters; to teach us how to make and prepare most of the colours we use. Here we have none equal to this task. If any useful discoveries are therefore made among us, they are the effects of chance, or else arise from that restless industry which is the principal characteristic of these colonies.

James. Oh! could I express myself as you do, my friend, I should not balance a single instant, I should rather be anxious to commence a correspondence which would do me credit.

Minister. You can write full as well as you need, and will improve very fast; trust to my prophecy, your letters, at least, will have the merit of coming from the edge of the great wilderness, three hundred miles from the sea, and three thousand miles over that sea: this will be no detriment to them, take my word for it. You intend one of your children for the gown, who knows but Mr. F. B. may give you some assistance when the lad comes to have concerns with the bishop; it is good for American farmers to have friends even in England. What he requires of you is but simple—what we speak out among ourselves we call conversation, and a letter is only conversation put down in black and white.

James. You quite persuade me—if he laughs at my awkwardness, surely he will be pleased with my ready compliance. On my part, it will be well meant let the execution be what it may. I will write enough, and so let him have the trouble of sifting the good from the bad, the useful from the trifling; let him select what he may want, and reject what may not answer his purpose. After all, it is but treating Mr. F. B. now that he is in London, as I treated him when he was in America under this roof; that is with the best things I had; given with a good intention; and the best manner I was able. Very different, James, very different indeed, said my wife, I like not thy comparison; our small house and cellar, our orchard and garden afforded what he wanted; one half of his time Mr. F. B., poor man, lived upon nothing but fruit-pies, or peaches and milk. Now these things were such as God had given us, myself and wench did the rest; we were not the creators of these victuals, we only cooked them as well and as neat as we could. The first thing, James, is to know what sort of materials thee hast within thy own self, and then whether thee canst dish them up.—Well, well, wife, thee art wrong for once; if I was filled with worldly vanity, thy rebuke would be timely, but thee knowest that I have but little of that. How shall I know what I am capable of till I try? Hadst thee never employed thyself in thy father's house to learn and to practise the many branches of house-keeping that thy parents were famous for, thee wouldst have made but a sorry wife for an American farmer; thee never shouldst have been mine. I married thee not for what thee hadst, but for what thee knewest; doest not thee observe what Mr. F. B. says beside; he tells me, that the art of writing is just like unto every other art of man; that it is acquired by habit, and by perseverance. That is singularly true, said our minister, he that shall write a letter every day of the week, will on Saturday perceive the sixth flowing from his pen much more readily than the first. I observed when I first entered into the ministry and began to preach the word, I felt perplexed and dry, my mind was like unto a parched soil, which produced nothing, not even weeds. By the blessing of heaven, and my perseverance in study, I grew richer in thoughts, phrases, and words; I felt copious, and now I can abundantly preach from any text that occurs to my mind. So will it be with you, neighbour James; begin therefore without delay; and Mr. F. B.'s letters may be of great service to you: he will, no doubt, inform you of many things: correspondence consists in reciprocal letters. Leave off your diffidence, and I will do my best to help you whenever I have any leisure. Well then, I am resolved, I said, to follow your counsel; my letters shall not be sent, nor will I receive any, without reading them to you and my wife; women are curious, they love to know their husband's secrets; it will not be the first thing which I have submitted to your joint opinions. Whenever you come to dine with us, these shall be the last dish on the table. Nor will they be the most unpalatable, answered the good man. Nature hath given you a tolerable share of sense, and that is one of her best gifts let me tell you. She has given you besides some perspicuity, which qualifies you to distinguish interesting objects; a warmth of imagination which enables you to think with quickness; you often extract useful reflections from objects which presented none to my mind: you have a tender and a well meaning heart, you love description, and your pencil, assure yourself, is not a bad one for the pencil of a farmer; it seems to be held without any labour; your mind is what we called at Yale college a *Tabula rasa,* where spontaneous and strong impressions are delineated with facility. Ah, neighbour! had you received but half the education of Mr. F. B. you had been a worthy correspondent indeed. But perhaps you will be a more entertaining one dressed in your simple American garb, than if you were clad in all the gowns of Cambridge. You will appear to him something like one of our wild American plants, irregularly luxuriant in its various branches, which an European scholar may probably think ill placed and useless. If our soil is not remarkable as yet for the excellence of its fruits, this exuberance is however a strong proof of fertility, which wants nothing but the progressive knowledge acquired by time to amend and to correct. It is easier to retrench than it is to add; I do not mean to flatter you, neighbour James, adulation would ill become my character, you may therefore believe what your pastor says. Were I in Europe I should be tired with perpetually seeing espaliers, plashed hedges, and trees dwarfed into pigmies. Do let Mr. F. B. see on paper a few American wild cherry trees, such as nature forms them here, in all her unconfined vigour, in all the amplitude of their extended limbs and spreading ramifications—let him see that we are possessed with strong vegetative embryos. After all, why should not a farmer be allowed to make use of his mental faculties as well as others; because a man works, is not he to think, and if he thinks usefully, why should not he in his leisure hours set down his thoughts? I have composed many a good sermon as I followed my plough. The eyes not being then engaged on any particular object, leaves the mind free for the introduction of many useful ideas. It is not in the noisy shop of a blacksmith or of a carpenter, that these studious moments can be enjoyed; it is as we silently till the ground, and muse along the odoriferous furrows of our low lands, uninterrupted either by stones or stumps; it is there that the salubrious effluvia of the earth animate our spirits and serve to inspire us; every other avocation of our farms are severe labours compared to this pleasing occupation: of all the tasks which mine imposes on me ploughing is the most agreeable, because I can think as I work; my mind is at leisure; my labour flows from instinct, as well as that of my horses; there is no kind of difference between us in our different shares of that operation; one of them keeps the furrow, the other avoids it; at the end of my field they turn either to the right or left as they are bid, whilst I thoughtlessly hold and guide the plough to which they are harnessed. Do therefore, neighbour, begin this correspondence, and persevere, difficulties will vanish in proportion as you draw near them; you'll be surprised at yourself by and by: when you come to look back you'll say as I have often said to myself; had I been diffident I had never proceeded thus far. Would you painfully till your stony up-land and neglect the fine rich bottom which lies before your door? Had you never tried, you never had learned how to mend and make your ploughs. It will be no small pleasure to your children to tell hereafter, that their father was not only one of the most industrious farmers in the country, but one of the best writers. When you have once begun, do as when you begin breaking up your summer fallow, you never consider what remains to be done, you view only what you have ploughed. Therefore, neighbour James, take my advice; it will go well with you, I am sure it will.——And do you really think so, Sir? Your counsel, which I have long followed, weighs much with me, I verily believe that I must write to Mr. F. B. by the first vessel.——If thee persistest in being such a foolhardy man, said my wife, for God's sake let it be kept a profound secret among us; if it were once known abroad that thee writest to a great and rich man over at London, there would be no end of the talk of the people; some would vow that thee art going to turn an author, others would pretend to foresee some great alterations in the welfare of thy family; some would say this, some would say that: Who would wish to become the subject of public talk? Weigh this matter well before thee beginnest, James—consider that a great deal of thy time, and of thy reputation is at stake as I may say. Wert thee to write as well as friend Edmund, whose speeches I often see in our papers, it would be the very self same thing; thee wouldst be equally accused of idleness, and vain notions not befitting thy condition. Our colonel would be often coming here to know what it is that thee canst write so much about. Some would imagine that thee wantest to become either an assemblyman or a magistrate, which God forbid; and that thee art telling the king's men abundance of things. Instead of being well looked upon as now, and living in peace with all the world, our neighbours would be making strange surmises: I had rather be as we are, neither better nor worse than the rest of our country folks. Thee knowest what I mean, though I should be sorry to deprive thee of any honest recreation. Therefore as I have said before, let it be as great a secret as if it was some heinous crime; the minister, I am sure, will not divulge it; as for my part, though I am a woman, yet I know what it is to be a wife.—I would not have thee, James, pass for what the world calleth a writer; no, not for a peck of gold, as the saying is. Thy father before thee was a plain dealing honest man, punctual in all things; he was one of yea and nay, of few words, all he minded was his farm and his work. I wonder from whence thee hast got this love of the pen? Had he spent his time in sending epistles to and fro, he never would have left thee this goodly plantation, free from debt. All I say is in good meaning; great people over sea may write to our town's folks, because they have nothing else to do. These Englishmen are strange people; because they can live upon what they call bank notes, without working, they think that all the world can do the same. This goodly country never would have been tilled and cleared with these notes. I am sure when Mr. F. B. was here, he saw thee sweat and take abundance of pains; he often told me how the Americans worked a great deal harder than the home Englishmen; for there he told us, that they have no trees to cut down, no fences to make, no negroes to buy and to clothe: and now I think on it, when wilt thee send him those trees he bespoke? But if they have no trees to cut down, they have gold in abundance, they say; for they rake it and scrape it from all parts far and near. I have often heard my grandfather tell how they live there by writing. By writing they send this cargo unto us, that to the West, and the other to the East Indies. But, James, thee knowest that it is not by writing that we shall pay the blacksmith, the minister, the weaver, the tailor, and the English shop. But as thee art an early man follow thine own inclinations; thee wantest some rest, I am sure, and why shouldst thee not employ it as it may seem meet unto thee.—However let it be a great secret; how wouldst thee bear to be called at our country meetings, the man of the pen? If this scheme of thine was once known, travellers as they go along would point out to our house, saying, here liveth the scribbling farmer; better hear them as usual observe, here liveth the warm substantial family, that never begrudgeth a meal of victuals, or a mess of oats, to any one that steps in. Look how fat and well clad their negroes are.

Thus, Sir, have I given you an unaffected and candid detail of the conversation which determined me to accept of your invitation. I thought it necessary thus to begin, and to let you into these primary secrets, to the end that you may not hereafter reproach me with any degree of presumption. You'll plainly see the motives which have induced me to begin, the fears which I have entertained, and the principles on which my diffidence hath been founded. I have now nothing to do but to prosecute my task—Remember you are to give me my subjects, and on no other shall I write, lest you should blame me for an injudicious choice—However incorrect my style, however unexpert my methods, however trifling my observations may hereafter appear to you, assure yourself they will all be the genuine dictates of my mind, and I hope will prove acceptable on that account. Remember that you have laid the foundation of this correspondence; you well know that I am neither a philosopher, politician, divine, nor naturalist, but a simple farmer. I flatter myself, therefore, that you'll receive my letters as conceived, not according to scientific rules to which I am a perfect stranger, but agreeable to the spontaneous impressions which each subject may inspire. This is the only line I am able to follow, the line which nature has herself traced for me; this was the covenant which I made with you, and with which you seemed to be well pleased. Had you wanted the style of the learned, the reflections of the patriot, the discussions of the politician, the curious observations of the naturalist, the pleasing garb of the man of taste, surely you would have applied to some of those men of letters with which our cities abound. But since on the contrary, and for what reason I know not, you wish to correspond with a cultivator of the earth, with a simple citizen, you must receive my letters for better or worse.

LETTER II

As YOU are the first enlightened European I have ever had the pleasure of being acquainted with, you will not be surprised that I should, according to your earnest desire and my promise, appear anxious of preserving your friendship and correspondence. By your accounts, I observe a material difference subsists between your husbandry, modes, and customs, and ours; everything is local; could we enjoy the advantages of the English farmer, we should be much happier, indeed, but this wish, like many others, implies a contradiction; and could the English farmer have some of those privileges we possess, they would be the first of their class in the world. Good and evil I see is to be found in all societies, and it is in vain to seek for any spot where those ingredients are not mixed. I therefore rest satisfied, and thank God that my lot is to be an American farmer, instead of a Russian boor, or an Hungarian peasant. I thank you kindly for the idea, however dreadful, which you have given me of their lot and condition; your observations have confirmed me in the justness of my ideas, and I am happier now than I thought myself before. It is strange that misery, when viewed in others, should become to us a sort of real good, though I am far from rejoicing to hear that there are in the world men so thoroughly wretched; they are no doubt as harmless, industrious, and willing to work as we are. Hard is their fate to be thus condemned to a slavery worse than that of our negroes. Yet when young I entertained some thoughts of selling my farm. I thought it afforded but a dull repetition of the same labours and pleasures. I thought the former tedious and heavy, the latter few and insipid; but when I came to consider myself as divested of my farm, I then found the world so wide, and every place so full, that I began to fear lest there would be no room for me. My farm, my house, my barn, presented to my imagination objects from which I adduced quite new ideas; they were more forcible than before. Why should not I find myself happy, said I, where my father was before? He left me no good books it is true, he gave me no other education than the art of reading and writing; but he left me a good farm, and his experience; he left me free from debts, and no kind of difficulties to struggle with.—I married, and this perfectly reconciled me to my situation; my wife rendered my house all at once cheerful and pleasing; it no longer appeared gloomy and solitary as before; when I went to work in my fields I worked with more alacrity and sprightliness; I felt that I did not work for myself alone, and this encouraged me much. My wife would often come with her knitting in her hand, and sit under the shady trees, praising the straightness of my furrows, and the docility of my horses; this swelled my heart and made everything light and pleasant, and I regretted that I had not married before.

I felt myself happy in my new situation, and where is that station which can confer a more substantial system of felicity than that of an American farmer, possessing freedom of action, freedom of thoughts, ruled by a mode of government which requires but little from us? I owe nothing, but a pepper corn to my country, a small tribute to my king, with loyalty and due respect; I know no other landlord than the lord of all land, to whom I owe the most sincere gratitude. My father left me three hundred and seventy-one acres of land, forty-seven of which are good timothy meadow, an excellent orchard, a good house, and a substantial barn. It is my duty to think how happy I am that he lived to build and to pay for all these improvements; what are the labours which I have to undergo, what are my fatigues when compared to his, who had everything to do, from the first tree he felled to the finishing of his house? Every year I kill from 1500 to 2000 weight of pork, 1200 of beef, half a dozen of good wethers in harvest: of fowls my wife has always a great stock: what can I wish more? My negroes are tolerably faithful and healthy; by a long series of industry and honest dealings, my father left behind him the name of a good man; I have but to tread his paths to be happy and a good man like him. I know enough of the law to regulate my little concerns with propriety, nor do I dread its power; these are the grand outlines of my situation, but as I can feel much more than I am able to express, I hardly know how to proceed.

When my first son was born, the whole train of my ideas were suddenly altered; never was there a charm that acted so quickly and powerfully; I ceased to ramble in imagination through the wide world; my excursions since have not exceeded the bounds of my farm, and all my principal pleasures are now centred within its scanty limits: but at the same time there is not an operation belonging to it in which I do not find some food for useful reflections. This is the reason, I suppose, that when you were here, you used, in your refined style, to denominate me the farmer of feelings; how rude must those feelings be in him who daily holds the axe or the plough, how much more refined on the contrary those of the European, whose mind is improved by education, example, books, and by every acquired advantage! Those feelings, however, I will delineate as well as I can, agreeably to your earnest request.

When I contemplate my wife, by my fire-side, while she either spins, knits, darns, or suckles our child, I cannot describe the various emotions of love, of gratitude, of conscious pride, which thrill in my heart and often overflow in involuntary tears. I feel the necessity, the sweet pleasure of acting my part, the part of an husband and father, with an attention and propriety which may entitle me to my good fortune. It is true these pleasing images vanish with the smoke of my pipe, but though they disappear from my mind, the impression they have made on my heart is indelible. When I play with the infant, my warm imagination runs forward, and eagerly anticipates his future temper and constitution. I would willingly open the book of fate, and know in which page his destiny is delineated; alas! where is the father who in those moments of paternal ecstasy can delineate one half of the thoughts which dilate his heart? I am sure I cannot; then again I fear for the health of those who are become so dear to me, and in their sicknesses I severely pay for the joys I experienced while they were well. Whenever I go abroad it is always involuntary. I never return home without feeling some pleasing emotion, which I often suppress as useless and foolish. The instant I enter on my own land, the bright idea of property, of exclusive right, of independence exalt my mind. Precious soil, I say to myself, by what singular custom of law is it that thou wast made to constitute the riches of the freeholder? What should we American farmers be without the distinct possession of that soil? It feeds, it clothes us, from it we draw even a great exuberancy, our best meat, our richest drink, the very honey of our bees comes from this privileged spot. No wonder we should thus cherish its possession, no wonder that so many Europeans who have never been able to say that such portion of land was theirs, cross the Atlantic to realise that happiness. This formerly rude soil has been converted by my father into a pleasant farm, and in return it has established all our rights; on it is founded our rank, our freedom, our power as citizens, our importance as inhabitants of such a district. These images I must confess I always behold with pleasure, and extend them as far as my imagination can reach: for this is what may be called the true and the only philosophy of an American farmer.

Pray do not laugh in thus seeing an artless countryman tracing himself through the simple modifications of his life; remember that you have required it, therefore with candour, though with diffidence, I endeavour to follow the thread of my feelings, but I cannot tell you all. Often when I plough my low ground, I place my little boy on a chair which screws to the beam of the plough—its motion and that of the horses please him, he is perfectly happy and begins to chat. As I lean over the handle, various are the thoughts which crowd into my mind. I am now doing for him, I say, what my father formerly did for me, may God enable him to live that he may perform the same operations for the same purposes when I am worn out and old! I relieve his mother of some trouble while I have him with me, the odoriferous furrow exhilarates his spirits, and seems to do the child a great deal of good, for he looks more blooming since I have adopted that practice; can more pleasure, more dignity be added to that primary occupation? The father thus ploughing with his child, and to feed his family, is inferior only to the emperor of China ploughing as an example to his kingdom. In the evening when I return home through my low grounds, I am astonished at the myriads of insects which I perceive dancing in the beams of the setting sun. I was before scarcely acquainted with their existence, they are so small that it is difficult to distinguish them; they are carefully improving this short evening space, not daring to expose themselves to the blaze of our meridian sun. I never see an egg brought on my table but I feel pene-

trated with the wonderful change it would have undergone but for my gluttony; it might have been a gentle
useful hen leading her chickens with a care and vigilance
which speaks shame to many women. A cock perhaps,
arrayed with the most majestic plumes, tender to its
mate, bold, courageous, endowed with an astonishing
instinct, with thoughts, with memory, and every distinguishing characteristic of the reason of man. I never
see my trees drop their leaves and their fruit in the
autumn, and bud again in the spring, without wonder;
the sagacity of those animals which have long been the
tenants of my farm astonish me: some of them seem to
surpass even men in memory and sagacity. I could
tell you singular instances of that kind. What then is
this instinct which we so debase, and of which we are
taught to entertain so diminutive an idea? My bees,
above any other tenants of my farm, attract my attention and respect; I am astonished to see that nothing
exists but what has its enemy, one species pursue and
live upon the other: unfortunately our kingbirds are
the destroyers of those industrious insects; but on the
other hand, these birds preserve our fields from the
depredation of crows which they pursue on the wing
with great vigilance and astonishing dexterity.

Thus divided by two interested motives, I have long
resisted the desire I had to kill them, until last year,
when I thought they increased too much, and my indulgence had been carried too far; it was at the time
of swarming when they all came and fixed themselves
on the neighbouring trees, from whence they caught
those that returned loaded from the fields. This made
me resolve to kill as many as I could, and I was just
ready to fire, when a bunch of bees as big as my fist,
issued from one of the hives, rushed on one of the birds,
and probably stung him, for he instantly screamed, and
flew, not as before, in an irregular manner, but in a

direct line. He was followed by the same bold phalanx, at a considerable distance, which unfortunately becoming too sure of victory, quitted their military array and disbanded themselves. By this inconsiderate step they lost all that aggregate of force which had made the bird fly off. Perceiving their disorder he immediately returned and snapped as many as he wanted; nay, he had even the impudence to alight on the very twig from which the bees had drove him. I killed him and immediately opened his craw, from which I took 171 bees; I laid them all on a blanket in the sun, and to my great surprise 54 returned to life, licked themselves clean, and joyfully went back to the hive; where they probably informed their companions of such an adventure and escape, as I believe had never happened before to American bees! I draw a great fund of pleasure from the quails which inhabit my farm; they abundantly repay me, by their various notes and peculiar tameness, for the inviolable hospitality I constantly show them in the winter. Instead of perfidiously taking advantage of their great and affecting distress, when nature offers nothing but a barren universal bed of snow, when irresistible necessity forces them to my barn doors, I permit them to feed unmolested; and it is not the least agreeable spectacle which that dreary season presents, when I see those beautiful birds, tamed by hunger, intermingling with all my cattle and sheep, seeking in security for the poor scanty grain which but for them would be useless and lost. Often in the angles of the fences where the motion of the wind prevents the snow from settling, I carry them both chaff and grain; the one to feed them, the other to prevent their tender feet from freezing fast to the earth as I have frequently observed them to do.

I do not know an instance in which the singular barbarity of man is so strongly delineated, as in the catching and murthering those harmless birds, at that cruel season of the year. Mr. ——, one of the most famous and extraordinary farmers that has ever done honour to the province of Connecticut, by his timely and humane assistance in a hard winter, saved this species from being entirely destroyed. They perished all over the country, none of their delightful whistlings were heard the next spring, but upon this gentleman's farm; and to his humanity we owe the continuation of their music. When the severities of that season have dispirited all my cattle, no farmer ever attends them with more pleasure than I do; it is one of those duties which is sweetened with the most rational satisfaction. I amuse myself in beholding their different tempers, actions, and the various effects of their instinct now powerfully impelled by the force of hunger. I trace their various inclinations, and the different effects of their passions, which are exactly the same as among men; the law is to us precisely what I am in my barn yard, a bridle and check to prevent the strong and greedy from oppressing the timid and weak. Conscious of superiority, they always strive to encroach on their neighbours; unsatisfied with their portion, they eagerly swallow it in order to have an opportunity of taking what is given to others, except they are prevented. Some I chide, others, unmindful of my admonitions, receive some blows. Could victuals thus be given to men without the assistance of any language, I am sure they would not behave better to one another, nor more philosophically than my cattle do.

The same spirit prevails in the stable; but there I have to do with more generous animals, there my well-known voice has immediate influence, and soon restores peace and tranquillity. Thus by superior knowledge I govern all my cattle as wise men are obliged to govern fools and the ignorant. A variety of other thoughts crowd on my mind at that peculiar instant, but they all vanish by the time I return home. If in a cold night I swiftly travel in my sledge, carried along at the rate of twelve miles an hour, many are the reflections excited by surrounding circumstances. I ask myself what sort of an agent is that which we call frost? Our minister compares it to needles, the points of which enter our pores. What is become of the heat of the summer; in what part of the world is it that the N. W. keeps these grand magazines of nitre? when I see in the morning a river over which I can travel, that in the evening before was liquid, I am astonished indeed! What is become of those millions of insects which played in our summer fields, and in our evening meadows; they were so puny and so delicate, the period of their existence was so short, that one cannot help wondering how they could learn, in that short space, the sublime art to hide themselves and their offspring in so perfect a manner as to baffle the rigour of the season, and preserve that precious embryo of life, that small portion of ethereal heat, which if once destroyed would destroy the species! Whence that irresistible propensity to sleep so common in all those who are severely attacked by the frost. Dreary as this season appears, yet it has like all others its miracles, it presents to man a variety of problems which he can never resolve; among the rest, we have here a set of small birds which never appear until the snow falls; contrary to all others, they dwell and appear to delight in that element.

It is my bees, however, which afford me the most pleasing and extensive themes; let me look at them when I will, their government, their industry, their quarrels, their passions, always present me with something new; for which reason, when weary with labour, my common place of rest is under my locust-tree, close by my bee-house. By their movements I can predict the weather, and can tell the day of their swarming; but the most difficult point is, when on the wing, to know whether they want to go to the woods or not. If they have previously pitched in some hollow trees, it is not the allurements of salt and water, of fennel, hickory leaves, etc., nor the finest box, that can induce them to stay; they will prefer those rude, rough habitations to the best polished mahogany hive. When that is the case with mine, I seldom thwart their inclinations; it is in freedom that they work: were I to confine them, they would dwindle away and quit their labour. In such excursions we only part for a while; I am generally sure to find them again the following fall. This elopement of theirs only adds to my recreations; I know how to deceive even their superlative instinct; nor do I fear losing them, though eighteen miles from my house, and lodged in the most lofty trees, in the most impervious of our forests. I once took you along with me in one of these rambles, and yet you insist on my repeating the detail of our operations: it brings back into my mind many of the useful and entertaining reflections with which you so happily beguiled our tedious hours.

After I have done sowing, by way of recreation, I prepare for a week's jaunt in the woods, not to hunt either the deer or the bears, as my neighbours do, but to catch the more harmless bees. I cannot boast that this chase is so noble, or so famous among men, but I find it less fatiguing, and full as profitable; and the last consideration is the only one that moves me. I take with me my dog, as a companion, for he is useless as to this game; my gun, for no man you know ought to enter the woods without one; my blanket, some provisions, some wax, vermilion, honey, and a small pocket compass. With these implements I proceed to such woods as are at a considerable distance from any settlements. I carefully examine whether they abound with large trees,

if so, I make a small fire on some flat stones, in a convenient place; on the fire I put some wax; close by this
fire, on another stone, I drop honey in distinct drops,
which I surround with small quantities of vermilion,
laid on the stone; and then I retire carefully to watch
whether any bees appear. If there are any in that
neighbourhood, I rest assured that the smell of the
burnt wax will unavoidably attract them; they will
soon find out the honey, for they are fond of preying on
that which is not their own; and in their approach they
will necessarily tinge themselves with some particles
of vermilion, which will adhere long to their bodies. I
next fix my compass, to find out their course, which they
keep invariably straight, when they are returning home
loaded. By the assistance of my watch, I observe how
long those are returning which are marked with vermilion. Thus possessed of the course, and, in some
measure, of the distance, which I can easily guess at, I
follow the first, and seldom fail of coming to the tree
where those republics are lodged. I then mark it; and
thus, with patience, I have found out sometimes eleven
swarms in a season; and it is inconceivable what a
quantity of honey these trees will sometimes afford.
It entirely depends on the size of the hollow, as the bees
never rest nor swarm till it is all replenished; for like
men, it is only the want of room that induces them to
quit the maternal hive. Next I proceed to some of the
nearest settlements, where I procure proper assistance
to cut down the trees, get all my prey secured, and then
return home with my prize. The first bees I ever procured were thus found in the woods, by mere accident;
for at that time I had no kind of skill in this method of
tracing them. The body of the tree being perfectly
sound, they had lodged themselves in the hollow of one
of its principal limbs, which I carefully sawed off and
with a good deal of labour and industry brought it home,

where I fixed it up again in the same position in which I found it growing. This was in April; I had five swarms that year, and they have been ever since very prosperous. This business generally takes up a week of my time every fall, and to me it is a week of solitary ease and relaxation.

The seed is by that time committed to the ground; there is nothing very material to do at home, and this additional quantity of honey enables me to be more generous to my home bees, and my wife to make a due quantity of mead. The reason, Sir, that you found mine better than that of others is, that she puts two gallons of brandy in each barrel, which ripens it, and takes off that sweet, luscious taste, which it is apt to retain a long time. If we find anywhere in the woods (no matter on whose land) what is called a bee-tree, we must mark it; in the fall of the year when we propose to cut it down, our duty is to inform the proprietor of the land, who is entitled to half the contents; if this is not complied with we are exposed to an action of trespass, as well as he who should go and cut down a bee-tree which he had neither found out nor marked.

We have twice a year the pleasure of catching pigeons, whose numbers are sometimes so astonishing as to obscure the sun in their flight. Where is it that they hatch? for such multitudes must require an immense quantity of food. I fancy they breed toward the plains of Ohio, and those about lake Michigan, which abound in wild oats; though I have never killed any that had that grain in their craws. In one of them, last year, I found some undigested rice. Now the nearest rice fields from where I live must be at least 560 miles; and either their digestion must be suspended while they are flying, or else they must fly with the celerity of the wind. We catch them with a net extended on the ground, to which they are allured by what we call *tame wild pigeons,* made blind, and fastened to a long string; his short flights, and his repeated calls, never fail to bring them down. The greatest number I ever catched was four-teen dozen, though much larger qauntities have often been trapped. I have frequently seen them at the market so cheap, that for a penny you might have as many as you could carry away; and yet from the extreme cheapness you must not conclude, that they are but an ordinary food; on the contrary, I think they are excel-lent. Every farmer has a tame wild pigeon in a cage at his door all the year round, in order to be ready when-ever the season comes for catching them.

The pleasure I receive from the warblings of the birds in the spring, is superior to my poor description, as the continual succession of their tuneful notes is for ever new to me. I generally rise from bed about that in-distinct interval, which, properly speaking, is neither night or day; for this is the moment of the most universal vocal choir. Who can listen unmoved to the sweet love tales of our robins, told from tree to tree? or to the shrill cat birds? The sublime accents of the thrush from on high always retard my steps that I may listen to the delicious music. The variegated appearances of the dew drops, as they hang to the different objects, must present even to a clownish imagination, the most volup-tuous ideas. The astonishing art which all birds display in the construction of their nests, ill provided as we may suppose them with proper tools, their neatness, their convenience, always make me ashamed of the slovenliness of our houses; their love to their dame, their incessant careful attention, and the peculiar songs they address to her while she tediously incubates their eggs, remind me of my duty could I ever forget it. Their affection to their helpless little ones, is a lively precept; and in short, the whole economy of what we proudly call the brute creation, is admirable in every circumstance; and vain man, though adorned with the additional gift of reason, might learn from the perfection of instinct, how to regulate the follies, and how to temper the errors which this second gift often makes him commit. This is a subject, on which I have often bestowed the most serious thoughts; I have often blushed within myself, and been greatly astonished, when I have compared the unerring path they all follow, all just, all proper, all wise, up to the necessary degree of perfection, with the coarse, the imperfect systems of men, not merely as governors and kings, but as masters, as husbands, as fathers, as citizens. But this is a sanctuary in which an ignorant farmer must not presume to enter.

If ever man was permitted to receive and enjoy some blessings that might alleviate the many sorrows to which he is exposed, it is certainly in the country, when he attentively considers those ravishing scenes with which he is everywhere surrounded. This is the only time of the year in which I am avaricious of every moment, I therefore lose none that can add to this simple and inoffensive happiness. I roam early throughout all my fields; not the least operation do I perform, which is not accompanied with the most pleasing observations; were I to extend them as far as I have carried them, I should become tedious; you would think me guilty of affectation, and I should perhaps represent many things as pleasurable from which you might not perhaps receive the least agreeable emotions. But, believe me, what I write is all true and real.

Some time ago, as I sat smoking a contemplative pipe in my piazza, I saw with amazement a remarkable instance of selfishness displayed in a very small bird, which I had hitherto respected for its inoffensiveness. Three nests were placed almost contiguous to each other in my piazza: that of a swallow was affixed in the corner next to the house, that of a phebe in the other, a wren possessed a little box which I had made on purpose, and hung between. Be not surprised at their tameness, all my family had long been taught to respect them as well as myself. The wren had shown before signs of dislike to the box which I had given it, but I knew not on what account; at last it resolved, small as it was, to drive the swallow from its own habitation, and to my very great surprise it succeeded. Impudence often gets the better of modesty, and this exploit was no sooner performed, than it removed every material to its own box with the most admirable dexterity; the signs of triumph appeared very visible, it fluttered its wings with uncommon velocity, an universal joy was perceivable in all its movements. Where did this little bird learn that spirit of injustice? It was not endowed with what we term reason! Here then is a proof that both those gifts border very near on one another; for we see the perfection of the one mixing with the errors of the other! The peaceable swallow, like the passive Quaker, meekly sat at a small distance and never offered the least resistance; but no sooner was the plunder carried away, than the injured bird went to work with unabated ardour, and in a few days the depredations were repaired. To prevent however a repetition of the same violence, I removed the wren's box to another part of the house.

In the middle of my new parlour I have, you may remember, a curious republic of industrious hornets; their nest hangs to the ceiling, by the same twig on which it was so admirably built and contrived in the woods. Its removal did not displease them, for they find in my house plenty of food; and I have left a hole open in one of the panes of the window, which answers all their purposes. By this kind usage they are become quite harmless; they live on the flies, which are very troublesome to us throughout the summer; they are constantly busy in catching them, even on the eyelids of my children. It is surprising how quickly they smear them with a sort of glue, lest they might escape, and when thus prepared, they carry them to their nests, as food for their young ones. These globular nests are most ingeniously divided into many stories, all provided with cells, and proper communications. The materials with which this fabric is built, they procure from the cottony furze, with which our oak rails are covered; this substance tempered with glue, produces a sort of pasteboard, which is very strong, and resists all the inclemencies of the weather. By their assistance, I am but little troubled with flies. All my family are so accustomed to their strong buzzing, that no one takes any notice of them; and though they are fierce and vindictive, yet kindness and hospitality has made them useful and harmless.

We have a great variety of wasps; most of them build their nests in mud, which they fix against the shingles of our roofs, as nigh the pitch as they can. These aggregates represent nothing, at first view, but coarse and irregular lumps, but if you break them, you will observe, that the inside of them contains a great number of oblong cells, in which they deposit their eggs, and in which they bury themselves in the fall of the year. Thus immured they securely pass through the severity of that season, and on the return of the sun are enabled to perforate their cells, and to open themselves a passage from these recesses into the sunshine. The yellow wasps, which build under ground, in our meadows, are much more to be dreaded, for when the mower unwittingly passes his scythe over their holes they immediately sally forth with a fury and velocity superior even to the strength of man. They make the boldest fly, and the only remedy is to lie down and cover our heads with hay, for it is only at the head they aim their blows;

nor is there any possibility of finishing that part of
the work until, by means of fire and brimstone, they
are all silenced. But though I have been obliged to
execute this dreadful sentence in my own defence, I
have often thought it a great pity, for the sake of a
little hay, to lay waste so ingenious a subterranean town,
furnished with every conveniency, and built with a most
surprising mechanism.

I never should have done were I to recount the many
objects which involuntarily strike my imagination in
the midst of my work, and spontaneously afford me
the most pleasing relief. These appear insignificant
trifles to a person who has travelled through Europe and
America, and is acquainted with books and with many
sciences; but such simple objects of contemplation suffice
me, who have no time to bestow on more extensive observations. Happily these require no study, they are
obvious, they gild the moments I dedicate to them,
and enliven the severe labours which I perform. At
home my happiness springs from very different objects;
the gradual unfolding of my children's reason, the study
of their dawning tempers attract all my paternal attention. I have to contrive little punishments for their
little faults, small encouragements for their good actions,
and a variety of other expedients dictated by various
occasions. But these are themes unworthy your perusal,
and which ought not to be carried beyond the walls
of my house, being domestic mysteries adapted only to
the locality of the small sanctuary wherein my family
resides. Sometimes I delight in inventing and executing
machines, which simplify my wife's labour. I have been
tolerably successful that way; and these, Sir, are the narrow circles within which I constantly revolve, and what
can I wish for beyond them? I bless God for all the good
he has given me; I envy no man's prosperity, and with
no other portion of happiness than that I may live to

teach the same philosophy to my children; and give each of them a farm, show them how to cultivate it, and be like their father, good substantial independent American farmers—an appellation which will be the most fortunate one a man of my class can possess, so long as our civil government continues to shed blessings on our husbandry. Adieu.

LETTER III

I wish I could be acquainted with the feelings and thoughts which must agitate the heart and present themselves to the mind of an enlightened Englishman, when he first lands on this continent. He must greatly rejoice that he lived at a time to see this fair country discovered and settled; he must necessarily feel a share of national pride, when he views the chain of settlements which embellishes these extended shores. When he says to himself, this is the work of my countrymen, who, when convulsed by factions, afflicted by a variety of miseries and wants, restless and impatient, took refuge here. They brought along with them their national genius, to which they principally owe what liberty they enjoy, and what substance they possess. Here he sees the industry of his native country displayed in a new manner, and traces in their works the embryos of all the arts, sciences, and ingenuity which flourish in Europe. Here he beholds fair cities, substantial villages, extensive fields, an immense country filled with decent houses, good roads, orchards, meadows, and bridges, where an hundred years ago all was wild, woody, and uncultivated! What a train of pleasing ideas this fair spectacle must suggest; it is a prospect which must inspire a good citizen with the most heartfelt pleasure. The difficulty consists in the manner of viewing so extensive a scene. He is arrived on a new continent; a modern society offers itself to his contemplation, different from what he had hitherto seen. It is not composed, as in Europe, of great lords who possess everything, and of a herd of people who have nothing. Here are no aristocratical

35

families, no courts, no kings, no bishops, no ecclesiastical dominion, no invisible power giving to a few a very visible one; no great manufacturers employing thousands, no great refinements of luxury. The rich and the poor are not so far removed from each other as they are in Europe. Some few towns excepted, we are all tillers of the earth, from Nova Scotia to West Florida. We are a people of cultivators, scattered over an immense territory, communicating with each other by means of good roads and navigable rivers, united by the silken bands of mild government, all respecting the laws, without dreading their power, because they are equitable. We are all animated with the spirit of an industry which is unfettered and unrestrained, because each person works for himself. If he travels through our rural districts he views not the hostile castle, and the haughty mansion, contrasted with the clay-built hut and miserable cabin, where cattle and men help to keep each other warm, and dwell in meanness, smoke, and indigence. A pleasing uniformity of decent competence appears throughout our habitations. The meanest of our log-houses is a dry and comfortable habitation. Lawyer or merchant are the fairest titles our towns afford; that of a farmer is the only appellation of the rural inhabitants of our country. It must take some time ere he can reconcile himself to our dictionary, which is but short in words of dignity, and names of honour. There, on a Sunday, he sees a congregation of respectable farmers and their wives, all clad in neat homespun, well mounted, or riding in their own humble waggons. There is not among them an esquire, saving the unlettered magistrate. There he sees a parson as simple as his flock, a farmer who does not riot on the labour of others. We have no princes, for whom we toil, starve, and bleed: we are the most perfect society now existing in the world. Here man is free as he ought to be; nor is this pleasing equality so transitory as many others are. Many ages will not see the shores of our great lakes replenished with inland nations, nor the unknown bounds of North America entirely peopled. Who can tell how far it extends? Who can tell the millions of men whom it will feed and contain? for no European foot has as yet travelled half the extent of this mighty continent!

The next wish of this traveller will be to know whence came all these people? they are a mixture of English, Scotch, Irish, French, Dutch, Germans, and Swedes. From this promiscuous breed, that race now called Americans have arisen. The eastern provinces must indeed be excepted, as being the unmixed descendants of Englishmen. I have heard many wish that they had been more intermixed also: for my part, I am no wisher, and think it much better as it has happened. They exhibit a most conspicuous figure in this great and variegated picture; they too enter for a great share in the pleasing perspective displayed in these thirteen provinces. I know it is fashionable to reflect on them, but I respect them for what they have done; for the accuracy and wisdom with which they have settled their territory; for the decency of their manners; for their early love of letters; their ancient college, the first in this hemisphere; for their industry; which to me who am but a farmer, is the criterion of everything. There never was a people, situated as they are, who with so ungrateful a soil have done more in so short a time. Do you think that the monarchical ingredients which are more prevalent in other governments, have purged them from all foul stains? Their histories assert the contrary.

In this great American asylum, the poor of Europe have by some means met together, and in consequence of various causes; to what purpose should they ask one another what countrymen they are? Alas, two thirds

of them had no country. Can a wretch who wanders
about, who works and starves, whose life is a continual
scene of sore affliction or pinching penury; can that
man call England or any other kingdom his country?
A country that had no bread for him, whose fields procured him no harvest, who met with nothing but the
frowns of the rich, the severity of the laws, with jails
and punishments; who owned not a single foot of the
extensive surface of this planet? No! urged by a
variety of motives, here they came. Every thing has
tended to regenerate them; new laws, a new mode of
living, a new social system; here they are become men:
in Europe they were as so many useless plants, wanting
vegetative mould, and refreshing showers; they withered,
and were mowed down by want, hunger, and war; but
now by the power of transplantation, like all other
plants they have taken root and flourished! Formerly
they were not numbered in any civil lists of their country, except in those of the poor; here they rank as citizens. By what invisible power has this surprising metamorphosis been performed? By that of the laws and
that of their industry. The laws, the indulgent laws,
protect them as they arrive, stamping on them the sym-
bol of adoption; they receive ample rewards for their
labours; these accumulated rewards procure them lands;
those lands confer on them the title of freemen, and
to that title every benefit is affixed which men can possibly require. This is the great operation daily performed
by our laws. From whence proceed these laws? From
our government. Whence the government? It is derived
from the original genius and strong desire of the people
ratified and confirmed by the crown. This is the great
chain which links us all, this is the picture which every
province exhibits, Nova Scotia excepted. There the
crown has done all; either there were no people who
had genius, or it was not much attended to: the con-

sequence is, that the province is very thinly inhabited indeed; the power of the crown in conjunction with the musketos has prevented men from settling there. Yet some parts of it flourished once, and it contained a mild harmless set of people. But for the fault of a few leaders, the whole were banished. The greatest political error the crown ever committed in America, was to cut off men from a country which wanted nothing but men!

What attachment can a poor European emigrant have for a country where he had nothing? The knowledge of the language, the love of a few kindred as poor as himself, were the only cords that tied him: his country is now that which gives him land, bread, protection, and consequence: *Ubi panis ibi patria,* is the motto of all emigrants. What then is the American, this new man? He is either an European, or the descendant of an European, hence that strange mixture of blood, which you will find in no other country. I could point out to you a family whose grandfather was an Englishman, whose wife was Dutch, whose son married a French woman, and whose present four sons have now four wives of different nations. *He* is an American, who, leaving behind him all his ancient prejudices and manners, receives new ones from the new mode of life he has embraced, the new government he obeys, and the new rank he holds. He becomes an American by being received in the broad lap of our great *Alma Mater.* Here individuals of all nations are melted into a new race of men, whose labours and posterity will one day cause great changes in the world. Americans are the western pilgrims, who are carrying along with them that great mass of arts, sciences, vigour, and industry which began long since in the east; they will finish the great circle. The Americans were once scattered all over Europe; here they are incorporated into one of the finest systems of population which has ever appeared, and which will hereafter become distinct by the power of the different climates they inhabit. The American ought therefore to love this country much better than that wherein either he or his forefathers were born. Here the rewards of his industry follow with equal steps the progress of his labour; his labour is founded on the basis of nature, *self-interest;* can it want a stronger allurement? Wives and children, who before in vain demanded of him a morsel of bread, now, fat and frolicsome, gladly help their father to clear those fields whence exuberant crops are to arise to feed and to clothe them all; without any part being claimed, either by a despotic prince, a rich abbot, or a mighty lord. Here religion demands but little of him; a small voluntary salary to the minister, and gratitude to God; can he refuse these? The American is a new man, who acts upon new principles; he must therefore entertain new ideas, and form new opinions. From involuntary idleness, servile dependence, penury, and useless labour, he has passed to toils of a very different nature, rewarded by ample subsistence.—This is an American.

British America is divided into many provinces, forming a large association, scattered along a coast 1500 miles extent and about 200 wide. This society I would fain examine, at least such as it appears in the middle provinces; if it does not afford that variety of tinges and gradations which may be observed in Europe, we have colours peculiar to ourselves. For instance, it is natural to conceive that those who live near the sea, must be very different from those who live in the woods; the intermediate space will afford a separate and distinct class.

Men are like plants; the goodness and flavour of the fruit proceeds from the peculiar soil and exposition in which they grow. We are nothing but what we derive from the air we breathe, the climate we inhabit, the government we obey, the system of religion we profess, and the nature of our employment. Here you will find but few crimes; these have acquired as yet no root among us. I wish I was able to trace all my ideas; if my ignorance prevents me from describing them properly, I hope I shall be able to delineate a few of the outlines, which are all I propose.

Those who live near the sea, feed more on fish than on flesh, and often encounter that boisterous element. This renders them more bold and enterprising; this leads them to neglect the confined occupations of the land. They see and converse with a variety of people, their intercourse with mankind becomes extensive. The sea inspires them with a love of traffic, a desire of transporting produce from one place to another; and leads them to a variety of resources which supply the place of labour. Those who inhabit the middle settlements, by far the most numerous, must be very different; the simple cultivation of the earth purifies them, but the indulgences of the government, the soft remonstrances of religion, the rank of independent freeholders, must necessarily inspire them with sentiments, very little known in Europe among people of the same class. What do I say? Europe has no such class of men; the early knowledge they acquire, the early bargains they make, give them a great degree of sagacity. As freemen they will be litigious; pride and obstinacy are often the cause of law suits; the nature of our laws and governments may be another. As citizens it is easy to imagine, that they will carefully read the newspapers, enter into every political disquisition, freely blame or censure governors and others. As farmers they will be careful and anxious to get as much as they can, because what they get is their own. As northern men they will love the cheerful cup. As Christians, religion curbs them not in their opinions; the general indulgence leaves every one to think for themselves in spiritual matters; the laws inspect our actions, our thoughts are left to God. Industry, good living, selfishness, litigiousness, country politics, the pride of freemen, religious indifference, are their characteristics. If you recede still farther from the sea, you will come into more modern settlements; they exhibit the same strong lineaments, in a ruder appearance. Religion seems to have still less influence, and their manners are less improved.

Now we arrive near the great woods, near the last inhabited districts; there men seem to be placed still farther beyond the reach of government, which in some measure leaves them to themselves. How can it pervade every corner; as they were driven there by misfortunes, necessity of beginnings, desire of acquiring large tracts of land, idleness, frequent want of economy, ancient debts; the re-union of such people does not afford a very pleasing spectacle. When discord, want of unity and friendship; when either drunkenness or idleness prevail in such remote districts; contention, inactivity, and wretchedness must ensue. There are not the same remedies to these evils as in a long established community. The few magistrates they have, are in general little better than the rest; they are often in a perfect state of war; that of man against man, sometimes decided by blows, sometimes by means of the law; that of man against every wild inhabitant of these venerable woods, of which they are come to dispossess them. There men appear to be no better than carnivorous animals of a superior rank, living on the flesh of wild animals when they can catch them, and when they are not able, they subsist on grain. He who would wish to see America in its proper light, and have a true idea of its feeble beginnings and barbarous rudiments, must visit our extended line of frontiers where the last settlers dwell, and where he may see the first labours of settlement, the mode of clearing the earth, in all their different appearances; where men are wholly left dependent on their native tempers, and on the spur of uncertain industry, which often fails when not sanctified by the efficacy of a few moral rules. There, remote from the power of example and check of shame, many families exhibit the most hideous parts of our society. They are a kind of forlorn hope, preceding by ten or twelve years the most respectable army of veterans which come after them. In that space, prosperity will polish some, vice and the law will drive off the rest, who uniting again with others like themselves will recede still farther; making room for more industrious people, who will finish their improvements, convert the loghouse into a convenient habitation, and rejoicing that the first heavy labours are finished, will change in a few years that hitherto barbarous country into a fine fertile, well regulated district. Such is our progress, such is the march of the Europeans toward the interior parts of this continent. In all societies there are off-casts; this impure part serves as our precursors or pioneers; my father himself was one of that class, but he came upon honest principles, and was therefore one of the few who held fast; by good conduct and temperance, he transmitted to me his fair inheritance, when not above one in fourteen of his contemporaries had the same good fortune.

Forty years ago this smiling country was thus inhabited; it is now purged, a general decency of manners prevails throughout, and such has been the fate of our best countries.

Exclusive of those general characteristics, each province has its own, founded on the government, climate, mode of husbandry, customs, and peculiarity of circumstances. Europeans submit insensibly to these great powers, and become, in the course of a few generations, not only Americans in general, but either Pennsylvanians, Virginians, or provincials under some other name. Whoever traverses the continent must easily observe those strong differences, which will grow more evident in time. The inhabitants of Canada, Massachusetts, the middle provinces, the southern ones will be as different as their climates; their only points of unity will be those of religion and language.

As I have endeavoured to show you how Europeans become Americans; it may not be disagreeable to show you likewise how the various Christian sects introduced, wear out, and how religious indifference becomes prevalent. When any considerable number of a particular sect happen to dwell contiguous to each other, they immediately erect a temple, and there worship the Divinity agreeably to their own peculiar ideas. Nobody disturbs them. If any new sect springs up in Europe it may happen that many of its professors will come and settle in America. As they bring their zeal with them, they are at liberty to make proselytes if they can, and to build a meeting and to follow the dictates of their consciences; for neither the government nor any other power interferes. If they are peaceable subjects, and are industrious, what is it to their neighbours how and in what manner they think fit to address their prayers to the Supreme Being? But if the sectaries are not settled close together, if they are mixed with other denominations, their zeal will cool for want of fuel, and will be extinguished in a little time. Then the Americans become as to religion, what they are as to country, allied to all. In them the name of Englishman, Frenchman, and European is lost, and in like manner, the strict modes of Christianity as practised in Europe are lost also. This effect will extend itself still farther hereafter, and though this may appear to you as a strange idea, yet it is a very true one. I shall be able perhaps hereafter to explain myself better; in the meanwhile, let the following example serve as my first justification.

Let us suppose you and I to be travelling; we observe that in this house, to the right, lives a Catholic, who prays to God as he has been taught, and believes in transubstantiation; he works and raises wheat, he has a large family of children, all hale and robust; his belief, his prayers offend nobody. About one mile farther on the same road, his next neighbour may be a good honest plodding German Lutheran, who addresses himself to the same God, the God of all, agreeably to the modes he has been educated in, and believes in consubstantiation; by so doing he scandalises nobody; he also works in his fields, embellishes the earth, clears swamps, etc. What has the world to do with his Lutheran principles? He persecutes nobody, and nobody persecutes him, he visits his neighbours, and his neighbours visit him. Next to him lives a seceder, the most enthusiastic of all sectaries; his zeal is hot and fiery, but separated as he is from others of the same complexion, he has no congregation of his own to resort to, where he might cabal and mingle religious pride with worldly obstinacy. He likewise raises good crops, his house is handsomely painted, his orchard is one of the fairest in the neighbourhood. How does it concern the welfare of the country, or of the province at large, what this man's religious sentiments are, or really whether he has any at all? He is a good farmer, he is a sober, peaceable, good citizen: William Penn himself would not wish for more. This is the visible character, the invisible one is only guessed at, and is nobody's business. Next again lives a Low Dutchman, who implicitly believes the rules laid down by the synod of Dort. He conceives no other idea of a clergyman than that of an hired man; if he does his work well he will pay him the stipulated sum; if not he will dismiss him, and do without his sermons, and let his church be shut up for years. But notwithstanding this coarse idea, you will find his house and farm to be the neatest in all the country; and you will judge by his waggon and fat horses, that he thinks more of the affairs of this world than of those of the next. He is sober and laborious, therefore he is all he ought to be as to the affairs of this life; as for those of the next, he must trust to the great Creator. Each of these people instruct their children as well as they can, but these instructions are feeble compared to those which are given to the youth of the poorest class in Europe. Their children will therefore grow up less zealous and more indifferent in matters of religion than their parents. The foolish vanity, or rather the fury of making Prose-lytes, is unknown here; they have no time, the seasons call for all their attention, and thus in a few years, this mixed neighbourhood will exhibit a strange religious medley, that will be neither pure Catholicism nor pure Calvinism. A very perceptible indifference even in the first generation, will become apparent; and it may hap-pen that the daughter of the Catholic will marry the son of the seceder, and settle by themselves at a distance from their parents. What religious education will they give their children? A very imperfect one. If there happens to be in the neighbourhood any place of wor-ship, we will suppose a Quaker's meeting; rather than not show their fine clothes, they will go to it, and some of them may perhaps attach themselves to that society. Others will remain in a perfect state of indifference; the children of these zealous parents will not be able to tell what their religious principles are, and their grandchil-dren still less. The neighbourhood of a place of worship generally leads them to it, and the action of going thither, is the strongest evidence they can give of their attachment to any sect. The Quakers are the only people who retain a fondness for their own mode of worship; for be they ever so far separated from each other, they hold a sort of communion with the society, and seldom

depart from its rules, at least in this country. Thus all
sects are mixed as well as all nations; thus religious
indifference is imperceptibly disseminated from one end
of the continent to the other; which is at present one of
the strongest characteristics of the Americans. Where
this will reach no one can tell, perhaps it may leave a
vacuum fit to receive other systems. Persecution, religious pride, the love of contradiction, are the food of
what the world commonly calls religion. These motives
have ceased here; zeal in Europe is confined; here it
evaporates in the great distance it has to travel; there
it is a grain of powder inclosed, here it burns away in
the open air, and consumes without effect.

But to return to our back settlers. I must tell you,
that there is something in the proximity of the woods,
which is very singular. It is with men as it is with the
plants and anmals that grow and live in the forests; they
are entirely different from those that live in the plains.
I will candidly tell you all my thoughts but you are not
to expect that I shall advance any reasons. By living
in or near the woods, their actions are regulated by the
wildness of the neighbourhood. The deer often come
to eat their grain, the wolves to destroy their sheep, the
bears to kill their hogs, the foxes to catch their poultry.
This surrounding hostility immediately puts the gun
into their hands; they watch these animals, they kill
some; and thus by defending their property, they soon
become professed hunters: this is the progress; once
hunters, farewell to the plough. The chase renders
them ferocious, gloomy, and unsociable; a hunter wants
no neighbour, he rather hates them, because he dreads
the competition. In a little time their success in the
woods makes them neglect their tillage. They trust to
the natural fecundity of the earth, and therefore do little;
carelessness in fencing often exposes what little they sow
to destruction; they are not at home to watch; in order

therefore to make up the deficiency, they go oftener to the woods. That new mode of life brings along with it a new set of manners, which I cannot easily describe. These new manners being grafted on the old stock, produce a strange sort of lawless profligacy, the impressions of which are indelible. The manners of the Indian natives are respectable, compared with this European medley. Their wives and children live in sloth and inactivity; and having no proper pursuits, you may judge what education the latter receive. Their tender minds have nothing else to contemplate but the example of their parents; like them they grow up a mongrel breed, half civilised, half savage, except nature stamps on them some constitutional propensities. That rich, that voluptuous sentiment is gone that struck them so forcibly; the possession of their freeholds no longer conveys to their minds the same pleasure and pride. To all these reasons you must add, their lonely situation, and you cannot imagine what an effect on manners the great distances they live from each other has! Consider one of the last settlements in its first view: of what is it composed? Europeans who have not that sufficient share of knowledge they ought to have, in order to prosper; people who have suddenly passed from oppression, dread of government, and fear of laws, into the unlimited freedom of the woods. This sudden change must have a very great effect on most men, and on that class particularly. Eating of wild meat, whatever you may think, tends to alter their temper: though all the proof I can adduce, is, that I have seen it: and having no place of worship to resort to, what little society this might afford is denied them. The Sunday meetings, exclusive of religious benefits, were the only social bonds that might have inspired them with some degree of emulation in neatness. Is it then surprising to see men thus situated, immersed in great and heavy labours, degenerate a little? It is rather a wonder the effect is not more diffusive. The Moravians and the Quakers are the only instances in exception to what I have advanced. The first never settle singly, it is a colony of the society which emigrates; they carry with them their forms, worship, rules, and decency: the others never begin so hard, they are always able to buy improvements, in which there is a great advantage, for by that time the country is recovered from its first barbarity. Thus our bad people are those who are half cultivators and half hunters; and the worst of them are those who have degenerated altogether into the hunting state. As old ploughmen and new men of the woods, as Europeans and new made Indians, they contract the vices of both; they adopt the moroseness and ferocity of a native, without his mildness, or even his industry at home. If manners are not refined, at least they are rendered simple and inoffensive by tilling the earth; all our wants are supplied by it, our time is divided between labour and rest, and leaves none for the commission of great misdeeds. As hunters it is divided between the toil of the chase, the idleness of repose, or the indulgence of inebriation. Hunting is but a licentious idle life, and if it does not always pervert good dispositions; yet, when it is united with bad luck, it leads to want: want stimulates that propensity to rapacity and injustice, too natural to needy men, which is the fatal gradation. After this explanation of the effects which follow by living in the woods, shall we yet vainly flatter ourselves with the hope of converting the Indians? We should rather begin with converting our back-settlers; and now if I dare mention the name of religion, its sweet accents would be lost in the immensity of these woods. Men thus placed are not fit either to receive or remember its mild instructions; they want temples and ministers, but as soon as men cease to remain at home, and begin to lead an erratic life, let them be either tawny or white, they cease to be its disciples.

Thus have I faintly and imperfectly endeavoured to trace our society from the sea to our woods! yet you must not imagine that every person who moves back, acts upon the same principles, or falls into the same degeneracy. Many families carry with them all their decency of conduct, purity of morals, and respect of religion; but these are scarce, the power of example is sometimes irresistible. Even among these back-settlers, their depravity is greater or less, according to what nation or province they belong. Were I to adduce proofs of this, I might be accused of partiality. If there happens to be some rich intervals, some fertile bottoms, in those remote districts, the people will there prefer tilling the land to hunting, and will attach themselves to it; but even on these fertile spots you may plainly perceive the inhabitants to acquire a great degree of rusticity and selfishness.

It is in consequence of this straggling situation, and the astonishing power it has on manners, that the back-settlers of both the Carolinas, Virginia, and many other parts, have been long a set of lawless people; it has been even dangerous to travel among them. Government can do nothing in so extensive a country, better it should wink at these irregularities, than that it should use means inconsistent with its usual mildness. Time will efface those stains: in proportion as the great body of population approaches them they will reform, and become polished and subordinate. Whatever has been said of the four New England provinces, no such degeneracy of manners has ever tarnished their annals; their back-settlers have been kept within the bounds of decency, and government, by means of wise laws, and by the influence of religion. What a detestable idea such people

must have given to the natives of the Europeans! They
trade with them, the worst of people are permitted to
do that which none but persons of the best characters
should be employed in. They get drunk with them, and
often defraud the Indians. Their avarice, removed from
the eyes of their superiors, knows no bounds; and aided
by the little superiority of knowledge, these traders deceive them, and even sometimes shed blood. Hence
those shocking violations, those sudden devastations
which have so often stained our frontiers, when hundreds of innocent people have been sacrificed for the
crimes of a few. It was in consequence of such behaviour, that the Indians took the hatchet against the
Virginians in 1774. Thus are our first steps trod, thus
are our first trees felled, in general, by the most vicious
of our people; and thus the path is opened for the
arrival of a second and better class, the true American
freeholders; the most respectable set of people in this
part of the world: respectable for their industry, their
happy independence, the great share of freedom they
possess, the good regulation of their families, and for
extending the trade and the dominion of our mother
country.

Europe contains hardly any other distinctions but
lords and tenants; this fair country alone is settled by
freeholders, the possessors of the soil they cultivate,
members of the government they obey, and the framers
of their own laws, by means of their representatives.
This is a thought which you have taught me to cherish;
our difference from Europe, far from diminishing, rather
adds to our usefulness and consequence as men and
subjects. Had our forefathers remained there, they
would only have crowded it, and perhaps prolonged
those convulsions which had shook it so long. Every
industrious European who transports himself here, may
be compared to a sprout growing at the foot of a great

tree; it enjoys and draws but a little portion of sap; wrench it from the parent roots, transplant it, and it will become a tree bearing fruit also. Colonists are therefore entitled to the consideration due to the most useful subjects; a hundred families barely existing in some parts of Scotland, will here in six years, cause an annual exportation of 10,000 bushels of wheat: 100 bushels being but a common quantity for an industrious family to sell, if they cultivate good land. It is here then that the idle may be employed, the useless become useful, and the poor become rich; but by riches I do not mean gold and silver, we have but little of those metals; I mean a better sort of wealth, cleared lands, cattle, good houses, good clothes, and an increase of people to enjoy them.

There is no wonder that this country has so many charms, and presents to Europeans so many temptations to remain in it. A traveller in Europe becomes a stranger as soon as he quits his own kingdom; but it is otherwise here. We know, properly speaking, no strangers; this is every person's country; the variety of our soils, situations, climates, governments, and produce, hath something which must please everybody. No sooner does an European arrive, no matter of what condition, than his eyes are opened upon the fair prospect; he hears his language spoken, he retraces many of his own country manners, he perpetually hears the names of families and towns with which he is acquainted; he sees happiness and prosperity in all places disseminated; he meets with hospitality, kindness, and plenty everywhere; he beholds hardly any poor, he seldom hears of punishments and executions; and he wonders at the elegance of our towns, those miracles of industry and freedom. He cannot admire enough our rural districts, our convenient roads, good taverns, and our many accommodations; he involuntarily loves a country where everything is so lovely.

When in England, he was a mere Englishman; here he stands on a larger portion of the globe, not less than its fourth part, and may see the productions of the north, in iron and naval stores; the provisions of Ireland, the grain of Egypt, the indigo, the rice of China. He does not find, as in Europe, a crowded society, where every place is over-stocked; he does not feel that perpetual collision of parties, that difficulty of beginning, that contention which oversets so many. There is room for everybody in America; has he any particular talent, or industry? he exerts it in order to procure a livelihood, and it succeeds. Is he a merchant? the avenues of trade are infinite; is he eminent in any respect? he will be employed and respected. Does he love a country life? pleasant farms present themselves; he may purchase what he wants, and thereby become an American farmer. Is he a labourer, sober and industrious? he need not go many miles, nor receive many informations before he will be hired, well fed at the table of his employer, and paid four or five times more than he can get in Europe. Does he want uncultivated lands? thousands of acres present themselves, which he may purchase cheap. Whatever be his talents or inclinations, if they are moderate, he may satisfy them. I do not mean that every one who comes will grow rich in a little time; no, but he may procure an easy, decent maintenance, by his industry. Instead of starving he will be fed, instead of being idle he will have employment; and these are riches enough for such men as come over here. The rich stay in Europe, it is only the middling and the poor that emigrate. Would you wish to travel in independent idleness, from north to south, you will find easy access, and the most cheerful reception at every house; society without ostentation, good cheer without pride, and every decent diversion which the country affords, with little expense. It is no wonder that the European who has lived here a few years, is desirous to remain; Europe with all its pomp, is not to be compared to this continent, for men of middle stations, or labourers.

An European, when he first arrives, seems limited in his intentions, as well as in his views; but he very suddenly alters his scale; two hundred miles formerly appeared a very great distance, it is now but a trifle; he no sooner breathes our air than he forms schemes, and embarks in designs he never would have thought of in his own country. There the plenitude of society confines many useful ideas, and often extinguishes the most laudable schemes which here ripen into maturity. Thus Europeans become Americans.

But how is this accomplished in that crowd of low, indigent people, who flock here every year from all parts of Europe? I will tell you; they no sooner arrive than they immediately feel the good effects of that plenty of provisions we possess: they fare on our best food, and they are kindly entertained; their talents, character, and peculiar industry are immediately inquired into; they find countrymen everywhere disseminated, let them come from whatever part of Europe. Let me select one as an epitome of the rest; he is hired, he goes to work, and works moderately; instead of being employed by a haughty person, he finds himself with his equal, placed at the substantial table of the farmer, or else at an inferior one as good; his wages are high, his bed is not like that bed of sorrow on which he used to lie: if he behaves with propriety, and is faithful, he is caressed, and becomes as it were a member of the family. He begins to feel the effects of a sort of resurrection; hitherto he had not lived, but simply vegetated; he now feels himself a man, because he is treated as such; the laws of his own country had overlooked him in his insignificancy; the laws of this cover him with their mantle. Judge what an alteration there must arise in

the mind and thoughts of this man; he begins to forget
his former servitude and dependence, his heart involuntarily swells and glows; this first swell inspires him with
those new thoughts which constitute an American. What
love can he entertain for a country where his existence
was a burthen to him; if he is a generous good man, the
love of this new adoptive parent will sink deep into
his heart. He looks around, and sees many a prosperous
person, who but a few years before was as poor as himself. This encourages him much, he begins to form
some little scheme, the first, alas, he ever formed in his
life. If he is wise he thus spends two or three years,
in which time he acquires knowledge, the use of tools,
the modes of working the lands, felling trees, etc. This
prepares the foundation of a good name, the most useful acquisition he can make. He is encouraged, he has
gained friends; he is advised and directed, he feels bold,
he purchases some land; he gives all the money he has
brought over, as well as what he has earned, and trusts
to the God of harvests for the discharge of the rest. His
good name procures him credit. He is now possessed
of the deed, conveying to him and his posterity the fee
simple and absolute property of two hundred acres of
land, situated on such a river. What an epocha in this
man's life! He is become a freeholder, from perhaps a
German boor—he is now an American, a Pennsylvanian,
an English subject. He is naturalised, his name is en-
rolled with those of the other citizens of the province.
Instead of being a vagrant, he has a place of residence;
he is called the inhabitant of such a county, or of such
a district, and for the first time in his life counts for
something; for hitherto he has been a cypher. I only repeat what I have heard many say, and no wonder their
hearts should glow, and be agitated with a multitude of
feelings, not easy to describe. From nothing to start into
being; from a servant to the rank of a master; from being

the slave of some despotic prince, to become a free man, invested with lands, to which every municipal blessing is annexed! What a change indeed! It is in consequence of that change that he becomes an American. This great metamorphosis has a double effect, it extinguishes all his European prejudices, he forgets that mechanism of subordination, that servility of disposition which poverty had taught him; and sometimes he is apt to forget too much, often passing from one extreme to the other. If he is a good man, he forms schemes of future prosperity, he proposes to educate his children better than he has been educated himself; he thinks of future modes of conduct, feels an ardour to labour he never felt before. Pride steps in and leads him to everything that the laws do not forbid: he respects them; with a heart-felt gratitude he looks toward the east, toward that insular government from whose wisdom all his new felicity is derived, and under whose wings and protection he now lives. These reflections constitute him the good man and the good subject. Ye poor Europeans, ye, who sweat, and work for the great—ye, who are obliged to give so many sheaves to the church, so many to your lords, so many to your government, and have hardly any left for yourselves—ye, who are held in less estimation than favourite hunters or useless lap-dogs—ye, who only breathe the air of nature, because it cannot be withheld from you; it is here that ye can conceive the possibility of those feelings I have been describing; it is here the laws of naturalisation invite every one to partake of our great labours and felicity, to till unrented, untaxed lands! Many, corrupted beyond the power of amendment, have brought with them all their vices, and disregarding the advantages held to them, have gone on in their former career of iniquity, until they have been overtaken and punished by our laws. It is not every emigrant who succeeds; no, it is only the sober, the honest, and industrious: happy those to whom this transition has served as a powerful spur to labour, to prosperity, and to the good establishment of children, born in the days of their poverty; and who had no other portion to expect but the rags of their parents, had it not been for their happy emigration. Others again, have been led astray by this enchanting scene; their new pride, instead of leading them to the fields, has kept them in idleness: the idea of possessing lands is all that satisfies them—though surrounded with fertility, they have mouldered away their time in inactivity, misinformed husbandry, and ineffectual endeavours. How much wiser, in general, the honest Germans than almost all other Europeans; they hire themselves to some of their wealthy landsmen, and in that apprenticeship learn everything that is necessary. They attentively consider the prosperous industry of others, which imprints in their minds a strong desire of possessing the same advantages. This forcible idea never quits them, they launch forth, and by dint of sobriety, rigid parsimony, and the most persevering industry, they commonly succeed. Their astonishment at their first arrival from Germany is very great—it is to them a dream; the contrast must be powerful indeed; they observe their countrymen flourishing in every place; they travel through whole counties where not a word of English is spoken; and in the names and the language of the people, they retrace Germany. They have been an useful acquisition to this continent, and to Pennsylvania in particular; to them it owes some share of its prosperity: to their mechanical knowledge and patience it owes the finest mills in all America, the best teams of horses, and many other advantages. The recollection of their former poverty and slavery never quits them as long as they live.

The Scotch and the Irish might have lived in their own country perhaps as poor, but enjoying more civil

advantages, the effects of their new situation do not
strike them so forcibly, nor has it so lasting an effect.
From whence the difference arises I know not, but out of
twelve families of emigrants of each country, generally
seven Scotch will succeed, nine German, and four Irish.
The Scotch are frugal and laborious, but their wives
cannot work so hard as German women, who on the
contrary vie with their husbands, and often share with
them the most severe toils of the field, which they understand better. They have therefore nothing to struggle
against, but the common casualties of nature. The
Irish do not prosper so well; they love to drink and to
quarrel; they are litigious, and soon take to the gun,
which is the ruin of everything; they seem beside to
labour under a greater degree of ignorance in husbandry
than the others; perhaps it is that their industry had
less scope, and was less exercised at home. I have heard
many relate, how the land was parcelled out in that
kingdom; their ancient conquest has been a great detriment to them, by over-setting their landed property.
The lands possessed by a few, are leased down *ad
infinitum,* and the occupiers often pay five guineas an
acre. The poor are worse lodged there than anywhere
else in Europe; their potatoes, which are easily raised,
are perhaps an inducement to laziness: their wages are
too low, and their whisky too cheap.

There is no tracing observations of this kind, without
making at the same time very great allowances, as there
are everywhere to be found, a great many exceptions.
The Irish themselves, from different parts of that kingdom, are very different. It is difficult to account for
this surprising locality, one would think on so small an
island an Irishman must be an Irishman: yet it is not
so, they are different in their aptitude, and in their
love of labour.

The Scotch on the contrary are all industrious and

saving; they want nothing more than a field to exert themselves in, and they are commonly sure of succeeding. The only difficulty they labour under is, that technical American knowledge which requires some time to obtain; it is not easy for those who seldom saw a tree, to conceive how it is to be felled, cut up, and split into rails and posts.

As I am fond of seeing and talking of prosperous families, I intend to finish this letter by relating to you the history of an honest Scotch Hebridean, who came here in 1774, which will show you in epitome what the Scotch can do, wherever they have room for the exertion of their industry. Whenever I hear of any new settlement, I pay it a visit once or twice a year, on purpose to observe the different steps each settler takes, the gradual improvements, the different tempers of each family, on which their prosperity in a great nature depends; their different modifications of industry, their ingenuity, and contrivance; for being all poor, their life requires sagacity and prudence. In the evening I love to hear them tell their stories, they furnish me with new ideas; I sit still and listen to their ancient misfortunes, observing in many of them a strong degree of gratitude to God, and the government. Many a well meant sermon have I preached to some of them. When I found laziness and inattention to prevail, who could refrain from wishing well to these new countrymen, after having undergone so many fatigues. Who could withhold good advice? What a happy change it must be, to descend from the high, sterile, bleak lands of Scotland, where everything is barren and cold, to rest on some fertile farms in these middle provinces! Such a transition must have afforded the most pleasing satisfaction.

The following dialogue passed at an out-settlement, where I lately paid a visit:

Well, friend, how do you do now; I am come fifty odd

miles on purpose to see you; how do you go on with your new cutting and slashing? Very well, good Sir, we learn the use of the axe bravely, we shall make it out; we have a belly full of victuals every day, our cows run about, and come home full of milk, our hogs get fat of themselves in the woods: Oh, this is a good country! God bless the king, and William Penn; we shall do very well by and by, if we keep our healths. Your loghouse looks neat and light, where did you get these shingles? One of our neighbours is a New-England man, and he showed us how to split them out of chestnut-trees. Now for a barn, but all in good time, here are fine trees to build with. Who is to frame it, sure you don't understand that work yet? A countryman of ours who has been in America these ten years, offers to wait for his money until the second crop is lodged in it. What did you give for your land? Thirty-five shillings per acre, payable in seven years. How many acres have you got? An hundred and fifty. That is enough to begin with; is not your land pretty hard to clear? Yes, Sir, hard enough, but it would be harder still if it were ready cleared, for then we should have no timber, and I love the woods much; the land is nothing without them. Have not you found out any bees yet? No, Sir; and if we had we should not know what to do with them. I will tell you by and by. You are very kind. Farewell, honest man, God prosper you; whenever you travel toward ——, inquire for J.S. He will entertain you kindly, provided you bring him good tidings from your family and farm. In this manner I often visit them, and carefully examine their houses, their modes of ingenuity, their different ways; and make them all relate all they know, and describe all they feel. These are scenes which I believe you would willingly share with me. I well remember your philanthropic turn of mind. Is it not better to contemplate under these humble roofs, the rudiments of future wealth and population, than to behold the accumulated bundles of litigious papers in the office of a lawyer? To examine how the world is gradually settled, how the howling swamp is converted into a pleasing meadow, the rough ridge into a fine field; and to hear the cheerful whistling, the rural song, where there was no sound heard before, save the yell of the savage, the screech of the owl or the hissing of the snake? Here an European, fatigued with luxury, riches, and pleasures, may find a sweet relaxation in a series of interesting scenes, as affecting as they are new. England, which now contains so many domes, so many castles, was once like this; a place woody and marshy; its inhabitants, now the favourite nation for arts and commerce, were once painted like our neighbours. The country will flourish in its turn, and the same observations will be made which I have just delineated. Posterity will look back with avidity and pleasure, to trace, if possible, the era of this or that particular settlement.

Pray, what is the reason that the Scots are in general more religious, more faithful, more honest, and industrious than the Irish? I do not mean to insinuate national reflections, God forbid! It ill becomes any man, and much less an American; but as I know men are nothing of themselves, and that they owe all their different modifications either to government or other local circumstances, there must be some powerful causes which constitute this great national difference.

Agreeable to the account which several Scotchmen have given me of the north of Britain, of the Orkneys, and the Hebride Islands, they seem, on many accounts, to be unfit for the habitation of men; they appear to be calculated only for great sheep pastures. Who then can blame the inhabitants of these countries for transporting themselves hither? This great continent must in time absorb the poorest part of Europe; and this will happen in proportion as it becomes better known; and as war, taxation, oppression, and misery increase there. The Hebrides appear to be fit only for the residence of male-factors, and it would be much better to send felons there than either to Virginia or Maryland. What a strange compliment has our mother country paid to two of the finest provinces in America! England has enter-tained in that respect very mistaken ideas; what was in-tended as a punishment, is become the good fortune of several; many of those who have been transported as felons, are now rich, and strangers to the stings of those wants that urged them to violations of the law: they are become industrious, exemplary, and useful citizens. The English government should purchase the most northern and barren of those islands; it should send over to us the honest, primitive Hebrideans, settle them here on good lands, as a reward for their virtue and ancient poverty; and replace them with a colony of her wicked sons. The severity of the climate, the inclemency of the seasons, the sterility of the soil, the tempestuousness of the sea, would afflict and punish enough. Could there be found a spot better adapted to retaliate the injury it had re-ceived by their crimes? Some of those islands might be considered as the hell of Great Britain, where all evil spirits should be sent. Two essential ends would be answered by this simple operation. The good people, by emigration, would be rendered happier; the bad ones would be placed where they ought to be. In a few years the dread of being sent to that wintry region would have a much stronger effect than that of transportation.— This is no place of punishment; were I a poor hopeless, breadless Englishman, and not restrained by the power of shame, I should be very thankful for the passage. It is of very little importance how, and in what manner an indigent man arrives; for if he is but sober, honest, and industrious, he has nothing more to ask of heaven. Let him go to work, he will have opportunities enough to earn a comfortable support, and even the means of procuring some land; which ought to be the utmost wish of every person who has health and hands to work. I knew a man who came to this country, in the literal sense of the expression, stark naked; I think he was a Frenchman, and a sailor on board an English man-of-war. Being discontented, he had stripped himself and swam ashore; where, finding clothes and friends, he settled afterwards at Maraneck, in the county of Chester, in the province of New York: he married and left a good farm to each of his sons. I knew another person who was but twelve years old when he was taken on the frontiers of Canada, by the Indians; at his arrival at Albany he was purchased by a gentleman, who generously bound him apprentice to a tailor. He lived to the age of ninety, and left behind him a fine estate and a numerous family, all well settled; many of them I am acquainted with.—Where is then the industrious European who ought to despair?

After a foreigner from any part of Europe is arrived, and become a citizen; let him devoutly listen to the voice of our great parent, which says to him, "Welcome to my shores, distressed European; bless the hour in which thou didst see my verdant fields, my fair navigable rivers, and my green mountains!—If thou wilt work, I have bread for thee; if thou wilt be honest, sober, and industrious, I have greater rewards to confer on thee—ease and independence. I will give thee fields to feed and clothe thee; a comfortable fireside to sit by, and tell thy children by what means thou hast prospered; and a decent bed to repose on. I shall endow thee beside with the immunities of a freeman. If thou wilt carefully educate thy children, teach them gratitude to God, and reverence to that government, that philanthropic government, which has collected here so many men and made them happy. I will also provide for thy progeny; and to every good man this ought to be the most holy, the most powerful, the most earnest wish he can possibly form, as well as the most consolatory prospect when he dies. Go thou and work and till; thou shalt prosper, provided thou be just, grateful, and industrious."

History of Andrew, the Hebridean

Let historians give the detail of our charters, the succession of our several governors, and of their administrations; of our political struggles, and of the foundation of our towns: let annalists amuse themselves with collecting anecdotes of the establishment of our modern provinces: eagles soar high—I, a feebler bird, cheerfully content myself with skipping from bush to bush, and living on insignificant insects. I am so habituated to draw all my food and pleasure from the surface of the earth which I till, that I cannot, nor indeed am I able to quit it—I therefore present you with the short history of a simple Scotchman; though it contain not a single remarkable event to amaze the reader; no tragical scene to convulse the heart, or pathetic narrative to draw tears from sympathetic eyes. All I wish to delineate is, the progressive steps of a poor man, advancing from indigence to ease; from oppression to freedom; from obscurity and contumely to some degree of consequence— not by virtue of any freaks of fortune, but by the gradual operation of sobriety, honesty, and emigration. These are the limited fields, through which I love to wander; sure to find in some parts, the smile of new-born happiness, the glad heart, inspiring the cheerful song, the glow of manly pride excited by vivid hopes and rising independence. I always return from my neighbourly excursions extremely happy, because there I see good living almost under every roof, and prosperous endeavours almost in every field. But you may say, why don't you describe some of the more ancient, opulent settlements of our country, where even the eye of an European has something to admire? It is true, our American fields are in general pleasing to behold, adorned and intermixed as they are with so many substantial houses, flourishing orchards, and copses of woodlands; the pride of our farms, the source of every good we possess. But what I might observe there is but natural and common; for to draw comfortable subsistence from well fenced cultivated fields, is easy to conceive. A father dies and leaves a decent house and rich farm to his son; the son modernises the one, and carefully tills the other; marries the daughter of a friend and neighbour: this is the common prospect; but though it is rich and pleasant, yet it is far from being so entertaining and instructive as the one now in my view.

I had rather attend on the shore to welcome the poor European when he arrives, I observe him in his first moments of embarrassment, trace him throughout his primary difficulties, follow him step by step, until he pitches his tent on some piece of land, and realises that energetic wish which has made him quit his native land, his kindred, and induced him to traverse a boisterous ocean. It is there I want to observe his first thoughts and feelings, the first essays of an industry, which hitherto has been suppressed. I wish to see men cut down the first trees, erect their new buildings, till their first fields, reap their first crops, and say for the first time in their lives, "This is our own grain, raised from American soil—on it we shall feed and grow fat, and convert the rest into gold and silver." I want to see how the happy effects of their sobriety, honesty, and industry are first displayed: and who would not take a pleasure in seeing these strangers settling as new countrymen, struggling with arduous difficulties, overcoming them, and becoming happy:

Landing on this great continent is like going to sea, they must have a compass, some friendly directing needle; or else they will uselessly err and wander for a long time, even with a fair wind: yet these are the struggles through which our forefathers have waded; and they have left us no other records of them, but the possession of our farms. The reflections I make on these new settlers recall to my mind what my grandfather did in his days; they fill me with gratitude to his memory as well as to that government, which invited him to come, and helped him when he arrived, as well as many others. Can I pass over these reflections without remembering thy name, O Penn! thou best of legislators; who by the wisdom of thy laws hast endowed human nature, within the bounds of thy province, with every dignity it can possibly enjoy in a civilised state; and showed by thy singular establishment, what all men might be if they would follow thy example!

In the year 1770, I purchased some lands in the county of ——, which I intended for one of my sons; and was obliged to go there in order to see them properly surveyed and marked out: the soil is good, but the country has a very wild aspect. However I observed with pleasure, that land sells very fast; and I am in hopes when the lad gets a wife, it will be a well-settled decent country. Agreeable to our customs, which indeed are those of nature, it is our duty to provide for our eldest children while we live, in order that our homesteads may be left to the youngest, who are the most helpless. Some people are apt to regard the portions given to daughters as so much lost to the family; but this is selfish, and is not agreeable to my way of thinking; they cannot work as men do; they marry young: I have given an honest European a farm to till for himself, rent free, provided he clears an acre of swamp every year, and that he quits it whenever my daughter shall marry. It will procure her a substantial husband, a good farmer—and that is all my ambition.

Whilst I was in the woods I met with a party of Indians; I shook hands with them, and I perceived they had killed a cub; I had a little Peach brandy, they perceived it also, we therefore joined company, kindled a large fire, and ate an hearty supper. I made their hearts glad, and we all reposed on good beds of leaves. Soon after dark, I was surprised to hear a prodigious hooting through the woods; the Indians laughed heartily. One of them, more skilful than the rest, mimicked the owls so exactly, that a very large one perched on a high tree over our fire. We soon brought him down; he measured five feet seven inches from one extremity of the wings to the other. By Captain —— I have sent you the talons, on which I have had the heads of small candlesticks fixed. Pray keep them on the table of your study for my sake.

Contrary to my expectation, I found myself under the necessity of going to Philadelphia, in order to pay the purchase money, and to have the deeds properly recorded. I thought little of the journey, though it was above two hundred miles, because I was well acquainted with many friends, at whose houses I intended to stop. The third night after I left the woods, I put up at Mr. ——'s, the most worthy citizen I know; he happened to lodge at my house when you were there.—He kindly inquired after your welfare, and desired I would make a friendly mention of him to you. The neatness of these good people is no phenomenon, yet I think this excellent family surpasses everything I know. No sooner did I lie down to rest than I thought myself in a most odoriferous arbour, so sweet and fragrant were the sheets. Next morning I found my host in the orchard destroying caterpillars. I think, friend B., said I, that thee art greatly departed from the good rules of the society; thee seemeth to have quitted that happy simplicity for which it hath hitherto been so remarkable. Thy rebuke, friend James, is a pretty heavy one; what motive canst thee have for thus accusing us? Thy kind wife made a mistake last evening, I said; she put me on a bed of roses, instead of a common one; I am not used to such delicacies. And is that all, friend James, that thee hast to reproach us with?—Thee wilt not call it luxury I hope? thee canst but know that it is the produce of our garden; and friend Pope sayeth, that "to enjoy is to obey." This is a most learned excuse indeed, friend B., and must be valued because it is founded upon truth. James, my wife hath done nothing more to thy bed than what is done all the year round to all the beds in the family; she sprinkles her linen with rose-water before she puts it under the press; it is her fancy, and I have nought to say. But thee shalt not escape so, verily I will send for her; thee and she must settle the matter, whilst I proceed on my work, before the sun gets too high.—Tom, go thou and call thy mistress Philadelphia. What, said I, is thy wife called by that name? I did not know that before. I'll tell thee, James, how it came to pass: her grandmother was the first female child born after William Penn landed with the rest of our brethren; and in compliment to the city he intended to build, she was called after the name he intended to give it; and so there is always one of the daughters of her family known by the name of Philadelphia. She soon came, and after a most friendly altercation, I gave up the point; breakfasted, departed, and in four days reached the city.

A week after news came that a vessel was arrived with Scotch emigrants. Mr. C. and I went to the dock to see them disembark. It was a scene which inspired me with a variety of thoughts: here are, said I to my friend, a number of people, driven by poverty, and other adverse causes, to a foreign land, in which they know nobody.

The name of a stranger, instead of implying relief, assistance, and kindness, on the contrary, conveys very different ideas. They are now distressed; their minds are racked by a variety of apprehensions, fears, and hopes. It was this last powerful sentiment which has brought them here. If they are good people, I pray that heaven may realise them. Whoever were to see them thus gathered again in five or six years, would behold a more pleasing sight, to which this would serve as a very powerful contrast. By their honesty, the vigour of their arms, and the benignity of government, their condition will be greatly improved; they will be well clad, fat, possessed of that manly confidence which property confers; they will become useful citizens. Some of the posterity may act conspicuous parts in our future American transactions. Most of them appeared pale and emaciated, from the length of the passage, and the indifferent provision on which they had lived. The number of children seemed as great as that of the people; they had all paid for being conveyed here. The captain told us they were a quiet, peaceable, and harmless people, who had never dwelt in cities. This was a valuable cargo; they seemed, a few excepted, to be in the full vigour of their lives. Several citizens, impelled either by spontaneous attachments, or motives of humanity, took many of them to their houses; the city, agreeable to its usual wisdom and humanity, ordered them all to be lodged in the barracks, and plenty of provisions to be given them. My friend pitched upon one also and led him to his house, with his wife, and a son about fourteen years of age. The majority of them had contracted for land the year before, by means of an agent; the rest depended entirely upon chance; and the one who followed us was of this last class. Poor man, he smiled on receiving the invitation, and gladly accepted it, bidding his wife and son do the same, in a language which I did not understand. He

gazed with uninterrupted attention on everything he
saw; the houses, the inhabitants, the negroes, and carriages: everything appeared equally new to him; and
we went slow, in order to give him time to feed on this
pleasing variety. Good God! said he, is this Philadelphia,
that blessed city of bread and provisions, of which we
have heard so much? I am told it was founded the same
year in which my father was born; why, it is finer than
Greenock and Glasgow, which are ten times as old. It
is so, said my friend to him, and when thee hast been
here a month, thee will soon see that it is the capital of
a fine province, of which thee art going to be a citizen:
Greenock enjoys neither such a climate nor such a soil.
Thus we slowly proceeded along, when we met several
large Lancaster six-horse waggons, just arrived from the
country. At this stupendous sight he stopped short, and
with great diffidence asked us what was the use of these
great moving houses, and where those big horses came
from? Have you none such at home, I asked him? Oh,
no; these huge animals would eat all the grass of our
island! We at last reached my friend's house, who in
the glow of well-meant hospitality, made them all three
sit down to a good dinner, and gave them as much cider
as they could drink. God bless this country, and the
good people it contains, said he; this is the best meal's
victuals I have made a long time.—I thank you kindly.

What part of Scotland dost thee come from, friend
Andrew, said Mr. C.? Some of us come from the main,
some from the island of Barra, he answered—I myself
am a Barra man. I looked on the map, and by its latitude, easily guessed that it must be an inhospitable climate. What sort of land have you got there, I asked him?
Bad enough, said he; we have no such trees as I see here,
no wheat, no kine, no apples. Then, I observed, that it
must be hard for the poor to live. We have no poor, he
answered, we are all alike, except our laird; but he can-

not help everybody. Pray what is the name of your laird? Mr. Neill, said Andrew; the like of him is not to be found in any of the isles; his forefathers have lived there thirty generations ago, as we are told. Now, gentlemen, you may judge what an ancient family estate it must be. But it is cold, the land is thin, and there were too many of us, which are the reasons that some are come to seek their fortunes here. Well, Andrew, what step do you intend to take in order to become rich? I do not know, Sir; I am but an ignorant man, a stranger besides—I must rely on the advice of good Christians, they would not deceive me, I am sure. I have brought with me a character from our Barra minister, can it do me any good here? Oh, yes; but your future success will depend entirely on your own conduct; if you are a sober man, as the certificate says, laborious, and honest, there is no fear but that you will do well. Have you brought any money with you, Andrew? Yes, Sir, eleven guineas and a half. Upon my word it is a considerable sum for a Barra man; how came you by so much money? Why seven years ago I received a legacy of thirty-seven pounds from an uncle, who loved me much; my wife brought me two guineas, when the laird gave her to me for a wife, which I have saved ever since. I have sold all I had; I worked in Glasgow for some time. I am glad to hear you are so saving and prudent; be so still; you must go and hire yourself with some good people; what can you do? I can thresh a little, and handle the spade. Can you plough? Yes, Sir, with the little breast plough I have brought with me. These won't do here, Andrew; you are an able man; if you are willing you will soon learn. I'll tell you what I intend to do; I'll send you to my house, where you shall stay two or three weeks, there you must exercise yourself with the axe, that is the principal tool the Americans want, and particularly the back-settlers. Can your wife spin? Yes, she can. Well then as soon as you are able to handle the axe, you shall go and live with Mr. P. R., a particular friend of mine, who will give you four dollars per month, for the first six, and the usual price of five as long as you remain with him. I shall place your wife in another house, where she shall receive half a dollar a week for spinning; and your son a dollar a month to drive the team. You shall have besides good victuals to eat, and good beds to lie on; will all this satisfy you, Andrew? He hardly understood what I said; the honest tears of gratitude fell from his eyes as he looked at me, and its expressions seemed to quiver on his lips.—Though silent, this was saying a great deal; there was besides something extremely moving to see a man six feet high thus shed tears; and they did not lessen the good opinion I had entertained of him. At last he told me, that my offers were more than he deserved, and that he would first begin to work for his victuals. No, no, said I, if you are careful and sober, and do what you can, you shall receive what I told you, after you have served a short apprenticeship at my house. May God repay you for all your kindnesses, said Andrew; as long as I live I shall thank you, and do what I can for you. A few days after I sent them all three to ——, by the return of some waggons, that he might have an opportunity of viewing, and convincing himself of the utility of those machines which he had at first so much admired.

The further descriptions he gave us of the Hebrides in general, and of his native island in particular; of the customs and modes of living of the inhabitants; greatly entertained me. Pray is the sterility of the soil the cause that there are no trees, or is it because there are none planted? What are the modern families of all the kings of the earth, compared to the date of that of Mr. Neill? Admitting that each generation should last but forty years, this makes a period of 1200; an extraordinary duration for the uninterrupted descent of any family! Agreeably to the description he gave us of those countries, they seem to live according to the rules of nature, which gives them but bare subsistence; their constitutions are uncontaminated by any excess or effeminacy, which their soil refuses. If their allowance of food is not too scanty, they must all be healthy by perpetual temperance and exercise; if so, they are amply rewarded for their poverty. Could they have obtained but necessary food, they would not have left it; for it was not in consequence of oppression, either from their patriarch or the government, that they had emigrated. I wish we had a colony of these honest people settled in some parts of this province; their morals, their religion, seem to be as simple as their manners. This society would present an interesting spectacle could they be transported on a richer soil. But perhaps that soil would soon alter everything; for our opinions, vices, and virtues, are altogether local: we are machines fashioned by every circumstance around us.

Andrew arrived at my house a week before I did, and I found my wife, agreeable to my instructions, had placed the axe in his hands, as his first task. For some time he was very awkward, but he was so docile, so willing, and grateful, as well as his wife, that I foresaw he would succeed. Agreeably to my promise, I put them all with different families, where they were well liked, and all parties were pleased. Andrew worked hard, lived well, grew fat, and every Sunday came to pay me a visit on a good horse, which Mr. P. R. lent him. Poor man, it took him a long time ere he could sit on the saddle and hold the bridle properly. I believe he had never before mounted such a beast, though I did not choose to ask him that question, for fear it might suggest some mortifying ideas. After having been twelve months at Mr. P. R.'s, and having received his own and his family's wages, which amounted to eighty-four dollars; he came to see me on a week-day, and told me, that he was a man of middle age, and would willingly have land of his own, in order to procure him a home, as a shelter against old age: that whenever this period should come, his son, to whom he would give his land, would then maintain him, and thus live altogether; he therefore required my advice and assistance. I thought his desire very natural and praiseworthy, and told him that I should think of it, but that he must remain one month longer with Mr. P. R., who had 3000 rails to split. He immediately consented. The spring was not far advanced enough yet for Andrew to begin clearing any land even supposing that he had made a purchase; as it is always necessary that the leaves should be out, in order that this additional combustible may serve to burn the heaps of brush more readily.

A few days after, it happened that the whole family of Mr. P. R. went to meeting, and left Andrew to take care of the house. While he was at the door, attentively reading the Bible, nine Indians just come from the mountains, suddenly made their appearance, and unloaded their packs of furs on the floor of the piazza. Conceive, if you can, what was Andrew's consternation at this extraordinary sight! From the singular appearance of these people, the honest Hebridean took them for a lawless band come to rob his master's house. He therefore, like a faithful guardian, precipitately withdrew and shut the doors, but as most of our houses are without locks, he was reduced to the necessity of fixing his knife over the latch, and then flew upstairs in quest of a broadsword he had brought from Scotland. The Indians, who were Mr. P. R.'s particular friends, guessed at his suspicions and fears; they forcibly lifted the door, and suddenly took possession of the house, got all the bread and meat they wanted, and sat themselves down by the fire. At this instant Andrew, with his broadsword in his hand, entered the room; the Indians earnestly looking at him, and attentively watching his motions. After a very few reflections, Andrew found that his weapon was useless, when opposed to nine tomahawks; but this did not diminish his anger, on the contrary; it grew greater on observing the calm impudence with which they were devouring the family provisions. Unable to resist, he called them names in broad Scotch, and ordered them to desist and be gone; to which the Indians (as they told me afterwards) replied in their equally broad idiom. It must have been a most unintelligible altercation between this honest Barra man, and nine Indians who did not much care for anything he could say. At last he ventured to lay his hands on one of them, in order to turn him out of the house. Here Andrew's fidelity got the better of his prudence; for the Indian, by his motions, threatened to scalp him, while the rest gave the war whoop. This horrid noise so effectually frightened poor Andrew, that, unmindful of his courage, of his broadsword, and his intentions, he rushed out, left them masters of the house, and disappeared. I have heard one of the Indians say since, that he never laughed so heartily in his life. Andrew at a distance, soon recovered from the fears which had been inspired by this infernal yell, and thought of no other remedy than to go to the meeting-house, which was about two miles distant. In the eagerness of his honest intentions, with looks of affright still marked on his countenance, he called Mr. P. R. out, and told him with great vehemence of style, that nine monsters were come to his house—some blue, some red, and some black; that they had little axes in their hands out of which they smoked; and that like highlanders, they had no breeches; that they were devouring all his victuals, and that God only knew what they would do more. Pacify yourself, said Mr. P. R., my house is as safe with these people, as if I was there myself; as for the victuals, they are heartily welcome, honest Andrew; they are not people of much ceremony; they help themselves thus whenever they are among their friends; I do so too in their wigwams, whenever I go to their village: you had better therefore step in and hear the remainder of the sermon, and when the meeting is over we will all go back in the waggon together.

At their return, Mr. P. R., who speaks the Indian language very well, explained the whole matter; the Indians renewed their laugh, and shook hands with honest Andrew, whom they made to smoke out of their pipes; and thus peace was made, and ratified according to the Indian custom, by the calumet.

Soon after this adventure, the time approached when I had promised Andrew my best assistance to settle him; for that purpose I went to Mr. A. V. in the county of ——, who, I was informed, had purchased a tract of land, contiguous to —— settlement. I gave him a faithful detail of the progress Andrew had made in the rural arts; of his honesty, sobriety, and gratitude, and pressed him to sell him an hundred acres. This I cannot comply with, said Mr. A. V., but at the same time I will do better; I love to encourage honest Europeans as much as you do, and to see them prosper: you tell me he has but one son; I will lease them an hundred acres for any term of years you please, and make it more valuable to your Scotchman than if he was posessed of the fee simple. By that means he may, with what little money he has, buy a plough, a team, and some stock; he will not be incumbered with debts and mortgages; what he raises will be his own; had he two or three sons as able as himself, then I should think it more eligible for him to purchase the fee simple. I join with you in opinion, and will bring Andrew along with me in a few days.

Well, honest Andrew, said Mr. A. V., in consideration of your good name, I will let you have an hundred acres of good arable land, that shall be laid out along a new road; there is a bridge already erected on the creek that passes through the land, and a fine swamp of about twenty acres. These are my terms, I cannot sell, but I will lease you the quantity that Mr. James, your friend, has asked; the first seven years you shall pay no rent, whatever you sow and reap, and plant and gather, shall be entirely your own; neither the king, government, nor church, will have any claim on your future property: the remaining part of the time you must give me twelve dollars and an half a year; and that is all you will have to pay me. Within the three first years you must plant fifty apple trees, and clear seven acres of swamp within the first part of the lease; it will be your own advantage: whatever you do more within that time, I will pay you for it, at the common rate of the country. The term of the lease shall be thirty years; how do you like it, Andrew? Oh, Sir, it is very good, but I am afraid, that the king or his ministers, or the governor, or some of our great men, will come and take the land from me; your son may say to me, by and by, this is my father's land, Andrew, you must quit it. No, no, said Mr. A. V., there is no such danger; the king and his ministers are too just to take the labour of a poor settler; here we have no great men, but what are subordinate to our laws; but to calm all your fears, I will give you a lease, so that none can make you afraid. If ever you are dissatisfied with the land, a jury of your own neighbourhood shall value all your improvements, and you shall be paid agreeably to their verdict. You may sell the lease, or if you die, you may previously dispose of it, as if the land was your own. Expressive, yet inarticulate joy, was mixed in his countenance, which seemed impressed with astonishment and confusion. Do you understand me well, said Mr. A. V.? No, Sir, replied Andrew, I know nothing of what you mean about lease, improvement, will, jury, etc. That is honest, we will explain these things to you by and by. It must be confessed that those were hard words, which he had never heard in his life; for by his own account, the ideas they convey would be totally useless in the island of Barra. No wonder, therefore, that he was embarrassed; for how could the man who had hardly a will of his own since he was born, imagine he could have one after his death? How could the person who never possessed anything, conceive that he could extend his new dominion over this land, even after he should be laid in his grave? For my part, I think Andrew's amazement did not imply any extraordinary degree of ignorance; he was an actor introduced upon a new scene, it required some time ere he could reconcile himself to the part he was to perform. However he was soon enlightened, and introduced into those mysteries with which we native Americans are but too well acquainted.

Here then is honest Andrew, invested with every municipal advantage they confer; become a freeholder, possessed of a vote, of a place of residence, a citizen of the province of Pennsylvania. Andrew's original hopes and the distant prospects he had formed in the island of Barra, were at the eve of being realised; we therefore can easily forgive him a few spontaneous ejaculations, which would be useless to repeat. This short tale is easily told; few words are sufficient to describe this sudden change of situation; but in his mind it was gradual, and took him above a week before he could be sure, that without disturbing any money he could possess lands. Soon after he prepared himself; I lent him a barrel of pork, and 200 lb. weight of meal, and made him purchase what was necessary besides.

He set out, and hired a room in the house of a settler who lived the most contiguous to his own land. His first work was to clear some acres of swamp, that he might have a supply of hay the following year for his two horses and cows. From the first day he began to work, he was indefatigable; his honesty procured him friends, and his industry the esteem of his new neighbours. One of them offered him two acres of cleared land, whereon he might plant corn, pumpkins, squashes, and a few potatoes, that very season. It is astonishing how quick men will learn when they work for themselves. I saw with pleasure two months after, Andrew holding a two-horse plough and tracing his furrows quite straight; thus the spade man of the island of Barra was become the tiller of American soil. Well done, said I, Andrew, well done; I see that God speeds and directs your works; I see prosperity delineated in all your furrows and head lands. Raise this crop of corn with attention and care, and then you will be master of the art.

As he had neither mowing nor reaping to do that year, I told him that the time was come to build his house; and that for the purpose I would myself invite the neighbourhood to a frolic; that thus he would have a large dwelling erected, and some upland cleared in one day. Mr. P. R., his old friend, came at the time appointed, with all his hands, and brought victuals in plenty: I did the same. About forty people repaired to the spot; the songs, and merry stories, went round the woods from cluster to cluster, as the people had gathered to their different works; trees fell on all sides, bushes were cut up and heaped; and while many were thus employed, others with their teams hauled the big logs to the spot which Andrew had pitched upon for the erection of his new dwelling. We all dined in the woods; in the afternoon the logs were placed with skids, and the usual contrivances: thus the rude house was raised, and above two acres of land cut up, cleared, and heaped.

Whilst all these different operations were performing, Andrew was absolutely incapable of working; it was to him the most solemn holiday he had ever seen; it would have been sacrilegious in him to have defiled it with menial labour. Poor man, he sanctified it with joy and thanksgiving, and honest libations—he went from one to the other with the bottle in his hand, pressing everybody to drink, and drinking himself to show the example. He spent the whole day in smiling, laughing, and uttering monosyllables: his wife and son were there also, but as they could not understand the language, their pleasure must have been altogether that of the imagination. The powerful lord, the wealthy merchant, on seeing the superb mansion finished, never can feel half the joy and real happiness which was felt and enjoyed on that day by this honest Hebridean: though this new dwelling, erected in the midst of the woods, was nothing more than a square inclosure, composed of twenty-four large clumsy logs, let in at the ends. When the work was finished, the company made the woods resound with the noise of their three cheers, and the honest wishes they formed for Andrew's prosperity. He could say nothing, but with thankful tears he shook hands with them all. Thus from the first day he had landed, Andrew marched towards this important event: this memorable day made the sun shine on that land on which he was to sow wheat and other grain. What swamp he had cleared lay before his door; the essence of future bread, milk, and meat, were scattered all round him. Soon after he hired a carpenter, who put on a roof and laid the floors; in a week more the house was properly plastered, and the chimney finished. He moved into it, and purchased two cows, which found plenty of food in the woods—his hogs had the same advantage. That very year, he and his son sowed three bushels of wheat, from which he reaped ninety-one and a half; for I had ordered him to keep an exact account of all he should raise. His first crop of other corn would have been as good, had it not been for the squirrels, which were enemies not to be dispersed by the broadsword. The fourth year I took an inventory of the wheat this man possessed, which I send you. Soon after, further settlements were made on that road, and Andrew, instead of being the last man towards the wilderness, found himself in a few years in the middle of a numerous society. He helped others as generously as others had helped him; and I have dined many times at his table with several of his neighbours. The second year he was made overseer of the road, and served on two petty juries, performing as a citizen all the duties required of him. The historiographer of some great prince or general, does not bring his hero victorious to the end of a successful campaign, with one half of the heart-felt pleasure with which I have conducted Andrew to the situation he now enjoys: he is independent and easy. Triumph and military honours do not always imply those two blessings. He is unencumbered with debts, services, rents, or any other dues; the success of a campaign, the laurels of war, must be purchased at the dearest rate, which makes every cool reflecting citizen to tremble and shudder. By the literal account hereunto annexed, you will easily be made acquainted with the happy effects which constantly flow, in this country, from sobriety and industry, when united with good land and freedom.

The account of the property he acquired with his own hands and those of his son, in four years, is under:

	DOLLARS
The value of his improvements and lease .	225
Six cows, at 13 dollars	78
Two breeding mares	50
The rest of the stock	100
Seventy-three bushels of wheat	66
Money due to him on notes	43
Pork and beef in his cellar	28
Wool and flax	19
Ploughs and other utensils of husbandry . .	31
£240 Pennsylvania currency—dollars .	640

LETTER IV

DESCRIPTION OF THE ISLAND OF NANTUCKET, WITH THE
MANNERS, CUSTOMS, POLICY, AND TRADE
OF THE INHABITANTS

THE greatest compliment that can be paid to the best
of kings, to the wisest ministers, or the most patriotic
rulers, is to think, that the reformation of political
abuses, and the happiness of their people are the primary objects of their attention. But alas! how disagreeable must the work of reformation be; how dreaded the
operation; for we hear of no amendment: on the contrary, the great number of European emigrants, yearly
coming over here, informs us, that the severity of taxes,
the injustice of laws, the tyranny of the rich, and the
oppressive avarice of the church; are as intolerable as
ever. Will these calamities have no end? Are not the
great rulers of the earth afraid of losing, by degrees,
their most useful subjects? This country, providentially
intended for the general asylum of the world, will flourish by the oppression of their people; they will every
day become better acquainted with the happiness we
enjoy, and seek for the means of transporting themselves
here, in spite of all obstacles and laws. To what purpose
then have so many useful books and divine maxims been
transmitted to us from preceding ages?—Are they all
vain, all useless? Must human nature ever be the sport
of the few, and its many wounds remain unhealed? How
happy are we here, in having fortunately escaped the
miseries which attended our fathers; how thankful ought
we to be, that they reared us in a land where sobriety
and industry never fail to meet with the most ample
rewards! You have, no doubt, read several histories of

this continent, yet there are a thousand facts, a thousand explanations overlooked. Authors will certainly convey to you a geographical knowledge of this country; they will acquaint you with the eras of the several settlements, the foundations of our towns, the spirit of our different charters, etc., yet they do not sufficiently disclose the genius of the people, their various customs, their modes of agriculture, the innumerable resources which the industrious have of raising themselves to a comfortable and easy situation. Few of these writers have resided here, and those who have, had not pervaded every part of the country, nor carefully examined the nature and principles of our association. It would be a task worthy a speculative genius, to enter intimately into the situation and characters of the people, from Nova Scotia to West Florida; and surely history cannot possibly present any subject more pleasing to behold. Sensible how unable I am to lead you through so vast a maze, let us look attentively for some small unnoticed corner; but where shall we go in quest of such a one? Numberless settlements, each distinguished by some peculiarities, present themselves on every side; all seem to realise the most sanguine wishes that a good man could form for the happiness of his race. Here they live by fishing on the most plentiful coasts in the world; there they fell trees, by the sides of large rivers, for masts and lumber; here others convert innumerable logs into the best boards; there again others cultivate the land, rear cattle, and clear large fields. Yet I have a spot in my view, where none of these occupations are performed, which will, I hope, reward us for the trouble of inspection; but though it is barren in its soil, insignificant in its extent, inconvenient in its situation, deprived of materials for building; it seems to have been inhabited merely to prove what mankind can do when happily governed! Here I can point out to you exertions of the most successful industry; instances of native sagacity unassisted by science; the happy fruits of a well directed perseverance. It is always a refreshing spectacle to me, when in my review of the various component parts of this immense *whole,* I observe the labours of its inhabitants singularly rewarded by nature; when I see them emerged out of their first difficulties, living with decency and ease, and conveying to their posterity that plentiful subsistence, which their fathers have so deservedly earned. But when their prosperity arises from the goodness of the climate, and fertility of the soil; I partake of their happiness, it is true; yet stay but a little while with them, as they exhibit nothing but what is natural and common. On the contrary, when I meet with barren spots fertilised, grass growing where none grew before; grain gathered from fields which had hitherto produced nothing better than brambles; dwellings raised where no building materials were to be found; wealth acquired by the most uncommon means: there I pause, to dwell on the favourite object of my speculative inquiries. Willingly do I leave the former to enjoy the odoriferous furrow, or their rich valleys, with anxiety repairing to the spot, where so many difficulties have been overcome; where extraordinary exertions have produced extraordinary effects, and where every natural obstacle has been removed by a vigorous industry.

I want not to record the annals of the island of Nantucket—its inhabitants have no annals, for they are not a race of warriors. My simple wish is to trace them throughout their progressive steps, from their arrival here to this present hour; to inquire by what means they have raised themselves from the most humble, the most insignificant beginnings, to the ease and the wealth they now possess; and to give you some idea of their customs, religion, manners, policy, and mode of living.

This happy settlement was not founded on intrusion,

forcible entries, or blood, as so many others have been; it drew its origin from necessity on the one side, and from good will on the other; and ever since, all has been a scene of uninterrupted harmony.—Neither political, nor religious broils; neither disputes with the natives, nor any other contentions, have in the least agitated or disturbed its detached society. Yet the first founders knew nothing either of Lycurgus or Solon; for this settlement has not been the work of eminent men or powerful legislators, forcing nature by the accumulated labours of art. This singular establishment has been effected by means of that native industry and perseverance common to all men, when they are protected by a government which demands but little for its protection; when they are permitted to enjoy a system of rational laws founded on perfect freedom. The mildness and humanity of such a government necessarily implies that confidence which is the source of the most arduous undertakings and permanent success. Would you believe that a sandy spot, of about twenty-three thousand acres, affording neither stones nor timber, meadows nor arable, yet can boast of an handsome town, consisting of more than 50 houses, should possess above 200 sail of vessels, constantly employ upwards of 2000 seamen, feed more than 15,000 sheep, 500 cows, 200 horses; and has several citizens worth £20,000 sterling! Yet all these facts are uncontroverted. Who would have imagined that any people should have abandoned a fruitful and extensive continent, filled with the riches which the most ample vegetation affords; replete with good soil, enamelled meadows, rich pastures, every kind of timber, and with all other materials necessary to render life happy and comfortable: to come and inhabit a little sandbank, to which nature had refused those advantages; to dwell on a spot where there scarcely grew a shrub to announce, by the budding of its leaves, the arrival of the spring, and to warn by their fall the proximity of winter. Had this island been contiguous to the shores of some ancient monarchy, it would only have been occupied by a few wretched fishermen, who, oppressed by poverty, would hardly have been able to purchase or build little fishing barks; always dreading the weight of taxes, or the servitude of men-of-war. Instead of that boldness of speculation for which the inhabitants of this island are so remarkable, they would fearfully have confined themselves, within the narrow limits of the most trifling attempts; timid in their excursions, they never could have extricated themselves from their first difficulties. This island, on the contrary, contains 5000 hardy people, who boldly derive their riches from the element that surrounds them, and have been compelled by the sterility of the soil to seek abroad for the means of subsistence. You must not imagine, from the recital of these facts, that they enjoyed any exclusive privileges or royal charters, or that they were nursed by particular immunities in the infancy of their settlement. No, their freedom, their skill, their probity, and perseverance, have accomplished everything, and brought them by degrees to the rank they now hold.

From this first sketch, I hope that my partiality to this island will be justified. Perhaps you hardly know that such an one exists in the neighbourhood of Cape Cod. What has happened here, has and will happen everywhere else. Give mankind the full rewards of their industry, allow them to enjoy the fruit of their labour under the peaceable shade of their vines and fig-trees, leave their native activity unshackled and free, like a fair stream without dams or other obstacles; the first will fertilise the very sand on which they tread, the other exhibit a navigable river, spreading plenty and cheerfulness wherever the declivity of the ground leads it. If these people are not famous for tracing the fragrant furrow on the plain, they plough the rougher ocean, they gather from its surface, at an immense distance, and with Herculean labours, the riches it affords; they go to hunt and catch that huge fish which by its strength and velocity one would imagine ought to be beyond the reach of man. This island has nothing deserving of notice but its inhabitants; here you meet with neither ancient monuments, spacious halls, solemn temples, nor elegant dwellings; not a citadel, nor any kind of fortification, not even a battery to rend the air with its loud peals on any solemn occasion. As for their rural improvements, they are many, but all of the most simple and useful kind.

The island of Nantucket lies in latitude 41° 10′. 60 miles S. from Cape Cod; 27 S. from Hyanes or Barnstable, a town on the most contiguous part of the great peninsula; 21 miles E. by S. from Cape Pog, on the vineyard; 50 E. by S. from Wood's Hole, on Elizabeth Island; 80 miles S. from Boston; 120 from Rhode Island; 800 N. from Bermudas. Sherborn is the only town on the island, which consists of about 530 houses, that have been framed on the main; they are lathed and plastered within, handsomely painted and boarded without; each has a cellar underneath, built with stones fetched also from the main: they are all of a similar construction and appearance; plain, and entirely devoid of exterior or interior ornament. I observed but one which was built of bricks, belonging to Mr. ——, but like the rest it is unadorned. The town stands on a rising sandbank, on the west side of the harbour, which is very safe from all winds. There are two places of worship, one for the society of Friends, the other for that of Presbyterians; and in the middle of the town, near the market-place, stands a simple building, which is the county court-house. The town regularly ascends toward the country, and in its vicinage they have several small fields and gardens yearly manured with the dung of their cows, and the soil of their streets. There are a good many cherry and peach trees planted in their streets and in many other places; the apple tree does not thrive well, they have therefore planted but few. The island contains no mountains, yet is very uneven, and the many rising grounds and eminences with which it is filled, have formed in the several valleys a great variety of swamps, where the Indian grass and the blue bent, peculiar to such soils, grow with tolerable luxuriancy. Some of the swamps abound with peat, which serves the poor instead of firewood. There are fourteen ponds on this island, all extremely useful, some lying transversely, almost across it, which greatly helps to divide it into partitions for the use of their cattle; others abound with peculiar fish and sea fowls. Their streets are not paved, but this is attended with little inconvenience, as it is never crowded with country carriages; and those they have in the town are seldom made use of but in the time of the coming in and before the sailing of their fleets. At my first landing I was much surprised at the disagreeable smell which struck me in many parts of the town; it is caused by the whale oil, and is unavoidable; the neatness peculiar to these people can neither remove nor prevent it. There are near the wharfs a great many storehouses, where their staple commodity is deposited, as well as the innumerable materials which are always wanted to repair and fit out so many whalemen. They have three docks, each three hundred feet long, and extremely convenient; at the head of which there are ten feet of water. These docks are built like those in Boston, of logs fetched from the continent, filled with stones, and covered with sand. Between these docks and the town, there is room sufficient for the landing of goods and for the passage of their numerous carts; for almost every man here has one: the wharfs to the north and south of the docks, are built of the same materials, and give a stranger, at his first landing, an high idea of the prosperity of these people; and there is room around these three docks for 300 sail of vessels. When their fleets have been successful, the bustle and hurry of business on this spot for some days after their arrival, would make you imagine, that Sherborn is the capital of a very opulent and large province. On that point of land, which forms the west side of the harbour, stands a very neat lighthouse; the opposite peninsula, called Coitou, secures it from the most dangerous winds. There are but few gardens and arable fields in the neighbourhood of the town, for nothing can be more sterile and sandy than this part of the island; they have, however, with unwearied perseverance, by bringing a variety of manure, and by cow-penning, enriched several spots where they raise Indian corn, potatoes, pumpkins, turnips, etc. On the highest part of this sandy eminence, four windmills grind the grain they raise or import; and contiguous to them their rope walk is to be seen, where full half of their cordage is manufactured. Between the shores of the harbour, the docks, and the town, there is a most excellent piece of meadow, inclosed and manured with such cost and pains as show how necessary and precious grass is at Nantucket. Towards the point of Shemah, the island is more level and the soil better; and there they have considerable lots well fenced and richly manured, where they diligently raise their yearly crops. There are but very few farms on this island, because there are but very few spots that will admit of cultivation without the assistance of dung and other manure; which is very expensive to fetch from the main. This island was patented in the year 1671, by twenty-seven proprietors, under the province of New York; which then claimed all the islands from the Neway Sink to Cape Cod. They found it so uni-

versally barren and so unfit for cultivation, that they
mutually agreed not to divide it, as each could neither
live on, nor improve that lot which might fall to his
share. They then cast their eyes on the sea, and finding
themselves obliged to become fishermen, they looked for
a harbour, and having found one, they determined to
build a town in its neighbourhood and to dwell together. For that purpose they surveyed as much ground
as would afford to each what is generally called here a
home lot. Forty acres were thought sufficient to answer
this double purpose; for to what end should they covet
more land than they could improve, or even inclose;
not being possessed of a single tree, in the whole extent
of their new dominion. This was all the territorial
property they allotted; the rest they agreed to hold in
common, and seeing that the scanty grass of the island
might feed sheep, they agreed that each proprietor
should be entitled to feed on it if he pleased 560 sheep.
By this agreement, the national flock was to consist of
15,120; that is the undivided part of the island was by
such means ideally divisible into as many parts or
shares; to which nevertheless no certain determinate
quantity of land was affixed: for they knew not how
much the island contained, nor could the most judicious
surveyor fix this small quota as to quality and quantity.
Further they agreed, in case the grass should grow better
by feeding, that then four sheep should represent a cow,
and two cows a horse: such was the method this wise
people took to enjoy in common their new settlement:
such was the mode of their first establishment, which
may be truly and literally called a pastoral one. Several
hundred of sheep-pasture titles have since been divided
on those different tracts, which are now cultivated; the
rest by inheritance and intermarriages have been so
subdivided that it is very common for a girl to have
no other portion but her outset and four sheep pastures

or the privilege of feeding a cow. But as this privilege is founded on an ideal, though real title to some unknown piece of land, which one day or another may be ascertained; these *sheep-pasture titles* should convey to your imagination, something more valuable and of greater credit than the mere advantage arising from the benefit of a cow, which in that case would be no more than a right of commonage. Whereas, here as labour grows cheaper, as misfortunes from their sea adventures may happen, each person possessed of a sufficient number of these sheep-pasture titles may one day realise them on some peculiar spot, such as shall be adjudged by the council of the proprietors to be adequate to their value; and this is the reason that these people very unwillingly sell those small rights, and esteem them more than you would imagine. They are the representation of a future freehold, they cherish in the mind of the possessor a latent, though distant, hope, that by his success in his next whale season, he may be able to pitch on some predilected spot, and there build himself a home, to which he may retire, and spend the latter end of his days in peace. A council of proprietors always exists in this island, who decide their territorial differences; their titles are recorded in the books of the county, which this town represents, as well as every conveyance of lands and other sales.

This island furnishes the naturalist with few or no objects worthy of observation; it appears to be the uneven summit of a sandy submarine mountain, covered here and there with sorrel, grass, a few cedar bushes, and scrubby oaks; their swamps are much more valuable for the peat they contain, than for the trifling pasture of their surface; those declining grounds which lead to the seashores abound with *beach grass,* a light fodder when cut and cured, but very good when fed green. On the east side of the island they have several tracts of salt grasses, which being carefully fenced, yield a considerable quantity of that wholesome fodder. Among the many ponds or lakes with which this island abounds, there are some which have been made by the intrusion of the sea, such as Wiwidiah, the Long, the Narrow, and several others; consequently those are salt and the others fresh. The former answer two considerable purposes, first by enabling them to fence the island with greater facility; at peculiar high tides a great number of fish enter into them, where they feed and grow large, and at some known seasons of the year the inhabitants assemble and cut down the small bars which the waves always throw up. By these easy means the waters of the pond are let out, and as the fish follow their native element, the inhabitants with proper nets catch as many as they want, in their way out, without any other trouble. Those which are most common, are the streaked bass, the blue fish, the tom-cod, the mackerel, the tew-tag, the herring, the flounder, eel, etc. Fishing is one of the greatest diversions the island affords. At the west end lies the harbour of Mardiket, formed by Smith Point on the south-west, by Eel Point on the north, and Tuckernuck Island on the north-west; but it is neither so safe nor has it so good anchoring ground, as that near which the town stands. Three small creeks run into it, which yield the bitterest eels I have ever tasted. Between the lots of Palpus on the east, Barry's Valley and Miacomet pond on the south, and the narrow pond on the west, not far from Shèmàh Point, they have a considerable tract of even ground, being the least sandy, and the best on the island. It is divided into seven fields, one of which is planted by that part of the community which are entitled to it. This is called the common plantation, a simple but useful expedient, for was each holder of this track to fence his property, it would require a prodigious quantity of posts and rails, which you must remember are to be purchased and fetched from the main. Instead of those private subdivisions each man's allotment of land is thrown into the general field which is fenced at the expense of the parties; within it every one does with his own portion of the ground whatever he pleases. This apparent community saves a very material expense, a great deal of labour, and perhaps raises a sort of emulation among them, which urges every one to fertilise his share with the greatest care and attention. Thus every seven years the whole of this tract is under cultivation, and enriched by manure and ploughing yields afterwards excellent pasture; to which the town cows, amounting to 500 are daily led by the town shepherd, and as regularly driven back in the evening. There each animal easily finds the house to which it belongs, where they are sure to be well rewarded for the milk they give, by a present of bran, grain, or some farinaceous preparation; their economy being very great in that respect. These are commonly called Tètoukèmah lots. You must not imagine that every person on the island is either a landholder, or concerned in rural operations; no, the greater part are at sea; busily employed in their different fisheries; others are mere strangers, who come to settle as craftsmen, mechanics, etc., and even among the natives few are possessed of determinate shares of land: for engaged in sea affairs, or trade, they are satisfied with possessing a few sheep pastures, by means of which they may have perhaps one or two cows. Many have but one, for the great number of children they have, has caused such sub-divisions of the original proprietorship as is sometimes puzzling to trace; and several of the most fortunate at sea, have purchased and realised a great number of these original pasture titles. The best land on the island is at Palpus, remarkable for nothing but a house of entertainment. Quayes is a small but valuable track, long since purchased by Mr. Coffin, where he has erected the best house on the island. By long attention, proximity of the sea, etc., this fertile spot has been well manured, and is now the garden of Nantucket. Adjoining to it on the west side there is a small stream, on which they have erected a fulling mill; on the east is the lot, known by the name of Squam, watered likewise by a small rivulet, on which stands another fulling mill. Here is fine loamy soil, producing excellent clover, which is mowed twice a year. These mills prepare all the cloth which is made here: you may easily suppose that having so large a flock of sheep, they abound in wool; part of this they export, and the rest is spun by their industrious wives and converted into substantial garments. To the south-east is a great division of the island, fenced by itself, known by the name of Siasconcèt lot. It is a very uneven track of ground, abounding with swamps; here they turn in their fat cattle, or such as they intend to stall-feed, for their winter's provisions. It is on the shores of this part of the island, near Pochick Rip, where they catch their best fish, such as sea bass, tew-tag, or black fish, cod, smelt, perch, shadine, pike, etc. They have erected a few fishing houses on this shore, as well as at Sankate's Head, and Suffakatchè Beach, where the fishermen dwell in the fishing season. Many red cedar bushes and beach grass grow on the peninsula of Coitou; the soil is light and sandy, and serves as a receptacle for rabbits. It is here that their sheep find shelter in the snow storms of the winter. At the north end of Nantucket, there is a long point of land, projecting far into the sea, called Sandy Point; nothing grows on it but plain grass; and this is the place from whence they often catch porpoises and sharks, by a very ingenious method. On this point they commonly drive their horses in the spring of the year, in order to feed on the grass it bears, which is useless when arrived at maturity. Between that point and the main island they have a valuable salt meadow, called Croskaty, with a pond of the same name famous for black ducks. Hence we must return to Squam, which abounds in clover and herds grass; those who possess it follow no maritime occupation, and therefore neglect nothing that can render it fertile and profitable. The rest of the undescribed part of the island is open, and serves as a common pasture for their sheep. To the west of the island is that of Tuckernuck, where in the spring their young cattle are driven to feed; it has a few oak bushes and two fresh-water ponds, abounding with teals, brandts, and many other sea fowls, brought to this island by the proximity of their sand banks and shallows; where thousands are seen feeding at low water. Here they have neither wolves nor foxes; those inhabitants therefore who live out of town, raise with all security as much poultry as they want; their turkeys are very large and excellent. In summer this climate is extremely pleasant; they are not exposed to the scorching sun of the continent, the heats being tempered by the sea breezes, with which they are perpetually refreshed. In the winter, however, they pay severely for those advantages; it is extremely cold; the northwest wind, the tyrant of this country, after having escaped from our mountains and forests, free from all impediment in its short passage, blows with redoubled force and renders this island bleak and uncomfortable. On the other hand, the goodness of their houses, the social hospitality of their firesides, and their good cheer, make them ample amends for the severity of the season; nor are the snows so deep as on the main. The necessary and unavoidable inactivity of that season, combined with the vegetative rest of nature, force mankind to suspend their toils: often at this season more than half the inhabitants of the island are at sea, fishing in milder latitudes.

This island, as has been already hinted, appears to

be the summit of some huge sandy mountain, affording some acres of dry land for the habitation of man; other submarine ones lie to the southward of this, at different depths and different distances. This dangerous region is well known to the mariners by the name of Nantucket Shoals: these are the bulwarks which so powerfully defend this island from the impulse of the mighty ocean, and repel the force of its waves; which, but for the accumulated barriers, would ere now have dissolved its foundations, and torn it in pieces. These are the banks which afforded to the first inhabitants of Nantucket their daily subsistence, as it was from these shoals that they drew the origin of that wealth which they now possess; and was the school where they first learned how to venture farther, as the fish of their coast receded. The shores of this island abound with the soft-shelled, the hard-shelled, and the great sea clams, a most nutritious shell-fish. Their sands, their shallows are covered with them; they multiply so fast, that they are a never-failing resource. These and the great variety of fish they catch, constitute the principal food of the inhabitants. It was likewise that of the aborigines, whom the first settlers found here; the posterity of whom still live together in decent houses along the shores of Miacomet pond, on the south side of the island. They are an industrious, harmless race, as expert and as fond of a seafaring life as their fellow inhabitants the whites. Long before their arrival they had been engaged in petty wars against one another; the latter brought them peace, for it was in quest of peace that they abandoned the main. This island was then supposed to be under the jurisdiction of New York, as well as the islands of the Vineyard, Elizabeth's, etc., but have been since adjudged to be a part of the province of Massachusetts Bay. This change of jurisdiction procured them that peace they wanted, and which their brethren had so

long refused them in the days of their religious frenzy:
thus have enthusiasm and persecution both in Europe
as well as here, been the cause of the most arduous undertakings, and the means of those rapid settlements
which have been made along these extended sea-shores.
This island, having been since incorporated with the
neighbouring province, is become one of its counties,
known by the name of Nantucket, as well as the island
of the Vineyard, by that of Duke's County. They enjoy
here the same municipal establishment in common with
the rest; and therefore every requisite officer, such as
sheriff, justice of the peace, supervisors, assessors, con-
stables, overseer of the poor, etc. Their taxes are pro-
portioned to those of the metropolis, they are levied
as with us by valuations, agreed on and fixed, according
to the laws of the province; and by assessments formed
by the assessors, who are yearly chosen by the people,
and whose office obliges them to take either an oath or
an affirmation. Two thirds of the magistrates they have
here are of the society of Friends.

Before I enter into the further detail of this people's
government, industry, mode of living, etc., I think it
necessary to give you a short sketch of the political
state the natives had been in, a few years preceding the
arrival of the whites among them. They are hastening
towards a total annihilation, and this may be perhaps
the last compliment that will ever be paid them by any
traveller. They were not extirpated by fraud, violence,
or injustice, as hath been the case in so many provinces;
on the contrary, they have been treated by these people
as brethren; the peculiar genius of their sect inspiring
them with the same spirit of moderation which was
exhibited at Pennsylvania. Before the arrival of the
Europeans, they lived on the fish of their shores; and
it was from the same resources the first settlers were
compelled to draw their first subsistence. It is uncertain

whether the original right of the Earl of Sterling, or that of the Duke of York, was founded on a fair purchase of the soil or not; whatever injustice might have been committed in that respect, cannot be charged to the account of those Friends who purchased from others who no doubt founded their right on Indian grants: and if their numbers are now so decreased, it must not be attributed either to tyranny or violence, but to some of those causes, which have uninterruptedly produced the same effects from one end of the continent to the other, wherever both nations have been mixed. This insignificant spot, like the sea-shores of the great peninsula, was filled with these people; the great plenty of clams, oysters, and other fish, on which they lived, and which they easily caught, had prodigiously increased their numbers. History does not inform us what particular nation the aborigines of Nantucket were of; it is however very probable that they anciently emigrated from the opposite coast, perhaps from the Hyannees, which is but twenty-seven miles distant. As they then spoke and still speak the Nattick, it is reasonable to suppose that they must have had some affinity with that nation; or else that the Nattick, like the Huron, in the north-western parts of this continent, must have been the most prevailing one in this region. Mr. Elliot, an eminent New England divine, and one of the first founders of that great colony, translated the Bible into this language, in the year 1666, which was printed soon after at Cambridge, near Boston; he translated also the catechism, and many other useful books, which are still very common on this island, and are daily made use of by those Indians who are taught to read. The young Europeans learn it with the same facility as their own tongues; and ever after speak it both with ease and fluency. Whether the present Indians are the decendants of the ancient natives of the island, or whether they are the remains of the many different nations which once inhabited the regions of Mashpè and Nobscusset, in the peninsula now known by the name of Cape Cod, no one can positively tell, not even themselves. The last opinion seems to be that of the most sensible people of the island. So prevailing is the disposition of man to quarrel, and shed blood; so prone is he to divisions and parties; that even the ancient natives of this little spot were separated into two communities, inveterately waging war against each other, like the more powerful tribes of the continent. What do you imagine was the cause of this national quarrel? All the coast of their island equally abounded with the same quantity of fish and clams; in that instance there could be no jealousy, no motives to anger; the country afforded them no game; one would think this ought to have been the country of harmony and peace. But behold the singular destiny of the human kind, ever inferior, in many instances, to the more certain instinct of animals; among which the individuals of the same species are always friends, though reared in different climates they understand the same language, they shed not each other's blood, they eat not each other's flesh. That part of these rude people who lived on the eastern shores of the island, had from time immemorial tried to destroy those who lived on the west; those latter inspired with the same evil genius, had not been behind hand in retaliating: thus was a perpetual war subsisting between these people, founded on no other reason, but the adventitious place of their nativity and residence. In process of time both parties became so thin and depopulated, that the few who remained, fearing lest their race should become totally extinct, fortunately thought of an expedient which prevented their entire annihilation. Some years before the Europeans came, they mutally agreed to settle a partition line which should divide the island from north to south; the people of the west agreed not to kill those of the east, except they were found transgressing over the western part of the line; those of the last entered into a reciprocal agreement. By these simple means peace was established among them, and this is the only record which seems to entitle them to the denomination of men. This happy settlement put a stop to their sanguinary depredations, none fell afterward but a few rash imprudent individuals; on the contrary, they multiplied greatly. But another misfortune awaited them; when the Europeans came they caught the smallpox, and their improper treatment of that disorder swept away great numbers: this calamity was succeeded by the use of rum; and these are the two principal causes which so much diminished their numbers, not only here but all over the continent. In some places whole nations have disappeared. Some years ago three Indian canoes, on their return to Detroit from the falls of Niagara, unluckily got the smallpox from the Europeans with whom they had traded. It broke out near the long point on Lake Erie, there they all perished; their canoes, and their goods, were afterwards found by some travellers journeying the same way; their dogs were still alive. Besides the smallpox, and the use of spirituous liquors, the two greatest curses they have received from us, there is a sort of physical antipathy, which is equally powerful from one end of the continent to the other. Wherever they happen to be mixed, or even to live in the neighbourhood of the Europeans, they become exposed to a variety of accidents and misfortunes to which they always fall victims: such are particular fevers, to which they were strangers before, and sinking into a singular sort of indolence and sloth. This has been invariably the case wherever the same association has taken place; as at Nattick, Mashpè, Soccanoket in the bounds of Falmouth, Nobscusset, Houra-

tonick, Monhauset, and the Vineyard. Even the Mo-
hawks themselves, who were once so populous, and such
renowned warriors, are now reduced to less than 200
since the European settlements have circumscribed the
territories which their ancestors had reserved. Three
years before the arrival of the Europeans at Cape Cod,
a frightful distemper had swept away a great many
along its coasts, which made the landing and intrusion
of our forefathers much easier than it otherwise might
have been. In the year 1763, above half of the Indians
of this island perished by a strange fever, which the
Europeans who nursed them never caught; they appear
to be a race doomed to recede and disappear before the
superior genius of the Europeans. The only ancient
custom of these people that is remembered is, that in
their mutual exchanges, forty sun-dried clams, strung
on a string, passed for the value of what might be
called a copper. They were strangers to the use and
value of wampum, so well known to those of the main.
The few families now remaining are meek and harmless;
their ancient ferocity is gone: they were early christianised by the New England missionaries, as well as those
of the Vineyard, and of several other parts of Massachusetts; and to this day they remain strict observers
of the laws and customs of that religion, being carefully
taught while young. Their sedentary life has led them
to this degree of civilisation much more effectually, than
if they had still remained hunters. They are fond of
the sea, and expert mariners. They have learned from
the Quakers the art of catching both the cod and whale,
in consequence of which, five of them always make part
of the complement of men requisite to fit out a whale-
boat. Many have removed hither from the Vineyard,
on which account they are more numerous on Nantucket, than anywhere else.

It is strange what revolution has happened among

them in less than two hundred years! What is become of those numerous tribes which formerly inhabited the extensive shores of the great bay of Massachusetts? Even from Numkeag (*Salem*), Saugus (*Lynn*), Shawmut (*Boston*), Pataxet, Napouset (*Milton*), Matapan (*Dorchester*), Winèsimèt (*Chelsea*), Poïasset, Pokànoket (*New Plymouth*), Suecanosset (*Falmouth*), Titicut (*Chatham*), Nobscusset (*Yarmouth*), Naussit (*Eastham*), Hyanneès (*Barnstable*), etc., and many others who lived on seashores of above three hundred miles in length; without mentioning those powerful tribes which once dwelt between the rivers Hudson, Connecticut, Piskàtàquà, and Kènnebèck, the Mèhikaudret, Mohiguine, Pèquods, Narragansets, Nianticks, Massachusetts, Wamponougs, Nipnets, Tarranteens, etc.—They are gone, and every memorial of them is lost; no vestiges whatever are left of those swarms which once inhabited this country, and replenished both sides of the great peninsula of Cape Cod: not even one of the posterity of the famous Masconomèo is left (the sachem of Cape Ann); not one of the descendants of Massasoit, father of Mètacomèt (*Philip*), and Wamsutta (*Alexander*), he who first conveyed some lands to the Plymouth Company. They have all disappeared either in the wars which the Europeans carried on against them, or else they have mouldered away, gathered in some of their ancient towns, in contempt and oblivion: nothing remains of them all, but one extraordinary monument, and even this they owe to the industry and religious zeal of the Europeans, I mean the Bible translated into the Nattick tongue. Many of these tribes giving way to the superior power of the whites, retired to their ancient villages, collecting the scattered remains of nations once populous; and in their grant of lands reserved to themselves and posterity certain portions, which lay contiguous to them. There forgetting their ancient manners, they dwelt in peace;

in a few years their territories were surrounded by the improvements of the Europeans; in consequence of which they grew lazy, inactive, unwilling, and unapt to imitate, or to follow any of our trades, and in a few generations, either totally perished or else came over to the Vineyard, or to this island, to re-unite themselves with such societies of their countrymen as would receive them. Such has been the fate of many nations, once warlike and independent; what we see now on the main, or on those islands, may be justly considered as the only remains of those ancient tribes. Might I be permitted to pay perhaps a very useless compliment to *those* at least who inhabited the great peninsula of Namset, now Cape Cod, with whose names and ancient situation I am well acquainted. This peninsula was divided into two great regions; that on the side of the bay was known by the name of Nobscusset, from one of its towns; the capital was called Nausit (*now Eastham*); hence the Indians of that region were called Nausit Indians, though they dwelt in the villages of Pamet, Nosset, Pashèe, Potomaket, Soktoowoket, Nobscusset (*Yarmouth*).

The region on the Atlantic side was called Mashpèe, and contained the tribes of Hyannèes, Costowet, Waquoit, Scootin, Saconasset, Mashpè, and Namset. Several of these Indian towns have been since converted into flourishing European settlements, known by different names; for as the natives were excellent judges of land, which they had fertilised besides with the shells of their fish, etc., the latter could not make a better choice; though in general this great peninsula is but a sandy pine track, a few good spots excepted. It is divided into seven townships, viz. Barnstable, Yarmouth, Harwich, Chatham, Eastham, Pamet, Namset, or Province town, at the extremity of the Cape. Yet these are very populous, though I am at a loss to conceive on what the inhabitants live, besides clams, oysters, and fish; their piny lands being the most ungrateful soil in the world. The minister of Namset or Province town, receives from the government of Massachusetts a salary of fifty pounds per annum; and such is the poverty of the inhabitants of that place, that, unable to pay him any money, each master of a family is obliged to allow him two hundred horse feet (*sea spin*) with which this primitive priest fertilises the land of his glebe, which he tills himself: for nothing will grow on these hungry soils without the assistance of this extraordinary manure, fourteen bushels of Indian corn being looked upon as a good crop. But it is time to return from a digression, which I hope you will pardon. Nantucket is a great nursery of seamen, pilots, coasters, and bank-fishermen; as a country belonging to the province of Massachusetts, it has yearly the benefit of a court of Common Pleas, and their appeal lies to the supreme court at Boston. I observed before, that the Friends compose two-thirds of the magistracy of this island; thus they are the proprietors of its territory, and the principal rulers of its inhabitants; but with all this apparatus of law, its coercive powers are seldom wanted or required. Seldom is it that any individual is amerced or punished; their jail conveys no terror; no man has lost his life here judicially since the foundation of this town, which is upwards of an hundred years. Solemn tribunals, public executions, humiliating punishments, are altogether unknown. I saw neither governors, nor any pageantry of state; neither ostentatious magistrates, nor any individuals clothed with useless dignity: no artificial phantoms subsist here either civil or religious; no gibbets loaded with guilty citizens offer themselves to your view; no soldiers are appointed to bayonet their compatriots into servile compliance. But how is a society composed of 5000 individuals preserved in the bonds of peace and tranquillity? How are the weak protected from the strong?—I will tell you. Idleness and poverty, the causes of so many crimes, are unknown here; each seeks in the prosecution of his lawful business that honest gain which supports them; every period of their time is full, either on shore or at sea. A probable expectation of reasonable profits, or of kindly assistance, if they fail of success, renders them strangers to licentious expedients. The simplicity of their manners shortens the catalogues of their wants; the law at a distance is ever ready to exert itself in the protection of those who stand in need of its assistance. The greatest part of them are always at sea, pursuing the whale or raising the cod from the surface of the banks: some cultivate their little farms with the utmost diligence; some are employed in exercising various trades; others again in providing every necessary resource in order to refit their vessels, or repair what misfortunes may happen, looking out for future markets, etc. Such is the rotation of those different scenes of business which fill the measure of their days; of that part of their lives at least which is enlivened by health, spirits, and vigour. It is but seldom that vice grows on a barren sand like this, which produces nothing without extreme labour. How could the common follies of society take root in so despicable a soil; they generally thrive on its exuberant juices: here there are none but those which administer to the useful, to the necessary, and to the indispensable comforts of life. This land must necessarily either produce health, temperance, and a great equality of conditions, or the most abject misery. Could the manners of luxurious countries be imported here, like an epidemical disorder they would destroy everything; the majority of them could not exist a month, they would be obliged to emigrate. As in all societies except that of the natives, some difference must necessarily exist between individual and individual, for there must be some more exalted than the rest either by their riches or their talents; so in *this,* there are what you might call the high, the middling, and the low; and this difference will always be more remarkable among people who live by sea excursions than among those who live by the cultivation of their land. The first run greater hazard, and adventure more: the profits and the misfortunes attending this mode of life must necessarily introduce a greater disparity than among the latter, where the equal divisions of the land offers no short road to superior riches. The only difference that may arise among them is that of industry, and perhaps of superior goodness of soil: the gradations I observed here, are founded on nothing more than the good or ill success of their maritime enterprises, and do not proceed from education; that is the same throughout every class, simple, useful, and unadorned like their dress and their houses. This necessary difference in their fortunes does not however cause those heart burnings, which in other societies generate crimes. The sea which surrounds them is equally open to all, and presents to all an equal title to the chance of good fortune. A collector from Boston is the only king's officer who appears on these shores to receive the trifling duties which this community owe to those who protect them, and under the shadow of whose wings they navigate to all parts of the world.

LETTER V

CUSTOMARY EDUCATION AND EMPLOYMENT OF THE INHABITANTS OF NANTUCKET

THE easiest way of becoming acquainted with the modes of thinking, the rules of conduct, and the prevailing manners of any people, is to examine what sort of education they give their children; how they treat them at home, and what they are taught in their places of public worship. At home their tender minds must be early struck with the gravity, the serious though cheerful deportment of their parents; they are inured to a principle of subordination, arising neither from sudden passions nor inconsiderate pleasure; they are gently held by an uniform silk cord, which unites softness and strength. A perfect equanimity prevails in most of their families, and bad example hardly ever sows in their hearts the seeds of future and similar faults. They are corrected with tenderness, nursed with the most affectionate care, clad with that decent plainness, from which they observe their parents never to depart: in short, by the force of example, which is superior even to the strongest instinct of nature, more than by precepts, they learn to follow the steps of their parents, to despise ostentatiousness as being sinful. They acquire a taste for neatness for which their fathers are so conspicuous; they learn to be prudent and saving; the very tone of voice with which they are always addressed, establishes in them that softness of diction, which ever after becomes habitual. Frugal, sober, orderly parents, attached to their business, constantly following some useful occupation, never guilty of riot, dissipation, or other irregularities, cannot fail of training up children to the same uniformity of life and manners. If they are left with fortunes, they are taught how to save them, and how to enjoy them with moderation and decency; if they have none, they know how to venture, how to work and toil as their fathers have done before them. If they fail of success, there are always in this island (and wherever this society prevails) established resources, founded on the most benevolent principles. At their meetings they are taught the few, the simple tenets of their sect; tenets as fit to render men sober, industrious, just, and merciful, as those delivered in the most magnificent churches and cathedrals: they are instructed in the most essential duties of Christianity, so as not to offend the Divinity by the commission of evil deeds; to dread his wrath and the punishments he has denounced; they are taught at the same time to have a proper confidence in his mercy while they deprecate his justice. As every sect, from their different modes of worship, and their different interpretations of some parts of the Scriptures, necessarily have various opinions and prejudices, which contribute something in forming their characters in society; so those of the Friends are well known: obedience to the laws, even to non-resistance, justice, goodwill to all, benevolence at home, sobriety, meekness, neatness, love of order, fondness and appetite for commerce. They are as remarkable here for those virtues as at Philadelphia, which is their American cradle, and the boast of that society. At schools they learn to read, and to write a good hand, until they are twelve years old; they are then in general put apprentices to the cooper's trade, which is the second essential branch of business followed here; at fourteen they are sent to sea, where in their leisure hours their companions teach them the art of navigation, which they have an opportunity of practising on the spot. They learn the great and useful art of working a ship in all the different situations which the sea and wind so often require; and surely there cannot be a better or a more useful school of that kind in the world. Then they go gradually through every station of rowers, steersmen, and harpooners; thus they learn to attack, to pursue, to overtake, to cut, to dress their huge game: and after having performed several such voyages, and perfected themselves in this business, they are fit either for the counting house or the chase.

The first proprietors of this island, or rather the first founders of this town, began their career of industry with a single whale-boat, with which they went to fish for cod; the small distance from their shores at which they caught it, enabled them soon to increase their business, and those early successes first led them to conceive that they might likewise catch the whales, which hitherto sported undisturbed on their banks. After many trials and several miscarriages, they succeeded; thus they proceeded, step by step; the profits of one successful enterprise helped them to purchase and prepare better materials for a more extensive one: as these were attended with little costs, their profits grew greater. The south sides of the island from east to west, were divided into four equal parts, and each part was assigned to a company of six, which though thus separated, still carried on their business in common. In the middle of this distance, they erected a mast, provided with a sufficient number of rounds, and near it they built a temporary hut, where five of the associates lived, whilst the sixth from his high station carefully looked toward the sea, in order to observe the spouting of the whales. As soon as any were discovered, the sentinel descended, the whale-boat was launched, and the company went forth in quest of their game. It may appear strange to you, that so slender a vessel as an *American whale-boat,* containing six diminutive beings, should dare to pursue and to attack, in its native element, the largest and strongest fish that nature has created. Yet by the exertions of an admirable dexterity, improved by a long practice, in which these people are become superior to any other whalemen; by knowing the temper of the whale after her first movement, and by many other useful observations; they seldom failed to harpoon it, and to bring the huge leviathan on the shores. Thus they went on until the profits they made, enabled them to purchase larger vessels, and to pursue them farther, when the whales quitted their coasts; those who failed in their enterprises, returned to the cod-fisheries, which had been their first school, and their first resource; they even began to visit the banks of Cape Breton, the isle of Sable, and all the other fishing places, with which this coast of America abounds. By degrees they went a-whaling to Newfoundland, to the Gulf of St. Lawrence, to the Straits of Belleisle, the coast of Labrador, Davis's Straits, even to Cape Desolation, in 70° of latitude; where the Danes carry on some fisheries in spite of the perpetual severities of the inhospitable climate. In process of time they visited the western islands, the latitude of 34° famous for that fish, the Brazils, the coast of Guinea. Would you believe that they have already gone to the Falkland Islands, and that I have heard several of them talk of going to the South Sea! Their confidence is so great, and their knowledge of this branch of business so superior to that of any other people, that they have acquired a monopoly of this commodity. Such were their feeble beginnings, such the infancy and the progress of their maritime schemes; such is now the degree of boldness and activity to which they are arrived in their manhood. After their examples several companies have been formed in many of our capitals, where every necessary article of provisions, implements, and timber, are to be found. But the industry exerted by the people of Nantucket, hath hitherto enabled them to rival all their competitors; consequently this is the greatest mart for oil, whalebone, and spermaceti, on the continent. It does not follow however that they are always successful, this would be an extraordinary field indeed, where the crops should never fail; many voyages do not repay the original cost of fitting out: they bear such misfortunes like true merchants, and as they never venture their all like gamesters, they try their fortunes again; the latter hope to win by chance alone, the former by industry, well judged speculation, and some hazard. I was there when Mr. —— had missed one of his vessels; she had been given over for lost by everybody, but happily arrived before I came away, after an absence of thirteen months. She had met with a variety of disappointments on the station she was ordered to, and rather than return empty, the people steered for the coast of Guinea, where they fortunately fell in with several whales, and brought home upward of 600 barrels of oil, beside bone. Those returns are sometimes disposed of in the towns on the continent, where they are exchanged for such commodities as are wanted; but they are most commonly sent to England, where they always sell for cash. When this is intended, a vessel larger than the rest is fitted out to be filled with oil on the spot where it is found and made, and thence she sails immediately for London. This expedient saves time, freight, and expense; and from that capital they bring back whatever they want. They employ also several vessels in transporting lumber to the West Indian Islands, from whence they procure in return the various productions of the country, which they afterwards exchange wherever they can hear of an advantageous market. Being extremely acute they well know how to improve all the advantages which the combination of so many branches of business constantly affords; the spirit of commerce, which is the simple art of a reciprocal supply of wants, is well understood here by everybody. They possess, like the generality of Americans, a large share of native penetration, activity, and good sense, which lead them to a variety of other secondary schemes too tedious to mention: they are well acquainted with the cheapest method of procuring lumber from Kennebeck river, Penobscot, etc., pitch and tar, from North Carolina; flour and biscuit, from Philadelphia; beef and pork, from Connecticut. They know how to exchange their cod fish and West-Indian produce, for those articles which they are continually either bringing to their island, or sending off to other places where they are wanted. By means of all these commercial negotiations, they have greatly cheapened the fitting out of their whaling fleets, and therefore much improved their fisheries. They are indebted for all these advantages not only to their national genius but to the poverty of their soil; and as proof of what I have so often advanced, look at the Vineyard (their neighbouring island) which is inhabited by a set of people as keen and as sagacious as themselves. Their soil being in general extremely fertile, they have fewer navigators; though they are equally well situated for the fishing business. As in my way back to Falmouth on the main, I visited this sister island, permit me to give you as concisely as I can, a short but true description of it; I am not so limited in the principal object of this journey, as to wish to confine myself to the single spot of Nantucket.

LETTER VI

THIS island is twenty miles in length, and from seven to eight miles in breadth. It lies nine miles from the continent, and with the Elizabeth Islands forms one of the counties of Massachusetts Bay, known by the name of Duke's County. Those latter, which are six in number, are about nine miles distant from the Vineyard, and are all famous for excellent dairies. A good ferry is established between the Edgar Town, and Falmouth on the main, the distance being nine miles. Martha's Vineyard is divided into three townships, viz. Edgar, Chilmark, and Tisbury; the number of inhabitants is computed at about 4000, 300 of which are Indians. Edgar is the best seaport, and the shire town, and as its soil is light and sandy, many of its inhabitants follow the example of the people of Nantucket. The town of Chilmark has no good harbour, but the land is excellent and no way inferior to any on the continent: it contains excellent pastures, convenient brooks for mills, stone for fencing, etc. The town of Tisbury is remarkable for the excellence of its timber, and has a harbour where the water is deep enough for ships of the line. The stock of the island is 20,000 sheep, 2000 neat cattle, beside horses and goats; they have also some deer, and abundance of sea-fowls. This has been from the beginning, and is to this day, the principal seminary of the Indians; they live on that part of the island which is called Chapoquidick, and were very early Christianised by the respectable family of the Mahews, the first proprietors of it. The first settler of that name conveyed by will to a favourite daughter a certain part of it, on which there grew many wild vines; thence it was called Martha's Vineyard, after her name, which in process of time extended to the whole island. The posterity of the ancient Aborigines remain here to this day, on lands which their forefathers reserved for themselves, and which are religiously kept from any encroachments. The New England people are remarkable for the honesty with which they have fulfilled, all over that province, those ancient covenants which in many others have been disregarded, to the scandal of those governments. The Indians there appeared, by the decency of their manners, their industry, and neatness, to be wholly Europeans, and nowise inferior to many of the inhabitants. Like them they are sober, laborious, and religious, which are the principal characteristics of the four New England provinces. They often go, like the young men of the Vineyard, to Nantucket, and hire themselves for whalemen or fishermen; and indeed their skill and dexterity in all sea affairs is nothing inferior to that of the whites. The latter are divided into two classes, the first occupy the land, which they till with admirable care and knowledge; the second, who are possessed of none, apply themselves to the sea, the general resource of mankind in this part of the world. This island therefore, like Nantucket, is become a great nursery which supplies with pilots and seamen the numerous coasters with which this extended part of America abounds. Go where you will from Nova Scotia to the Mississippi, you will find almost everywhere some natives of these two islands employed in seafaring occupations. Their climate is so favourable to population, that marriage is the object of every man's earliest wish; and it is a blessing so easily obtained that great numbers are obliged to quit their native land and go to some other countries in

quest of subsistence. The inhabitants are all Presbyterians, which is the established religion of Massachusetts; and here let me remember with gratitude the
hospitable treatment I received from B. Norton, Esq.,
the colonel of the island, as well as from Dr. Mahew, the
lineal descendant of the first proprietor. Here are to be
found the most expert pilots, either for the great bay,
their sound, Nantucket shoals, or the different ports in
their neighbourhood. In stormy weather they are always
at sea, looking out for vessels, which they board with
singular dexterity, and hardly ever fail to bring safe to
their intended harbour. Gay-Head, the western point
of this island, abounds with a variety of ochres of
different colours, with which the inhabitants paint their
houses.

The vessels most proper for whale fishing are brigs
of about 150 tons burthen, particularly when they are
intended for distant latitudes; they always man them
with thirteen hands, in order that they may row two
whale-boats; the crews of which must necessarily consist of six, four at the oars, one standing on the bows
with the harpoon, and the other at the helm. It is also
necessary that there should be two of these boats, that
if one should be destroyed in attacking the whale, the
other, which is never engaged at the same time, may
be ready to save the hands. Five of the thirteen are
always Indians; the last of the complement remains on
board to steer the vessel during the action. They have
no wages; each draws a certain established share in
partnership with the proprietor of the vessel; by which
economy they are all proportionately concerned in the
success of the enterprise, and all equally alert and
vigilant. None of these whalemen ever exceed the age of
forty: they look on those who are past that period not
to be possessed of all that vigour and agility which
so adventurous a business requires. Indeed if you at-

.tentively consider the immense disproportion between the object assailed and the assailants; if you think on the diminutive size, and weakness of their frail vehicle; if you recollect the treachery of the element on which this scene is transacted; the sudden and unforeseen accidents of winds, etc., you will readily acknowledge that it must require the most consummate exertion of all the strength, agility, and judgment, of which the bodies and minds of men are capable, to undertake these adventurous encounters.

As soon as they arrive in those latitudes where they expect to meet with whales, a man is sent up to the mast head; if he sees one, he immediately cries out AWAITE PAWANA, *here is a whale;* they all remain still and silent until he repeats PAWANA, *a whale,* when in less than six minutes the two boats are launched, filled with every implement necessary for the attack. They row toward the whale with astonishing velocity; and as the Indians early became their fellow-labourers in this new warfare, you can easily conceive how the Nattick expressions became familiar on board the whale-boats. Formerly it often happened that whale vessels were manned with none but Indians and the master; recollect also that the Nantucket people understand the Nattick, and that there are always five of these people on board. There are various ways of approaching the whale, according to their peculiar species; and this previous knowledge is of the utmost consequence. When these boats are arrived at a reasonable distance, one of them rests on its oars and stands off, as a witness of the approaching engagement; near the bows of the other the harpooner stands up, and on him principally depends the success of the enterprise. He wears a jacket closely buttoned, and round his head a handkerchief tightly bound: in his hands he holds the dreadful weapon, made of the best steel, marked sometimes with the name of their town, and sometimes with that of their vessel; to the shaft of which the end of a cord of due length, coiled up with the utmost care in the middle of the boat, is firmly tied; the other end is fastened to the bottom of the boat. Thus prepared they row in profound silence, leaving the whole conduct of the enterprise to the harpooner and to the steersman, attentively following their directions. When the former judges himself to be near enough to the whale, that is, at the distance of about fifteen feet, he bids them stop; perhaps she has a calf, whose safety attracts all the attention of the dam, which is a favourable circumstance; perhaps she is of a dangerous species, and it is safest to retire, though their ardour will seldom permit them; perhaps she is asleep, in that case he balances high the harpoon, trying in this important moment to collect all the energy of which he is capable. He launches it forth—she is struck: from her first movements they judge of her temper, as well as of their future success. Sometimes in the immediate impulse of rage, she will attack the boat and demolish it with one stroke of her tail; in an instant the frail vehicle disappears and the assailants are immersed in the dreadful element. Were the whale armed with the jaws of a shark, and as voracious, they never would return home to amuse their listening wives with the interesting tale of the adventure. At other times she will dive and disappear from human sight; and everything must give way to her velocity, or else all is lost. Sometimes she will swim away as if untouched, and draw the cord with such swiftness that it will set the edge of the boat on fire by the friction. If she rises before she has run out the whole length, she is looked upon as a sure prey. The blood she has lost in her flight, weakens her so much, that if she sinks again, it is but for a short time; the boat follows her course with almost equal speed. She soon re-appears; tired at last with convulsing the element; which she tinges with her blood, she dies, and floats on the surface. At other times it may happen that she is not dangerously wounded, though she carries the harpoon fast in her body; when she will alternately dive and rise, and swim on with unabated vigour. She then soon reaches beyond the length of the cord, and carries the boat along with amazing velocity: this sudden impediment sometimes will retard her speed, at other times it only serves to rouse her anger, and to accelerate her progress. The harpooner, with the axe in his hands, stands ready. When he observes that the bows of the boat are greatly pulled down by the diving whale, and that it begins to sink deep and to take much water, he brings the axe almost in contact with the cord; he pauses, still flattering himself that she will relax; but the moment grows critical, unavoidable danger approaches: sometimes men more intent on gain, than on the preservation of their lives, will run great risks; and it is wonderful how far these people have carried their daring courage at this awful moment! But it is vain to hope, their lives must be saved, the cord is cut, the boat rises again. If after thus getting loose, she re-appears, they will attack and wound her a second time. She soon dies, and when dead she is towed alongside of their vessel, where she is fastened.

The next operation is to cut with axes and spades, every part of her body which yields oil; the kettles are set a boiling, they fill their barrels as fast as it is made; but as this operation is much slower than that of *cutting up*, they fill the hold of their ship with those fragments, lest a storm should arise and oblige them to abandon their prize. It is astonishing what a quantity of oil some of these fish will yield, and what profit it affords to those who are fortunate enough to overtake them. The river St. Lawrence whale, which is the only one I am well acquainted with, is seventy-five feet long, sixteen deep, twelve in the length of its bone, which commonly weighs 3000 lbs., twenty in the breadth of their tails and produces 180 barrels of oil: I once saw 16 boiled out of the tongue only. After having once vanquished this leviathan, there are two enemies to be dreaded beside the wind; the first of which is the shark: that fierce voracious fish, to which nature has given such dreadful offensive weapons, often comes alongside, and in spite of the people's endeavours, will share with them their prey; at night particularly. They are very mischievious, but the second enemy is much more terrible and irresistible; it is the killer, sometimes called the thrasher, a species of whales about thirty feet long. They are possessed of such a degree of agility and fierceness, as often to attack the largest spermaceti whales, and not seldom to rob the fishermen of their prey; nor is there any means of defence against so potent an adversary. When all their barrels are full, for everything is done at sea, or when their limited time is expired and their stores almost expended, they return home, freighted with their valuable cargo; unless they have put it on board a vessel for the European market. Such are, as briefly as I can relate them, the different branches of the economy practised by these bold navigators, and the method with which they go such distances from their island to catch this huge game.

The following are the names and principal characteristics of the various species of whales known to these people:

The St. Lawrence whale, just described.

The disko, or Greenland ditto.

The right whale, or seven feet bone, common on the coasts of this country, about sixty feet long.

The spermaceti whale, found all over the world, and of all sizes; the longest are sixty feet, and yield about 100 barrels of oil.

The hump-backs, on the coast of Newfoundland, from forty to seventy feet in length.

The finn-back, an American whale, never killed, as being too swift.

The sulphur-bottom, river St. Lawrence, ninety foot long; they are but seldom killed, as being extremely swift.

The grampus, thirty feet long, never killed on the same account.

The killer or thrasher, about thirty feet; they often kill the other whales with which they are at perpetual war.

The black fish whale, twenty feet, yields from eight to ten barrels.

The porpoise, weighing about 160 lb.

In 1769 they fitted out 125 whalemen; the first fifty that returned brought with them 11,000 barrels of oil. In 1770 they fitted out 135 vessels for the fisheries, at thirteen hands each; four West-Indiamen, twelve hands; twenty-five wood vessels, four hands; eighteen coasters, five hands; fifteen London traders, eleven hands. All these amount to 2158 hands, employed in 197 vessels. Trace their progressive steps between the possession of a few whale-boats, and that of such a fleet!

The moral conduct, prejudices, and customs of a people who live two-thirds of their time at sea, must naturally be very different from those of their neighbours, who live by cultivating the earth. That long abstemiousness to which the former are exposed, the breathing of saline air, the frequent repetitions of danger, the boldness acquired in surmounting them, the very impulse of the winds, to which they are exposed; all these, one would imagine must lead them, when on shore, to no small desire of inebriation, and a more eager pursuit of those pleasures, of which they have been so long deprived, and which they must soon forego. There are many appetites that may be gratified on shore, even by the poorest man, but which must remain unsatisfied at sea. Yet notwithstanding the powerful effects of all these causes, I observed here, at the return of their fleets, no material irregularities; no tumultuous drinking assemblies: whereas in our continental towns, the thoughtless seaman indulges himself in the coarsest pleasures; and vainly thinking that a week of debauchery can compensate for months of abstinence, foolishly lavishes in a few days of intoxication, the fruits of half a year's labour. On the contrary all was peace here, and a general decency prevailed throughout; the reason I believe is, that almost everybody here is married, for they get wives very young; and the pleasure of returning to their families absorbs every other desire. The motives that lead them to the sea, are very different from those of most other sea-faring men; it is neither idleness nor profligacy that sends them to that element; it is a settled plan of life, a well founded hope of earning a livelihood; it is because their soil is bad, that they are early initiated to this profession, and were they to stay at home, what could they do? The sea therefore becomes to them a kind of patrimony; they go to whaling with as much pleasure and tranquil indifference, with as strong an expectation of success, as a landsman undertakes to clear a piece of swamp. The first is obliged to advance his time, and labour, to procure oil on the surface of the sea; the second advances the same to procure himself grass from grounds that produced nothing before but hassocks and bogs. Among those who do not use the sea, I observed the same calm appearance as among the inhabitants on the continent; here I found, without gloom, a decorum and reserve, so natural to them, that I thought myself in Philadelphia. At my landing I was cordially received by those to whom I was recommended, and treated with unaffected hospitality by such others with whom I became acquainted; and I can tell you, that it is impossible for any traveller to dwell here one month without knowing the heads of the principal families. Wherever I went I found a simplicity of diction and manners, rather more primitive and rigid than I expected; and I soon perceived that it proceeded from their secluded situation, which has prevented them from mixing with others. It is therefore easy to conceive how they have retained every degree of peculiarity for which this sect was formerly distinguished. Never was a bee-hive more faithfully employed in gathering wax, bee-bread, and honey, from all the neighbouring fields, than are the members of this society; every one in the town follows some particular occupation with great diligence, but without that servility of labour which I am informed prevails in Europe. The mechanic seemed to be descended from as good parentage, was as well dressed and fed, and held in as much estimation as those who employed him; they were once nearly related; their different degrees of prosperity is what has caused the various shades of their community. But this accidental difference has introduced, as yet, neither arrogance nor pride on the one part, nor meanness and servility on the other. All their houses are neat, convenient, and comfortable; some of them are filled with two families, for when the husbands are at sea, the wives require less house-room. They all abound with the most substantial furniture, more valuable from its usefulness than from any ornamental appearance. Wherever I went, I found good cheer, a welcome reception; and after the second visit I felt myself as much at my ease as if I had been an old acquaintance of the family. They had as great plenty of everything as if their island had been part of the golden quarter of Virginia (a valuable track of land on Cape Charles): I could hardly persuade myself that I had quitted the adjacent continent, where everything abounds, and that I was on a barren sandbank, fertilised with whale oil only. As their rural improvements are but trifling, and only of the useful kind, and as the best of them are at a considerable distance from the town, I amused myself for several days in conversing with the most intelligent of the inhabitants of both sexes, and making myself acquainted with the various branches of their industry; the different objects of their trade; the nature of that sagacity which, deprived as they are of every necessary material, produce, etc., yet enables them to flourish, to live well, and sometimes to make considerable fortunes. The whole is an enigma to be solved only by coming to the spot and observing the national genius which the original founders brought with them, as well as their unwearied patience and perseverance. They have all, from the highest to the lowest, a singular keenness of judgment, unassisted by any academical light; they all possess a large share of good sense, improved upon the experience of their fathers; and this is the surest and best guide to lead us through the path of life, because it approaches nearest to the infallibility of instinct. Shining talents and University knowledge, would be entirely useless here, nay, would be dangerous; it would pervert their plain judgment, it would lead them out of that useful path which is so well adapted to their situation; it would make them more adventurous, more presumptuous, much less cautious, and therefore less successful. It is pleasing to hear some of them tracing a father's progress and their own, through the different vicissitudes of good and adverse fortune. I have often, by their fire-sides, travelled with them the whole length of their career, from their earliest steps, from their first commercial adventure, from the possession of a single whale-boat, up to that of a dozen large vessels! This does not imply, however, that every one who began with a whale-boat, has ascended to a like pitch of fortune; by no means, the same casualty, the same combination of good and evil which attends human affairs in every other part of the globe, prevails here: a great prosperity is not the lot of every man, but there are many and various gradations; if they all do not attain riches, they all attain an easy subsistence. After all, is it not better to be possessed of a single whale-boat, or a few sheep pastures; to live free and independent under the mildest governments, in a healthy climate, in a land of charity and benevolence; than to be wretched as so many are in Europe, possessing nothing but their industry: tossed from one rough wave to another; engaged either in the most servile labours for the smallest pittance, or fettered with the links of the most irksome dependence, even without the hopes of rising?

The majority of those inferior hands which are employed in this fishery, many of the mechanics, such as coopers, smiths, caulkers, carpenters, etc., who do not belong to the society of Friends, are Presbyterians, and originally came from the main. Those who are possessed of the greatest fortunes at present belong to the former; but they all began as simple whalemen: it is even looked upon as honourable and necessary for the son of the wealthiest man to serve an apprenticeship to the same bold, adventurous business which has enriched his father; they go several voyages, and these early excursions never fail to harden their constitutions, and introduce them to the knowledge of their future means of subsistence.

LETTER VII

As I observed before, every man takes a wife as soon as he chooses, and that is generally very early; no portion is required, none is expected; no marriage articles are drawn up among us, by skilful lawyers, to puzzle and lead posterity to the bar, or to satisfy the pride of the parties. We give nothing with our daughters, their education, their health, and the customary out-set, are all that the fathers of numerous families can afford: as the wife's fortune consists principally in her future economy, modesty, and skilful management; so the husband's is founded on his abilities to labour, on his health, and the knowledge of some trade or business. Their mutual endeavours, after a few years of constant application, seldom fail of success, and of bringing them the means to rear and support the new race which accompanies the nuptial bed. Those children born by the sea-side, hear the roaring of its waves as soon as they are able to listen; it is the first noise with which they become acquainted, and by early plunging in it they acquire that boldness, that presence of mind, and dexterity, which makes them ever after such expert seamen. They often hear their fathers recount the adventures of their youth, their combats with the whales; and these recitals imprint on their opening minds an early curiosity and taste for the same life. They often cross the sea to go to the main, and learn even in those short voyages how to qualify themselves for longer and more dangerous ones; they are therefore deservedly conspicuous for their maritime knowledge and experience, all over the continent. A man born here is distinguishable by his gait from among

126

an hundred other men, so remarkable are they for a pliability of sinews, and a peculiar agility, which attends them even to old age. I have heard some persons attribute this to the effects of the whale oil, with which they are so copiously anointed in the various operations it must undergo ere it is fit either for the European market or the candle manufactory.

But you may perhaps be solicitous to ask, what becomes of that exuberancy of population which must arise from so much temperance, from healthiness of climate, and from early marriage? You may justly conclude that their native island and town can contain but a limited number. Emigration is both natural and easy to a maritime people, and that is the very reason why they are always populous, problematical as it may appear. They yearly go to different parts of this continent, constantly engaged in sea affairs; as our internal riches increase, so does our external trade, which consequently requires more ships and more men: sometimes they have emigrated like bees, in regular and connected swarms. Some of the Friends (by which word I always mean the people called Quakers) fond of a contemplative life, yearly visit the several congregations which this society has formed throughout the continent. By their means a sort of correspondence is kept up among them all; they are generally good preachers, friendly censors, checking vice wherever they find it predominating; preventing relaxations in any parts of their ancient customs and worship. They everywhere carry admonition and useful advice; and by thus travelling they unavoidably gather the most necessary observations concerning the various situations of particular districts, their soils, their produce, their distance from navigable rivers, the price of land, etc. In consequence of informations of this kind, received at Nantucket in the year 1766, a considerable number of them purchased a large track of land in the

county of Orange, in North Carolina, situated on the
several spring heads of *Deep River,* which is the western
branch of Cape Fear, or North-West River. The advantage of being able to convey themselves by sea, to
within forty miles of the spot, the richness of the soil.
etc., made them cheerfully quit an island on which there
was no longer any room for them. There they have
founded a beautiful settlement, known by the name of
New Garden, contiguous to the famous one which the
Moravians have at Bethabara, Bethamia, and Salem, on
Yadkin River. No spot of earth can be more beautiful;
it is composed of gentle hills, of easy declivities, excellent low lands, accompanied by different brooks which
traverse this settlement. I never saw a soil that rewards
men so early for their labours and disbursements; such
in general with very few exceptions, are the lands which
adjoin the innumerable heads of all the large rivers
which fall into the Chesapeak, or flow through the provinces of North and South Carolina, Georgia, etc. It is
perhaps the most pleasing, the most bewitching country
which the continent affords; because while it preserves
an easy communication with the sea-port towns, at some
seasons of the year, it is perfectly free from the conta-
gious air often breathed in those flat countries, which
are more contiguous to the Atlantic. These lands are as
rich as those over the Alleghany; the people of New
Garden are situated at the distance of between 200 and
300 miles from Cape Fear; Cape Fear is at least 450 from
Nantucket: you may judge therefore that they have but
little correspondence with this their little metropolis,
except it is by means of the itinerant Friends. Others
have settled on the famous river Kennebeck, in that territory of the province of Massachusetts, which is known
by the name of Sagadahock. Here they have softened the
labours of clearing the heaviest timbered land in America, by means of several branches of trade which their

fair river, and proximity to the sea affords them. Instead of entirely consuming their timber, as we are obliged to do, some parts of it are converted into useful articles for exportation, such as staves, scantlings, boards, hoops, poles, etc. For that purpose they keep a correspondence with their native island, and I know many of the principal inhabitants of Sherburn, who, though merchants, and living at Nantucket, yet possess valuable farms on that river; from whence they draw great part of their subsistence, meat, grain, fire-wood, etc. The title of these lands is vested in the ancient Plymouth Company, under the powers of which the Massachusetts was settled; and that company which resides in Boston, are still the granters of all the vacant lands within their limits.

Although this part of the province is so fruitful, and so happily situated, yet it has been singularly overlooked and neglected: it is surprising that the excellence of that soil which lies on the river should not have caused it to be filled before now with inhabitants; for the settlements from thence to Penobscot are as yet but in their infancy. It is true that immense labour is required to make room for the plough, but the peculiar strength and quality of the soil never fails most amply to reward the industrious possessor; I know of no soil in this country more rich or more fertile. I do not mean that sort of transitory fertility which evaporates with the sun, and disappears in a few years; here on the contrary, even their highest grounds are covered with a rich moist swamp mould, which bears the most luxuriant grass, and never-failing crops of grain.

If New Gardens exceeds this settlement by the softness of its climate, the fecundity of its soil, and a greater variety of produce from less labour; it does not breed men equally hardy, nor capable to encounter dangers and fatigues. It leads too much to idleness and effeminacy; for great is the luxuriance of that part of America, and the ease with which the earth is cultivated. Were I to begin life again, I would prefer the country of Kennebeck to the other, however bewitching; the navigation of the river for above 200 miles, the great abundance of fish it contains, the constant healthiness of the climate, the happy severities of the winters always sheltering the earth with a voluminous coat of snow, the equally happy necessity of labour: all these reasons would greatly preponderate against the softer situations of Carolina; where mankind reaps too much, does not toil enough, and is liable to enjoy too fast the benefits of life. There are many I know who would despise my opinion, and think me a bad judge; let those go and settle at the Ohio, the Monongahela, Red Stone Creek, etc., let them go and inhabit the extended shores of that superlative river; I with equal cheerfulness would pitch my tent on the rougher shores of Kennebeck; this will always be a country of health, labour, and strong activity, and those are characteristics of society which I value more than greater opulence and voluptuous ease.

Thus though this fruitful hive constantly sends out swarms, as industrious as themselves, yet it always remains full without having any useless drones: on the contrary it exhibits constant scenes of business and new schemes; the richer an individual grows, the more extensive his field of action becomes; he that is near ending his career, drudges on as well as he who has just begun it; nobody stands still. But is it not strange, that after having accumulated riches, they should never wish to exchange their barren situation for a more sheltered, more pleasant one on the main? Is it not strange, that after having spent the morning and the meridian of their days amidst the jarring waves, weary with the toils of a laborious life, they should not wish to enjoy the evenings of those days of industry in a larger society, on some spots of terra firma, where the severity of the winters is balanced by a variety of more pleasing scenes, not to be found here? But the same magical power of habit and custom which makes the Laplander, the Siberian, the Hottentot, prefer their climates, their occupations, and their soil, to more beneficial situations, leads these good people to think, that no other spot on the globe is so analagous to their inclinations as Nantucket. Here their connections are formed; what would they do at a distance removed from them? Live sumptuously, you will say, procure themselves new friends, new acquaintances, by their splendid tables, by their ostentatious generosity, and by affected hospitality. These are thoughts that have never entered into their heads; they would be filled with horror at the thought of forming wishes and plans so different from that simplicity, which is their general standard in affluence as well as in poverty. They abhor the very idea of expending in useless waste and vain luxuries, the fruits of prosperous labour; they are employed in establishing their sons and in many other useful purposes: strangers to the honours of monarchy they do not aspire to the possession of affluent fortunes, with which to purchase sounding titles, and frivolous names!

Yet there are not at Nantucket so many wealthy people as one would imagine after having considered their great successes, their industry, and their knowledge. Many die poor, though hardly able to reproach Fortune with a frown; others leave not behind them that affluence which the circle of their business and of their prosperity naturally promised. The reason of this is, I believe, the peculiar expense necessarily attending their tables; for as their island supplies the town with little or nothing (a few families excepted) every one must procure what they want from the main. The very hay their horses consume, and every other article necessary to support a family, though cheap in a country of so great abundance as Massachusetts; yet the necessary waste and expenses attending their transport, render these commodities dear. A vast number of little vessels from the main, and from the Vineyard, are constantly resorting here, as to a market. Sherburn is extremely well supplied with everything, but this very constancy of supply, necessarily drains off a great deal of money. The first use they make of their oil and bone is to exchange it for bread and meat, and whatever else they want; the necessities of a large family are very great and numerous, let its economy be what it will; they are so often repeated, that they perpetually draw off a considerable branch of the profits. If by any accidents those profits are interrupted, the capital must suffer; and it very often happens that the greatest part of their property is floating on the sea.

There are but two congregations in this town. They assemble every Sunday in meeting houses, as simple as the dwelling of the people; and there is but one priest on the whole island. What would a good Portuguese observe?—But one single priest to instruct a whole island, and to direct their consciences! It is even so; each individual knows how to guide his own, and is content to do it, as well as he can. This lonely clergyman is a Presbyterian minister, who has a very large and respectable congregation; the other is composed of Quakers, who you know admit of no particular person, who in consequence of being ordained becomes exclusively entitled to preach, to catechise, and to receive certain salaries for his trouble. Among them, every one may expound the Scriptures, who thinks he is called so to do; beside, as they admit of neither sacrament, baptism, nor any other outward forms whatever, such a man would be useless. Most of these people are continually at sea, and have often the most urgent reasons to worship the Parent of Nature in the midst of the storms which they encounter. These two sects live in perfect peace and harmony with each other; those ancient times of religious discords are now gone (I hope never to return) when each thought it meritorious, not only to damn the other, which would have been nothing, but to persecute and murther one another, for the glory of that Being, who requires no more of us, than that we should love one another and live! Every one goes to that place of worship which he likes best, and thinks not that his neighbour does wrong by not following him; each busily employed in their temporal affairs, is less vehement about spiritual ones, and fortunately you will find at Nantucket neither idle drones, voluptuous devotees, ranting enthusiasts, nor sour demagogues. I wish I had it in my power to send the most persecuting bigot I could find in —— to the whale fisheries; in less than three or four years you would find him a much more tractable man, and therefore a better Christian.

Singular as it may appear to you, there are but two medical professors on the island; for of what service can physic be in a primitive society, where the excesses of inebriation are so rare? What need of galenical medicines, where fevers, and stomachs loaded by the loss of the digestive powers, are so few? Temperance, the calm of passions, frugality, and continual exercise, keep them healthy, and preserve unimpaired that constitution which they have received from parents as healthy as themselves; who in the unpolluted embraces of the earliest and chastest love, conveyed to them the soundest bodily frame which nature could give. But as no habitable part of this globe is exempt from some diseases, proceeding either from climate or modes of living; here they are sometimes subject to consumptions and to fevers. Since the foundation of that town no epidemical distempers have appeared, which at times cause such depopulations in other countries; many of them are extremely well acquainted with the Indian methods of

curing simple diseases, and practise them with success.
You will hardly find anywhere a community, composed
of the same number of individuals, possessing such uninterrupted health, and exhibiting so many green old
men, who show their advanced age by the maturity of
their wisdom, rather than by the wrinkles of their faces;
and this is indeed one of the principal blessings of the
island, which richly compensates their want of the richer
soils of the south; where iliac complaints and bilious
fevers, grow by the side of the sugar cane, the ambrosial
ananas, etc. The situation of this island, the purity of
the air, the nature of their marine occupations, their
virtue and moderation, are the causes of that vigour and
health which they possess. The poverty of their soil has
placed them, I hope, beyond the danger of conquest, or
the wanton desire of extirpation. Were they to be driven
from this spot, the only acquisition of the conquerors
would be a few acres of land, inclosed and cultivated;
a few houses, and some movables. The genius, the industry of the inhabitants would accompany them; and
it is those alone which constitute the sole wealth of their
island. Its present fame would perish, and in a few years
it would return to its pristine state of barrenness and
poverty: they might perhaps be allowed to transport
themselves in their own vessels to some other spot or
island, which they would soon fertilise by the same
means with which they have fertilised this.

One single lawyer has of late years found means to
live here, but his best fortune proceeds more from having married one of the wealthiest heiresses of the island,
than from the emoluments of his practice: however he
is sometimes employed in recovering money lent on the
main, or in preventing those accidents to which the con-
tentious propensity of its inhabitants may sometimes expose them. He is seldom employed as the means of self-
defence, and much seldomer as the channel of attack; to

which they are strangers, except the fraud is manifest, and the danger imminent. Lawyers are so numerous in all populous towns, that I am surprised they never thought before of establishing themselves here: they are plants that will grow in any soil that is cultivated by the hands of others; and when once they have taken root they will extinguish every other vegetable that grows around them. The fortunes they daily acquire in every province, from the misfortunes of their fellow-citizens, are surprising! The most ignorant, the most bungling member of that profession, will, if placed in the most obscure part of the country, promote litigiousness, and amass more wealth without labour, than the most opulent farmer, with all his toils. They have so dexterously interwoven their doctrines and quirks with the laws of the land, or rather they are become so necessary an evil in our present constitutions, that it seems unavoidable and past all remedy. What a pity that our forefathers, who happily extinguished so many fatal customs, and expunged from their new government so many errors and abuses, both religious and civil, did not also prevent the introduction of a set of men so dangerous! In some provinces, where every inhabitant is constantly employed in tilling and cultivating the earth, they are the only members of society who have any knowledge; let these provinces attest what iniquitous use they have made of that knowledge. They are here what the clergy were in past centuries with you; the reformation which clipped the clerical wings, is the boast of that age, and the happiest event that could possibly happen; a reformation equally useful is now wanted, to relieve us from the shameful shackles and the oppressive burthen under which we groan; this perhaps is impossible; but if mankind would not become too happy, it were an event most devoutly to be wished.

Here, happily, unoppressed with any civil bondage,

this society of fishermen and merchants live, without any military establishments, without governors or any masters but the laws; and their civil code is so light, that it is never felt. A man may pass (as many have done whom I am acquainted with) through the various scenes of a long life, may struggle against a variety of adverse fortune, peaceably enjoy the good when it comes, and never in that long interval, apply to the law either for redress or assistance. The principal benefit it confers is the general protection of individuals, and this protection is purchased by the most moderate taxes, which are cheerfully paid, and by the trifling duties incident in the course of their lawful trade (for they despise contraband). Nothing can be more simple than their municipal regulations, though similar to those of the other counties of the same province; because they are more detached from the rest, more distinct in their manners, as well as in the nature of the business they pursue, and more unconnected with the populous province to which they belong. The same simplicity attends the worship they pay to the Divinity; their elders are the only teachers of their congregations, the instructors of their youth, and often the example of their flock. They visit and comfort the sick; after death, the society bury them with their fathers, without pomp, prayers, or ceremonies; not a stone or monument is erected, to tell where any person was buried; their memory is preserved by tradition. The only essential memorial that is left of them, is their former industry, their kindness, their charity, or else their most conspicuous faults.

The Presbyterians live in great charity with them, and with one another; their minister as a true pastor of the gospel, inculcates to them the doctrines it contains, the rewards it promises, the punishments it holds out to those who shall commit injustice. Nothing can be more disencumbered likewise from useless ceremonies and trifling forms than their mode of worship; it might with great propriety have been called a truly primitive one, had that of the Quakers never appeared. As fellow Christians, obeying the same legislator, they love and mutually assist each other in all their wants; as fellow labourers they unite with cordiality and without the least rancour in all their temporal schemes: no other emulation appears among them but in their sea excursions, in the art of fitting out their vessels; in that of sailing, in harpooning the whale, and in bringing home the greatest harvest. As fellow subjects they cheerfully obey the same laws, and pay the same duties: but let me not forget another peculiar characteristic of this community: there is not a slave I believe on the whole island, at least among the Friends; whilst slavery prevails all around them, this society alone, lamenting that shocking insult offered to humanity, have given the world a singular example of moderation, disinterestedness, and Christian charity, in emancipating their negroes. I shall explain to you farther, the singular virtue and merit to which it is so justly entitled by having set before the rest of their fellow-subjects, so pleasing, so edifying a reformation. Happy the people who are subject to so mild a government; happy the government which has to rule over such harmless, and such industrious subjects!

While we are clearing forests, making the face of nature smile, draining marshes, cultivating wheat, and converting it into flour; they yearly skim from the surface of the sea riches equally necessary. Thus, had I leisure and abilities to lead you through this continent, I could show you an astonishing prospect very little known in Europe; one diffusive scene of happiness reaching from the sea-shores to the last settlements on the borders of the wilderness: an happiness, interrupted only by the folly of individuals, by our spirit of litigiousness, and by those unforeseen calamities, from which no human society can possibly be exempted. May the citizens of Nantucket dwell long here in uninterrupted peace, undisturbed either by the waves of the surrounding element, or the political commotions which sometimes agitate our continent.

LETTER VIII

PECULIAR CUSTOMS AT NANTUCKET

THE manners of *the Friends* are entirely founded on that simplicity which is their boast, and their most distinguished characteristic; and those manners have acquired the authority of laws. Here they are strongly attached to plainness of dress, as well as to that of language; insomuch that though some part of it may be ungrammatical, yet should any person who was born and brought up here, attempt to speak more correctly, he would be looked upon as a fop or an innovator. On the other hand, should a stranger come here and adopt their idiom in all its purity (as they deem it) this accomplishment would immediately procure him the most cordial reception; and they would cherish him like an ancient member of their society. So many impositions have they suffered on this account, that they begin now indeed to grow more cautious. They are so tenacious of their ancient habits of industry and frugality, that if any of them were to be seen with a long coat made of English cloth, on any other than the *first-day* (Sunday), he would be greatly ridiculed and censured; he would be looked upon as a careless spendthrift, whom it would be unsafe to trust, and in vain to relieve. A few years ago two *single-horse chairs* were imported from Boston, to the great offence of these prudent citizens; nothing appeared to them more culpable than the use of such gaudy painted vehicles, in contempt of the more useful and more simple *single-horse carts* of their fathers. This piece of extravagant and unknown luxury almost caused a schism, and set every tongue a-going; some predicted the approaching ruin of those families that had imported them; others feared the dangers of example; never since the foundation of the town had there happened anything which so much alarmed this primitive community. One of the possessors of these profane chairs, filled with repentance, wisely sent it back to the continent; the other, more obstinate and perverse, in defiance to all remonstrances, persisted in the use of his chair until by degrees they became more reconciled to it; though I observed that the wealthiest and the most respectable people still go to meeting or to their farms in a *single-horse cart* with a decent awning fixed over it: indeed, if you consider their sandy soil, and the badness of their roads, these appear to be the best contrived vehicles for this island.

Idleness is the most heinous sin that can be committed in Nantucket: an idle man would soon be pointed out as an object of compassion: for idleness is considered as another word for want and hunger. This principle is so thoroughly well understood, and is become so universal, so prevailing a prejudice, that literally speaking, they are never idle. Even if they go to the market-place, which is (if I may be allowed the expression) the coffee-house of the town, either to transact business, or to converse with their friends; they always have a piece of cedar in their hands, and while they are talking, they will, as it were instinctively, employ themselves in converting it into something useful, either in making bungs or spoyls for their oil casks, or other useful articles. I must confess, that I have never seen more ingenuity in the use of the knife; thus the most idle moments of their lives become usefully employed. In the many hours of leisure which their long cruises afford them, they cut and carve a variety of boxes and pretty toys, in wood, adapted to different uses; which they bring home as testimonies of remembrance to their wives or sweethearts. They have showed me a variety of little bowls and other imple-

ments, executed cooper-wise, with the greatest neatness
and elegance. You will be pleased to remember they are
all brought up to the trade of coopers, be their future
intentions or fortunes what they may; therefore almost
every man in this island has always two knives in his
pocket, one much larger than the other; and though
they hold everything that is called *fashion* in the utmost
contempt, yet they are as difficult to please, and as extravagant in the choice and price of their knives, as any
young buck in Boston would be about his hat, buckles,
or coat. As soon as a knife is injured, or superseded by
a more convenient one, it is carefully laid up in some
corner of their desk. I once saw upwards of fifty thus
preserved at Mr. ——'s, one of the worthiest men on this
island; and among the whole, there was not one that
perfectly resembled another. As the sea excursions are
often very long, their wives in their absence are necessarily obliged to transact business, to settle accounts, and
in short, to rule and provide for their families. These
circumstances being often repeated, give women the
abilities as well as a taste for that kind of superinten-
dency, to which, by their prudence and good management, they seem to be in general very equal. This
employment ripens their judgment, and justly entitles
them to a rank superior to that of other wives; and this
is the principal reason why those of Nantucket as well
as those of Montreal [1] are so fond of society, so affable,
and so conversant with the affairs of the world. The
men at their return, weary with the fatigues of the sea,
full of confidence and love, cheerfully give their consent
to every transaction that has happened during their absence, and all is joy and peace. "Wife, thee hast done

[1] Most of the merchants and young men of Montreal spend the
greatest part of their time in trading with the Indians, at an
amazing distance from Canada; and it often happens that they
are three years together absent from home.

well," is the general approbation they receive, for their application and industry. What would the men do without the agency of these faithful mates? The absence of so many of them at particular seasons, leaves the town quite desolate; and this mournful situation disposes the women to go to each other's house much oftener than when their husbands are at home: hence the custom of incessant visiting has infected every one, and even those whose husbands do not go abroad. The house is always cleaned before they set out, and with peculiar alacrity they pursue their intended visit, which consists of a social chat, a dish of tea, and an hearty supper. When the good man of the house returns from his labour, he peaceably goes after his wife and brings her home; meanwhile the young fellows, equally vigilant, easily find out which is the most convenient house, and there they assemble with the girls of the neighbourhood. Instead of cards, musical instruments, or songs, they relate stories of their whaling voyages, their various sea adventures, and talk of the different coasts and people they have visited. "The island of Catharine in the Brazil," says one, "is a very droll island, it is inhabited by none but men; women are not permitted to come in sight of it; not a woman is there on the whole island. Who among us is not glad it is not so here? The Nantucket girls and boys beat the world." At this innocent sally the titter goes round, they whisper to one another their spontaneous reflections: puddings, pies, and custards never fail to be produced on such occasions; for I believe there never were any people in their circumstances, who live so well, even to superabundance. As inebriation is unknown, and music, singing, and dancing, are held in equal detestation, they never could fill all the vacant hours of their lives without the repast of the table. Thus these young people sit and talk, and divert themselves as well as they can; if any one has lately returned from a cruise, he is generally the speaker of the night; they often all laugh and talk together, but they are happy, and would not exchange their pleasures for those of the most brilliant assemblies in Europe. This lasts until the father and mother return; when all retire to their respective homes, the men re-conducting the partners of their affections.

Thus they spend many of the youthful evenings of their lives; no wonder therefore, that they marry so early. But no sooner have they undergone this ceremony than they cease to appear so cheerful and gay; the new rank they hold in the society impresses them with more serious ideas than were entertained before. The title of master of a family necessarily requires more solid behaviour and deportment; the new wife follows in the trammels of Custom, which are as powerful as the tyranny of fashion; she gradually advises and directs; the new husband soon goes to sea, he leaves her to learn and exercise the new government, in which she is entered. Those who stay at home are full as passive in general, at least with regard to the inferior departments of the family. But you must not imagine from this account that the Nantucket wives are turbulent, of high temper, and difficult to be ruled; on the contrary, the wives of Sherburn in so doing, comply only with the prevailing custom of the island: the husbands, equally submissive to the ancient and respectable manners of their country, submit, without ever suspecting that there can be any impropriety. Were they to behave otherwise, they would be afraid of subverting the principles of their society by altering its ancient rules; thus both parties are perfectly satisfied, and all is peace and concord. The richest person now in the island owes all his present prosperity and success to the ingenuity of his wife: this is a known fact which is well recorded; for while he was performing his first cruises, she traded with pins and needles, and kept a schoo!. Afterward she purchased more considerable articles, which she sold with so much judgment, that she laid the foundation of a system of business, that she has ever since prosecuted with equal dexterity and success. She wrote to London, formed connections, and, in short, became the only ostensible instrument of that house, both at home and abroad. Who is he in this country, and who is a citizen of Nantucket or Boston, who does not know *Aunt Kesiah?* I must tell you that she is the wife of Mr. C————n, a very respectable man, who, well pleased with all her schemes, trusts to her judgment, and relies on her sagacity, with so entire a confidence, as to be altogether passive to the concerns of his family. They have the best country seat on the island, at Quayes, where they live with hospitality, and in perfect union. He seems to be altogether the contemplative man.

To this dexterity in managing the husband's business whilst he is absent, the Nantucket wives unite a great deal of industry. They spin, or cause to be spun in their houses, abundance of wool and flax; and would be for ever disgraced and looked upon as idlers if all the family were not clad in good, neat, and sufficient homespun cloth. *First Days* are the only seasons when it is lawful for both sexes to exhibit some garments of English manufacture; even *these* are of the most moderate price, and of the gravest colours: there is no kind of difference in their dress, they are all clad alike, and resemble in that respect the members of one family.

A singular custom prevails here among the women, at which I was greatly surprised; and am really at a loss how to account for the original cause that has introduced in this primitive society so remarkable a fashion, or rather so extraordinary a want. They have adopted these many years the Asiatic custom of taking a dose of opium every morning; and so deeply rooted is it, that they would be at a loss how to live without this indulgence; they would rather be deprived of any necessary than forego their favourite luxury. This is much more prevailing among the women than the men, few of the latter having caught the contagion; though the sheriff, whom I may call the first person in the island, who is an eminent physician beside, and whom I had the pleasure of being well acquainted with, has for many years submitted to this custom. He takes three grains of it every day after breakfast, without the effects of which, he often told me, he was not able to transact any business.

It is hard to conceive how a people always happy and healthy, in consequence of the exercise and labour they undergo, never oppressed with the vapours of idleness, yet should want the fictitious effects of opium to preserve that cheerfulness to which their temperance, their climate, their happy situation so justly entitle them. But where is the society perfectly free from error or folly; the least imperfect is undoubtedly that where the greatest good preponderates; and agreeable to this rule, I can truly say, that I never was acquainted with a less vicious, or more harmless one.

The majority of the present inhabitants are the descendants of the twenty-seven first proprietors, who patented the island; of the rest, many others have since come over among them, chiefly from the Massachusetts: here are neither Scotch, Irish, nor French, as is the case in most other settlements; they are an unmixed English breed. The consequence of this extended connection is, that they are all in some degree related to each other: you must not be surprised therefore when I tell you, that they always call each other cousin, uncle or aunt; which are become such common appellations, that no other are made use of in their daily intercourse: you would be deemed stiff and affected were you to refuse conforming yourself to this ancient custom, which truly depicts the image of a large family. The many who reside here that have not the least claim of relationship with any one in the town, yet by the power of custom make use of no other address in their conversation. Were you here yourself but a few days, you would be obliged to adopt the same phraseology, which is far from being disagreeable, as it implies a general acquaintance and friendship, which connects them all in unity and peace.

Their taste for fishing has been so prevailing, that it has engrossed all their attention, and even prevented them from introducing some higher degree of perfection in their agriculture. There are many useful improvements which might have meliorated their soil; there are many trees which if transplanted here would have thriven extremely well, and would have served to shelter as well as decorate the favourite spots they have so carefully manured. The red cedar, the locust,[1] the button wood, I am persuaded would have grown here rapidly and to a great size, with many others; but their thoughts are turned altogether toward the sea. The Indian corn begins to yield them considerable crops, and the wheat sown on its stocks is become a very profitable grain; rye will grow with little care; they might raise if they would, an immense quantity of buck-wheat.

Such an island inhabited as I have described, is not the place where gay travellers should resort, in order to enjoy that variety of pleasures the more splendid towns of this continent afford. Not that they are wholly deprived of what we might call recreations, and innocent pastimes; but opulence, instead of luxuries and extravagancies, produces nothing more here than an increase of business, an additional degree of hospitality, greater neatness in the preparation of dishes, and better wines.

[1] A species of what we call here the two-thorn acacia: it yields the most valuable timber we have, and its shade is very beneficial to the growth and goodness of the grass.

They often walk and converse with each other, as I have observed before; and upon extraordinary occasions, will take a ride to Palpus, where there is an house of entertainment; but these rural amusements are conducted upon the same plan of moderation, as those in town. They are so simple as hardly to be described; the pleasure of going and returning together; of chatting and walking about, of throwing the bar, heaving stones, etc., are the only entertainments they are acquainted with. This is all they practise, and all they seem to desire. The house at Palpus is the general resort of those who possess the luxury of a horse and chaise, as well as of those who still retain, as the majority do, a predilection for their primitive vehicle. By resorting to that place they enjoy a change of air, they taste the pleasures of exercise; perhaps an exhilarating bowl, not at all improper in this climate, affords the chief indulgence known to these people, on the days of their greatest festivity. The mounting a horse must afford a most pleasing exercise to those men who are so much at sea. I was once invited to that house, and had the satisfaction of conducting thither one of the many beauties of that island (for it abounds with handsome women) dressed in all the bewitching attire of the most charming simplicity: like the rest of the company, she was cheerful without loud laughs, and smiling without affectation. They all appeared gay without levity. I had never before in my life seen so much unaffected mirth, mixed with so much modesty. The pleasures of the day were enjoyed with the greatest liveliness and the most innocent freedom; no disgusting pruderies, no coquettish airs tarnished this enlivening assembly: they behaved according to their native dispositions, the only rules of decorum with which they were acquainted. What would an European visitor have done here without a fiddle, without a dance, without cards? He would have called it an insipid assembly, and ranked this among the dullest days he had ever spent. This rural excursion had a very great affinity to those practised in our province, with this difference only, that we have no objection to the sportive dance, though conducted by the rough accents of some self-taught African fiddler. We returned as happy as we went; and the brightness of the moon kindly lengthened a day which had past, like other agreeable ones, with singular rapidity.

In order to view the island in its longest direction from the town, I took a ride to the easternmost parts of it, remarkable only for the Pochick Rip, where their best fish are caught. I past by the Tetoukèmah lots, which are the fields of the community; the fences were made of cedar posts and rails, and looked perfectly straight and neat; the various crops they enclosed were flourishing: thence I descended into Barrey's Valley, where the *blue* and the *spear* grass looked more abundant than I had seen on any other part of the island; thence to Gib's Pond; and arrived at last at Siàsconcèt. Several dwellings had been erected on this wild shore, for the purpose of sheltering the fishermen in the season of fishing; I found them all empty, except that particular one to which I had been directed. It was like the others, built on the highest part of the shore, in the face of the great ocean; the soil appeared to be composed of no other stratum but sand, covered with a thinly scattered herbage. What rendered this house still more worthy of notice in my eyes, was, that it had been built on the ruins of one of the ancient huts, erected by the first settlers, for observing the appearance of the whales. Here lived a single family without a neighbour; I had never before seen a spot better calculated to cherish contemplative ideas; perfectly unconnected with the great world, and far removed from its perturbations. The ever raging ocean was all that presented itself to the view of this family; it irresistibly attracted my whole attention: my eyes were involuntarily directed to the horizontal line of that watery surface, which is ever in motion, and ever threatening destruction to these shores. My ears were stunned with the roar of its waves rolling one over the other, as if impelled by a superior force to overwhelm the spot on which I stood. My nostrils involuntarily inhaled the saline vapours which arose from the dispersed particles of the foaming billows, or from the weeds scattered on the shores. My mind suggested a thousand vague reflections, pleasing in the hour of their spontaneous birth, but now half forgot, and all indistinct: and who is the landman that can behold without affright so singular an element, which by its impetuosity seems to be destroyer of this poor planet, yet at particular times accumulates the scattered fragments and produces islands and continents fit for men to dwell on! Who can observe the regular vicissitudes of its waters without astonishment; now swelling themselves in order to penetrate through every river and opening, and thereby facilitate navigation; at other times retiring from the shores, to permit man to collect that variety of shell fish which is the support of the poor? Who can see the storms of wind, blowing sometimes with an impetuosity sufficiently strong even to move the earth, without feeling himself affected beyond the sphere of common ideas? Can this wind which but a few days ago refreshed our American fields, and cooled us in the shade, be the same element which now and then so powerfully convulses the waters of the sea, dismasts vessels, causes so many shipwrecks, and such extensive desolations? How diminutive does a man appear to himself when filled with these thoughts, and standing as I did on the verge of the ocean! This family lived entirely by fishing, for the plough has not dared yet to disturb the parched surface of the neighbouring plain; and to

what purpose could this operation be performed! Where
is it that mankind will not find safety, peace, and abundance, with freedom and civil happiness? Nothing was
wanting here to make this a most philosophical retreat,
but a few ancient trees, to shelter contemplation in its
beloved solitude. There I saw a numerous family of
children of various ages—the blessings of an early marriage; they were ruddy as the cherry, healthy as the fish
they lived on, hardy as the pine knots: the eldest were
already able to encounter the boisterous waves, and shuddered not at their approach; early initiating themselves
in the mysteries of that seafaring career, for which they
were all intended: the younger, timid as yet, on the edge
of a less agitated pool, were teaching themselves with
nut-shells and pieces of wood, in imitation of boats, how
to navigate in a future day the larger vessels of their
father, through a rougher and deeper ocean. I stayed
two days there on purpose to become acquainted with
the different branches of their economy, and their manner of living in this singular retreat. The clams, the
oysters of the shores, with the addition of Indian Dumplings,[1] constituted their daily and most substantial food.
Larger fish were often caught on the neighbouring rip;
these afforded them their greatest dainties; they had likewise plenty of smoked bacon. The noise of the wheels
announced the industry of the mother and daughters;
one of them had been bred a weaver, and having a loom
in the house, found means of clothing the whole family;
they were perfectly at ease, and seemed to want for
nothing. I found very few books among these people,
who have very little time for reading; the Bible and a
few school tracts, both in the Nattick and English languages, constituted their most numerous libraries. I
saw indeed several copies of Hudibras, and Josephus;

[1] Indian Dumplings are a peculiar preparation of Indian meal,
boiled in large lumps.

but no one knows who first imported them. It is something extraordinary to see this people, professedly so grave, and strangers to every branch of literature, reading with pleasure the former work, which should seem to require some degree of taste, and antecedent historical knowledge. They all read it much, and can by memory repeat many passages; which yet I could not discover that they understood the beauties of. Is it not a little singular to see these books in the hands of fishermen, who are perfect strangers almost to any other? Josephus's history is indeed intelligible, and much fitter for their modes of education and taste; as it describes the history of a people from whom we have received the prophecies which we believe, and the religious laws which we follow.

Learned travellers, returned from seeing the paintings and antiquities of Rome and Italy, still filled with the admiration and reverence they inspire, would hardly be persuaded that so contemptible a spot, which contains nothing remarkable but the genius and the industry of its inhabitants, could ever be an object worthy attention. But I, having never seen the beauties which Europe contains, cheerfully satisfy myself with attentively examining what my native country exhibits: if we have neither ancient amphitheatres, gilded palaces, nor elevated spires; we enjoy in our woods a substantial happiness which the wonders of art cannot communicate. None among us suffer oppression either from government or religion; there are very few poor except the idle, and fortunately the force of example, and the most ample encouragement, soon create a new principle of activity, which had been extinguished perhaps in their native country, for want of those opportunities which so often compel honest Europeans to seek shelter among us. The means of procuring subsistence in Europe are limited; the army may be full, the navy may abound with seamen, the land perhaps wants no additional labourers, the manufacturer is overcharged with supernumerary hands; what then must become of the unemployed? Here, on the contrary, human industry has acquired a boundless field to exert itself in—a field which will not be fully cultivated in many ages!

LETTER IX

CHARLES-TOWN is, in the north, what Lima is in the south; both are Capitals of the richest provinces of their respective hemispheres: you may therefore conjecture, that both cities must exhibit the appearances necessarily resulting from riches. Peru abounding in gold, Lima is filled with inhabitants who enjoy all those gradations of pleasure, refinement, and luxury, which proceed from wealth. Carolina produces commodities, more valuable perhaps than gold, because they are gained by greater industry; it exhibits also on our northern stage, a display of riches and luxury, inferior indeed to the former, but far superior to what are to be seen in our northern towns. Its situation is admirable, being built at the confluence of two large rivers, which receive in their course a great number of inferior streams; all navigable in the spring, for flat boats. Here the produce of this extensive territory concentres; here therefore is the seat of the most valuable exportation; their wharfs, their docks, their magazines, are extremely convenient to facilitate this great commercial business. The inhabitants are the gayest in America; it is called the centre of our beau monde, and is always filled with the richest planters of the province, who resort hither in quest of health and pleasure. Here are always to be seen a great number of valetudinarians from the West Indies, seeking for the renovation of health, exhausted by the debilitating nature of their sun, air, and modes of living. Many of these West Indians have I seen, at thirty, loaded with the infirmities of old age; for nothing is more common in those countries of wealth, than for persons to lose the abilities of enjoying the comforts of life, at a time when we northern men just begin to taste the fruits of our labour and prudence. The round of pleasure, and the expenses of those citizens' tables, are much superior to what you would imagine: indeed the growth of this town and province has been astonishingly rapid. It is a pity that the narrowness of the neck on which it stands prevents it from increasing; and which is the reason why houses are so dear. The heat of the climate, which is sometimes very great in the interior parts of the country, is always temperate in Charles-Town; though sometimes when they have no sea breezes the sun is too powerful. The climate renders excesses of all kinds very dangerous, particularly those of the table; and yet, insensible or fearless of danger, they live on, and enjoy a short and a merry life: the rays of their sun seem to urge them irresistibly to dissipation and pleasure: on the contrary, the women, from being abstemious, reach to a longer period of life, and seldom die without having had several husbands. An European at his first arrival must be greatly surprised when he sees the elegance of their houses, their sumptuous furniture, as well as the magnificence of their tables. Can he imagine himself in a country, the establishment of which is so recent?

The three principal classes of inhabitants are, lawyers, planters, and merchants; this is the province which has afforded to the first the richest spoils, for nothing can exceed their wealth, their power, and their influence. They have reached the *ne plus ultra* of worldly felicity; no plantation is secured, no title is good, no will is valid, but what they dictate, regulate, and approve. The whole mass of provincial property is become tributary to this society; which, far above priests and bishops, disdain to be satisfied with the poor Mosaical portion of the tenth. I appeal to the many inhabitants, who, while contending perhaps for their right to a few hundred acres, have lost by the mazes of the law their whole patrimony. These men are more properly law givers than interpreters of the law; and have united here, as well as in most other provinces, the skill and dexterity of the scribe with the power and ambition of the prince: who can tell where this may lead in a future day? The nature of our laws, and the spirit of freedom, which often tends to make us litigious, must necessarily throw the greatest part of the property of the colonies into the hands of these gentlemen. In another century, the law will possess in the north, what now the church possesses in Peru and Mexico.

While all is joy, festivity, and happiness in Charles-Town, would you imagine that scenes of misery over-spread in the country? Their ears by habit are become deaf, their hearts are hardened; they neither see, hear, nor feel for the woes of their poor slaves, from whose painful labours all their wealth proceeds. Here the horrors of slavery, the hardship of incessant toils, are unseen; and no one thinks with compassion of those showers of sweat and of tears which from the bodies of Africans, daily drop, and moisten the ground they till. The cracks of the whip urging these miserable beings to excessive labour, are far too distant from the gay Capital to be heard. The chosen race eat, drink, and live happy, while the unfortunate one grubs up the ground, raises indigo, or husks the rice; exposed to a sun full as scorching as their native one; without the support of good food, without the cordials of any cheering liquor. This great contrast has often afforded me subjects of the most conflicting meditation. On the one side, behold a people enjoying all that life affords most bewitching and pleasurable, without labour, without fatigue, hardly subjected to the trouble of wishing. With gold, dug from Peruvian mountains, they order vessels to the coasts of

Guinea; by virtue of that gold, wars, murders, and devastations are committed in some harmless, peaceable African neighbourhood, where dwelt innocent people, who
even knew not but that all men were black. The
daughter torn from her weeping mother, the child from
the wretched parents, the wife from the loving husband;
whole families swept away and brought through storms
and tempests to this rich metropolis! There, arranged
like horses at a fair, they are branded like cattle, and
then driven to toil, to starve, and to languish for a few
years on the different plantations of these citizens. And
for whom must they work? For persons they know not,
and who have no other power over them than that of
violence, no other right than what this accursed metal
has given them! Strange order of things! Oh, Nature,
where art thou?—Are not these blacks thy children as
well as we? On the other side, nothing is to be seen but
the most diffusive misery and wretchedness, unrelieved
even in thought or wish! Day after day they drudge on
without any prospect of ever reaping for themselves;
they are obliged to devote their lives, their limbs, their
will, and every vital exertion to swell the wealth of
masters; who look not upon them with half the kindness
and affection with which they consider their dogs and
horses. Kindness and affection are not the portion of
those who till the earth, who carry the burdens, who
convert the logs into useful boards. This reward, simple
and natural as one would conceive it, would border on
humanity; and planters must have none of it!

If negroes are permitted to become fathers, this fatal
indulgence only tends to increase their misery: the poor
companions of their scanty pleasures are likewise the
companions of their labours; and when at some critical
seasons they could wish to see them relieved, with tears
in their eyes they behold them perhaps doubly oppressed,
obliged to bear the burden of nature—a fatal present—

as well as that of unabated tasks. How many have I seen cursing the irresistible propensity, and regretting, that by having tasted of those harmless joys, they had become the authors of double misery to their wives. Like their masters, they are not permitted to partake of those ineffable sensations with which nature inspires the hearts of fathers and mothers; they must repel them all, and become callous and passive. This unnatural state often occasions the most acute, the most pungent of their afflictions; they have no time, like us, tenderly to rear their helpless off-spring, to nurse them on their knees, to enjoy the delight of being parents. Their paternal fondness is embittered by considering, that if their children live, they must live to be slaves like themselves; no time is allowed them to exercise their pious office, the mothers must fasten them on their backs, and, with this double load, follow their husbands in the fields, where they too often hear no other sound than that of the voice or whip of the taskmaster, and the cries of their infants, broiling in the sun. These unfortunate creatures cry and weep like their parents, without a possibility of relief; the very instinct of the brute, so laudable, so irresistible, runs counter here to their master's interest; and to that god, all the laws of nature must give way. Thus planters get rich; so raw, so unexperienced am I in this mode of life, that were I to be possessed of a plantation, and my slaves treated as in general they are here, never could I rest in peace; my sleep would be perpetually disturbed by a retrospect of the frauds committed in Africa, in order to entrap them; frauds surpassing in enormity everything which a common mind can possibly conceive. I should be thinking of the barbarous treatment they meet with on ship-board; of their anguish, of the despair necessarily inspired by their situation, when torn from their friends and relations; when delivered into the hands of a people differently coloured, whom they cannot understand; carried in a strange machine over an ever agitated element, which they had never seen before; and finally delivered over to the severities of the whippers, and the excessive labours of the field. Can it be possible that the force of custom should ever make me deaf to all these reflections, and as insensible to the injustice of that trade, and to their miseries, as the rich inhabitants of this town seem to be? What then is man; this being who boasts so much of the excellence and dignity of his nature, among that variety of inscrutable mysteries, of unsolvable problems, with which he is surrounded? The reason why man has been thus created, is not the least astonishing! It is said, I know that they are much happier here than in the West Indies; because land being cheaper upon this continent than in those islands, the fields allowed them to raise their subsistence from, are in general more extensive. The only possible chance of any alleviation depends on the humour of the planters, who, bred in the midst of slaves, learn from the example of their parents to despise them; and seldom conceive either from religion or philosophy, any ideas that tend to make their fate less calamitous; except some strong native tenderness of heart, some rays of philanthropy, overcome the obduracy contracted by habit.

I have not resided here long enough to become insensible of pain for the objects which I every day behold. In the choice of my friends and acquaintance, I always endeavour to find out those whose dispositions are somewhat congenial with my own. We have slaves likewise in our northern provinces; I hope the time draws near when they will be all emancipated: but how different their lot, how different their situation, in every possible respect! They enjoy as much liberty as their masters, they are as well clad, and as well fed; in health and sickness they are tenderly taken care of; they live under the same roof, and are, truly speaking, a part of our families. Many of them are taught to read and write, and are well instructed in the principles of religion; they are the companions of our labours, and treated as such; they enjoy many perquisites, many established holidays, and are not obliged to work more than white people. They marry where inclination leads them; visit their wives every week; are as decently clad as the common people; they are indulged in educating, cherishing, and chastising their children, who are taught subordination to them as to their lawful parents: in short, they participate in many of the benefits of our society, without being obliged to bear any of its burdens. They are fat, healthy, and hearty, and far from repining at their fate; they think themselves happier than many of the lower class whites: they share with their masters the wheat and meat provision they help to raise; many of those whom the good Quakers have emancipated have received that great benefit with tears of regret, and have never quitted, though free, their former masters and benefactors.

But is it really true, as I have heard it asserted here, that those blacks are incapable of feeling the spurs of emulation, and the cheerful sound of encouragement? By no means; there are a thousand proofs existing of their gratitude and fidelity: those hearts in which such noble dispositions can grow, are then like ours, they are susceptible of every generous sentiment, of every useful motive of action; they are capable of receiving lights, of imbibing ideas that would greatly alleviate the weight of their miseries. But what methods have in general been made use of to obtain so desirable an end? None; the day in which they arrive and are sold, is the first of their labours; labours, which from that hour admit of no respite; for though indulged by law with relaxation on Sundays, they are obliged to employ that time which is intended for rest, to till their little plantations. What can be expected from wretches in such circumstances? Forced from their native country, cruelly treated when on board, and not less so on the plantations to which they are driven; is there anything in this treatment but what must kindle all the passions, sow the seeds of inveterate resentment, and nourish a wish of perpetual revenge? They are left to the irresistible effects of those strong and natural propensities; the blows they receive, are they conducive to extinguish them, or to win their affections? They are neither soothed by the hopes that their slavery will ever terminate but with their lives; or yet encouraged by the goodness of their food, or the mildness of their treatment. The very hopes held out to mankind by religion, that consolatory system, so useful to the miserable, are never presented to them; neither moral nor physical means are made use of to soften their chains; they are left in their original and untutored state; that very state wherein the natural propensities of revenge and warm passions are so soon kindled. Cheered by no one single motive that can impel the will, or excite their efforts; nothing but terrors and punishments are presented to them; death is denounced if they run away; horrid delaceration if they speak with their native freedom; perpetually awed by the terrible cracks of whips, or by the fear of capital punishments, while even those punishments often fail of their purpose.

A clergyman settled a few years ago at George-Town, and feeling as I do now, warmly recommended to the planters, from the pulpit, a relaxation of severity; he introduced the benignity of Christianity, and pathetically made use of the admirable precepts of that system to melt the hearts of his congregation into a greater degree of compassion toward their slaves than had been hitherto customary; "Sir," said one of his hearers, "we pay you a genteel salary to read to us the prayers of the liturgy, and to explain to us such parts of the Gospel as the rule of the church directs; but we do not want you to teach us what we are to do with our blacks." The clergyman found it prudent to withhold any farther admonition. Whence this astonishing right, or rather this barbarous custom, for most certainly we have no kind of right beyond that of force? We are told, it is true, that slavery cannot be so repugnant to human nature as we at first imagine, because it has been practised in all ages, and in all nations: the Lacedemonians themselves, those great assertors of liberty, conquered the Helotes with the design of making them their slaves; the Romans, whom we consider as our masters in civil and military policy, lived in the exercise of the most horrid oppression; they conquered to plunder and to enslave. What a hideous aspect the face of the earth must then have exhibited! Provinces, towns, districts, often depopulated! their inhabitants driven to Rome, the greatest market in the world, and there sold by thousands! The Roman dominions were tilled by the hands of unfortunate people, who had once been, like their victors, free, rich, and possessed of every benefit society can confer; until they became subject to the cruel right of war, and to lawless force. Is there then no superintending power who conducts the moral operations of the world, as well as the physical? The same sublime hand which guides the planets round the sun with so much exactness, which preserves the arrangement of the whole with such exalted wisdom and paternal care, and prevents the vast system from falling into confusion; doth it abandon mankind to all the errors, the follies, and the miseries, which their most frantic rage, and their most dangerous vices and passions can produce?

The history of the earth! Doth it present anything but crimes of the most heinous nature, committed from one end of the world to the other? We observe avarice, rapine, and murder, equally prevailing in all parts. History perpetually tells us of millions of people abandoned to the caprice of the maddest princes, and of whole nations devoted to the blind fury of tyrants. Countries destroyed; nations alternately buried in ruins by other nations; some parts of the world beautifully cultivated, returned again to the pristine state; the fruits of ages of industry, the toil of thousands in a short time destroyed by a few! If one corner breathes in peace for a few years, it is, in turn subjected, torn, and levelled; one would almost believe the principles of action in man, considered as the first agent of this planet, to be poisoned in their most essential parts. We certainly are not that class of beings which we vainly think ourselves to be; man an animal of prey, seems to have rapine and the love of bloodshed implanted in his heart; nay, to hold it the most honourable occupation in society: we never speak of a hero of mathematics, a hero of knowledge of humanity; no, this illustrious appelation is reserved for the most successful butchers of the world. If Nature has given us a fruitful soil to inhabit, she has refused us such inclinations and propensities as would afford us the full enjoyment of it. Extensive as the surface of this planet is, not one half of it is yet cultivated, not half replenished; she created man, and placed him either in the woods or plains, and provided him with passions which must for ever oppose his happiness; everything is submitted to the power of the strongest; men, like the elements, are always at war; the weakest yield to the most potent; force, subtlety, and malice, always triumph over unguarded honesty and simplicity. Benignity, moderation, and justice, are virtues adapted only to the humble paths of life: we love to talk of virtue and to admire its beauty, while in the shade of solitude and retirement; but when we step forth into active life, if it happen to be in competition with any passion or desire, do we observe it to prevail? Hence so many religious impostors have triumphed over the credulity of mankind, and have rendered their frauds the creeds of succeeding generations, during the course of many ages; until worn away by time, they have been replaced by new ones. Hence the most unjust war, if supported by the greatest force, always succeeds; hence the most just ones, when supported only by their justice, as often fail. Such is the ascendancy of power; the supreme arbiter of all the revolutions which we observe in this planet: so irresistible is power, that it often thwarts the tendency of the most forcible causes, and prevents their subsequent salutary effects, though ordained for the good of man by the Governor of the universe. Such is the perverseness of human nature; who can describe it in all its latitude?

In the moments of our philanthropy we often talk of an indulgent nature, a kind parent, who for the benefit of mankind has taken singular pains to vary the genera of plants, fruits, grain, and the different productions of the earth; and has spread peculiar blessings in each climate. This is undoubtedly an object of contemplation which calls forth our warmest gratitude; for so singularly benevolent have those parental intentions been, that where barrenness of soil or severity of climate prevail, there she has implanted in the heart of man, sentiments which overbalance every misery, and supply the place of every want. She has given to the inhabitants of these regions, an attachment to their savage rocks and wild shores, unknown to those who inhabit the fertile fields of the temperate zone. Yet if we attentively view this globe, will it not appear rather a place of punishment, than of delight? And what misfortune! that those punishments should fall on the innocent, and its few delights be enjoyed by the most unworthy. Famine, diseases, elementary convulsions, human feuds, dissensions, etc., are the produce of every climate; each climate produces besides, vices, and miseries peculiar to its latitude. View the frigid sterility of the north, whose famished inhabitants hardly acquainted with the sun, live and fare worse than the bears they hunt: and to which they are superior only in the faculty of speaking. View the arctic and antarctic regions, those huge voids, where nothing lives; regions of eternal snow: where winter in all his horrors has established his throne, and arrested every creative power of nature. Will you call the miserable stragglers in these countries by the name of men? Now contrast this rigid power of the north and south with that of the sun; examine the parched lands of the torrid zone, replete with sulphureous exhalations; view those countries of Asia subject to pestilential infections which lay nature waste; view this globe often convulsed both from within and without; pouring forth from several mouths, rivers of boiling matter, which are imperceptibly leaving immense subterranean graves, wherein millions will one day perish! Look at the poisonous soil of the equator, at those putrid slimy tracks, teeming with horrid monsters, the enemies of the human race; look next at the sandy continent, scorched perhaps by the fatal approach of some ancient comet, now the abode of desolation. Examine the rains, the convulsive storms of those climates, where masses of sulphur, bitumen, and electrical fire, combining their dreadful powers, are incessantly hovering and bursting over a globe threatened with dissolution. On this little shell, how very few are the spots where man can live and flourish? even under those mild climates which seem to breathe peace and happiness, the poison of slavery, the fury of despotism, and the rage of superstition, are all combined against man! There only the few live and rule, whilst the many starve and utter ineffectual complaints: there, human nature appears more debased, perhaps than in the less favoured climates. The fertile plains of Asia, the rich low lands of Egypt and of Diarbeck, the fruitful fields bordering on the Tigris and the Euphrates, the extensive country of the East Indies in all its separate districts; all these must to the geographical eye, seem as if intended for terrestrial paradises: but though surrounded with the spontaneous riches of nature, though her kindest favours seem to be shed on those beautiful regions with the most profuse hand; yet there in general we find the most wretched people in the world. Almost everywhere, liberty so natural to mankind is refused, or rather enjoyed but by their tyrants; the word slave, is the appellation of every rank, who adore as a divinity, a being worse than themselves; subject to every caprice, and to every lawless rage which unrestrained power can give. Tears are shed, perpetual groans are heard, where only the accents of peace, alacrity, and gratitude should resound. There the very delirium of tyranny tramples on the best gifts of nature, and sports with the fate, the happiness, the lives of millions: there the extreme fertility of the ground always indicates the extreme misery of the inhabitants!

Everywhere one part of the human species are taught the art of shedding the blood of the other; of setting fire to their dwellings; of levelling the works of their industry: half of the existence of nations regularly employed in destroying other nations. What little political felicity is to be met with here and there, has cost oceans of blood to purchase; as if good was never to be the portion of unhappy man. Republics, kingdoms, monarchies, founded either on fraud or successful violence, increase by pursuing the steps of the same policy, until they are destroyed in their turn, either by the influence of their own crimes, or by more successful but equally criminal enemies.

If from this general review of human nature, we

descend to the examination of what is called civilised society; there the combination of every natural and artificial want, makes us pay very dear for what little share of political felicity we enjoy. It is a strange heterogeneous assemblage of vices and virtues, and of a variety of other principles, for ever at war, for ever jarring, for ever producing some dangerous, some distressing extreme. Where do you conceive then that nature intended we should be happy? Would you prefer the state of men in the woods, to that of men in a more improved situation? Evil preponderates in both; in the first they often eat each other for want of food, and in the other they often starve each other for want of room. For my part, I think the vices and miseries to be found in the latter, exceed those of the former; in which real evil is more scarce, more supportable, and less enormous. Yet we wish to see the earth peopled; to accomplish the happiness of kingdoms, which is said to consist in numbers. Gracious God! to what end is the introduction of so many beings into a mode of existence in which they must grope amidst as many errors, commit as many crimes, and meet with as many diseases, wants, and sufferings!

The following scene will I hope account for these melancholy reflections, and apologise for the gloomy thoughts with which I have filled this letter: my mind is, and always has been, oppressed since I became a witness to it. I was not long since invited to dine with a planter who lived three miles from ——, where he then resided. In order to avoid the heat of the sun, I resolved to go on foot, sheltered in a small path, leading through a pleasant wood. I was leisurely travelling along, attentively examining some peculiar plants which I had collected, when all at once I felt the air strongly agitated, though the day was perfectly calm and sultry. I immediately cast my eyes toward the cleared ground, from which I was but at a small distance, in order to see whether it was not occasioned by a sudden shower; when at that instant a sound resembling a deep rough voice, uttered, as I thought, a few inarticulate monosyllables. Alarmed and surprised, I precipitately looked all round, when I perceived at about six rods distance something resembling a cage, suspended to the limbs of a tree; all the branches of which appeared covered with large birds of prey, fluttering about, and anxiously endeavouring to perch on the cage. Actuated by an involuntary motion of my hands, more than by any design of my mind, I fired at them; they all flew to a short distance, with a most hideous noise: when, horrid to think and painful to repeat, I perceived a negro, suspended in the cage, and left there to expire! I shudder when I recollect that the birds had already picked out his eyes, his cheek bones were bare; his arms had been attacked in several places, and his body seemed covered with a multitude of wounds. From the edges of the hollow sockets and from the lacerations with which he was disfigured, the blood slowly dropped, and tinged the ground beneath. No sooner were the birds flown, than swarms of insects covered the whole body of this unfortunate wretch, eager to feed on his mangled flesh and to drink his blood. I found myself suddenly arrested by the power of affright and terror; my nerves were convulsed; I trembled, I stood motionless, involuntarily contemplating the fate of this negro, in all its dismal latitude. The living spectre, though deprived of his eyes, could still distinctly hear, and in his uncouth dialect begged me to give him some water to allay his thirst. Humanity herself would have recoiled back with horror; she would have balanced whether to lessen such reliefless distress, or mercifully with one blow to end this dreadful scene of agonising torture! Had I had a ball in my gun, I certainly should have despatched him; but finding myself unable to perform so kind an office, I sought, though trembling, to relieve him as well as I could. A shell ready fixed to a pole, which had been used by some negroes, presented itself to me; I filled it with water, and with trembling hands I guided it to the quivering lips of the wretched sufferer. Urged by the irresistible power of thirst, he endeavoured to meet it, as he instinctively guessed its approach by the noise it made in passing through the bars of the cage. "Tankè, you whitè man, tankè you, putè somè poison and givè me." "How long have you been hanging there?" I asked him. "Two days, and me no die; the birds, the birds; aaah me!" Oppressed with the reflections which this shocking spectacle afforded me, I mustered strength enough to walk away, and soon reached the house at which I intended to dine. There I heard that the reason for this slave being thus punished, was on account of his having killed the overseer of the plantation. They told me that the laws of self-preservation rendered such executions necessary; and supported the doctrine of slavery with the arguments generally made use of to justify the practice; with the repetition of which I shall not trouble you at present.—Adieu.

LETTER X

WHY would you prescribe this task; you know that what we take up ourselves seems always lighter than what is imposed on us by others. You insist on my saying something about our snakes; and in relating what I know concerning them, were it not for two singularities, the one of which I saw, and the other I received from an eye-witness, I should have but very little to observe. The southern provinces are the countries where nature has formed the greatest variety of alligators, snakes, serpents; and scorpions, from the smallest size, up to the *pine barren*, the largest species known here. We have but two, whose stings are mortal, which deserve to be mentioned; as for the black one, it is remarkable for nothing but its industry, agility, beauty, and the art of enticing birds by the power of its eyes. I admire it much, and never kill it, though its formidable length and appearance often get the better of the philosophy of some people, particularly of Europeans. The most dangerous one is the *pilot*, or *copperhead;* for the poison of which no remedy has yet been discovered. It bears the first name because it always precedes the rattlesnake; that is, quits its state of torpidity in the spring a week before the other. It bears the second name on account of its head being adorned with many copper-coloured spots. It lurks in rocks near the water, and is extremely active and dangerous. Let man beware of it! I have heard only of one person who was stung by a copperhead in this country. The poor wretch instantly swelled in a most dreadful manner; a multitude of spots of different hues alternately appeared and vanished, on different parts of his body; his eyes were filled with madness and rage, he cast them on all present with the most vindictive looks: he thrust out his tongue as the snakes do; he hissed through his teeth with inconceivable strength, and became an object of terror to all by-standers. To the lividness of a corpse he united the desperate force of a maniac; they hardly were able to fasten him, so as to guard themselves from his attacks; when in the space of two hours death relieved the poor wretch from his struggles, and the spectators from their apprehensions. The poison of the rattlesnake is not mortal in so short a space, and hence there is more time to procure relief; we are acquainted with several antidotes with which almost every family is provided. They are extremely inactive, and if not touched, are perfectly inoffensive. I once saw, as I was travelling, a great cliff which was full of them; I handled several, and they appeared to be dead; they were all entwined together, and thus they remain until the return of the sun. I found them out, by following the track of some wild hogs which had fed on them; and even the Indians often regale on them. When they find them asleep, they put a small forked stick over their necks, which they keep immovably fixed on the ground; giving the snake a piece of leather to bite: and this they pull back several times with great force, until they observe their two poisonous fangs torn out. Then they cut off the head, skin the body, and cook it as we do eels; and their flesh is extremely sweet and white. I once saw a *tamed one,* as gentle as you can possibly conceive a reptile to be; it took to the water and swam whenever it pleased; and when the boys to whom it belonged called it back, their summons was readily obeyed. It had been deprived of its fangs by the preceding method; they often stroked it with a soft brush, and this friction seemed to cause the most pleasing sensations, for it would turn on its back to enjoy it, as a cat does before the fire. One of this species was the cause, some years ago, of a most deplorable accident which I shall relate to you, as I had it from the widow and mother of the victims. A Dutch farmer of the Minisink went to mowing, with his negroes, in his boots, a precaution used to prevent being stung. Inadvertently he trod on a snake, which immediately flew at his legs; and as it drew back in order to renew its blow, one of his negroes cut it in two with his scythe. They prosecuted their work, and returned home; at night the farmer pulled off his boots and went to bed; and was soon after attacked with a strange sickness at his stomach; he swelled, and before a physician could be sent for, died. The sudden death of this man did not cause much inquiry; the neighbourhood wondered, as is usual in such cases, and without any further examination the corpse was buried. A few days after, the son put on his father's boots, and went to the meadow; at night he pulled them off, went to bed, and was attacked with the same symptoms about the same time, and died in the morning. A little before he expired the doctor came, but was not able to assign what could be the cause of so singular a disorder; however, rather than appear wholly at a loss before the country people, he pronounced both father and son to have been bewitched. Some weeks after, the widow sold all the movables for the benefit of the younger children; and the farm was released. One of the neighbours, who bought the boots, presently put them on, and was attacked in the same manner as the other two had been; but this man's wife being alarmed by what had happened in the former family, despatched one of her negroes for an eminent physician, who fortunately having heard something of the dreadful affair, guessed at the cause, applied oil, etc. and recovered the man. The boots which had been so fatal, were then carefully examined; and he found that the two fangs of the snake had been left in the leather, after being wrenched out of their sockets by the strength with which the snake had drawn back its head. The bladders which contained the poison and several of the small nerves were still fresh, and adhered to the boot. The unfortunate father and son had been poisoned by pulling off these boots, in which action they imperceptibly scratched their legs with the points of the fangs, through the hollow of which, some of this astonishing poison was conveyed. You have no doubt heard of their rattles, if you have not seen them; the only observation I wish to make is, that the rattling is loud and distinct when they are angry; and on the contrary, when pleased, it sounds like a distant trepidation, in which nothing distinct is heard. In the thick settlements, they are now become very scarce; for wherever they are met with, open war is declared against them; so that in a few years there will be none left but on our mountains. The black snake on the contrary always diverts me because it excites no idea of danger. Their swiftness is astonishing; they will sometimes equal that of a horse; at other times they will climb up trees in quest of our tree toads; or glide on the ground at full length. On some occasions they present themselves half in the reptile state, half erect; their eyes and their heads in the erect posture appear to great advantage: the former display a fire which I have often admired, and it is by these they are enabled to fascinate birds and squirrels. When they have fixed their eyes on an animal, they become immovable; only turning their head sometimes to the right and sometimes to the left, but still with their sight invariably directed to the object. The distracted victim, instead of flying its enemy, seems to be arrested by some invincible power; it screams; now approaches, and then recedes; and after skipping about with unaccountable agitation, finally rushes into the jaws of the snake, and is swallowed, as soon as it is covered with a slime or glue to make it slide easily down the throat of the devourer.

One anecdote I must relate, the circumstances of which are as true as they are singular. One of my constant walks when I am at leisure, is in my lowlands, where I have the pleasure of seeing my cattle, horses, and colts. Exuberant grass replenishes all my fields, the best representative of our wealth; in the middle of that tract I have cut a ditch eight feet wide, the banks of which nature adorns every spring with the wild salendine, and other flowering weeds, which on these luxuriant grounds shoot up to a great height. Over this ditch I have erected a bridge, capable of bearing a loaded waggon; on each side I carefully sow every year some grains of hemp, which rise to the height of fifteen feet, so strong and so full of limbs as to resemble young trees: I once ascended one of them four feet above the ground. These produce natural arbours, rendered often still more compact by the assistance of an annual creeping plant which we call a vine, that never fails to entwine itself among their branches, and always produces a very desirable shade. From this simple grove I have amused myself an hundred times in observing the great number of humming birds with which our country abounds: the wild blossoms everywhere attract the attention of these birds, which like bees subsist by suction. From this retreat I distinctly watch them in all their various attitudes; but their flight is so rapid, that you cannot distinguish the motion of their wings. On this little bird nature has profusely lavished her most splendid colours; the most perfect azure, the most beautiful gold, the most dazzling red, are for ever in contrast, and help to embellish the plumes of his majestic head. The richest palette of the most luxuriant painter could

never invent anything to be compared to the variegated
tints, with which this insect bird is arrayed. Its bill
is as long and as sharp as a coarse sewing needle; like
the bee, nature has taught it to find out in the calix of
flowers and blossoms, those mellifluous particles that
serve it for sufficient food; and yet it seems to leave
them untouched, undeprived of anything that our eyes
can possibly distinguish. When it feeds, it appears as if
immovable though continually on the wing; and sometimes, from what motives I know not, it will tear and
lacerate flowers into a hundred pieces: for, strange to
tell, they are the most irascible of the feathered tribe.
Where do passions find room in so diminutive a body?
They often fight with the fury of lions, until one of
the combatants falls a sacrifice and dies. When fatigued,
it has often perched within a few feet of me, and on
such favourable opportunities I have surveyed it with
the most minute attention. Its little eyes appear like
diamonds, reflecting light on every side: most elegantly
finished in all parts it is a miniature work of our great
parent; who seems to have formed it the smallest, and
at the same time the most beautiful of the winged
species.

As I was one day sitting solitary and pensive in my
primitive arbour, my attention was engaged by a strange
sort of rustling noise at some paces distant. I looked all
around without distinguishing anything, until I climbed
one of my great hemp stalks; when to my astonishment,
I beheld two snakes of considerable length, the one pursuing the other with great celerity through a hemp stub-
ble field. The aggressor was of the black kind, six feet
long; the fugitive was a water snake, nearly of equal
dimensions. They soon met, and in the fury of their
first encounter, they appeared in an instant firmly
twisted together; and whilst their united tails beat the
ground, they mutually tried with open jaws to lacerate

each other. What a fell aspect did they present! their heads were compressed to a very small size, their eyes flashed fire; and after this conflict had lasted about five minutes, the second found means to disengage itself from the first, and hurried toward the ditch. Its antagonist instantly assumed a new posture, and half creeping and half erect, with a majestic mien, overtook and attacked the other again, which placed itself in the same attitude, and prepared to resist. The scene was uncommon and beautiful; for thus opposed they fought with their jaws, biting each other with the utmost rage; but notwithstanding this appearance of mutual courage and fury, the water snake still seemed desirous of retreating toward the ditch, its natural element. This was no sooner perceived by the keen-eyed black one, than twisting its tail twice round a stalk of hemp, and seizing its adversary by the throat, not by means of its jaws, but by twisting its own neck twice round that of the water snake, pulled it back from the ditch. To prevent a defeat the latter took hold likewise of a stalk on the bank, and by the acquisition of that point of resistance became a match for its fierce antagonist. Strange was this to behold; two great snakes strongly adhering to the ground mutually fastened together by means of the writhings which lashed them to each other, and stretched at their full length, they pulled but pulled in vain; and in the moments of greatest exertions that part of their bodies which was entwined, seemed extremely small, while the rest appeared inflated, and now and then convulsed with strong undulations, rapidly following each other. Their eyes seemed on fire, and ready to start out of their heads; at one time the conflict seemed decided; the water snake bent itself into two great folds, and by that operation rendered the other more than commonly outstretched; the next minute the new struggles of the black one gained an unexpected superiority, it acquired two great folds likewise, which necessarily extended the body of its adversary in proportion as it had contracted its own. These efforts were alternate; victory seemed doubtful, inclining sometimes to the one side and sometimes to the other; until at last the stalk to which the black snake fastened, suddenly gave way, and in consequence of this accident they both plunged into the ditch. The water did not extinguish their vindictive rage; for by their agitations I could trace, though not distinguish, their mutual attacks. They soon re-appeared on the surface twisted together, as in their first onset; but the black snake seemed to retain its wonted superiority, for its head was exactly fixed above that of the other, which it incessantly pressed down under the water, until it was stifled, and sunk. The victor no sooner perceived its enemy incapable of farther resistance, than abandoning it to the current, it returned on shore and disappeared.

LETTER XI

FROM MR. IW—N AL—Z, A RUSSIAN GENTLEMAN; DESCRIB-
ING THE VISIT HE PAID AT MY REQUEST TO MR. JOHN BERT-
RAM, THE CELEBRATED PENNSYLVANIAN BOTANIST

EXAMINE this flourishing province, in whatever light you
will, the eyes as well as the mind of an European traveller are equally delighted; because a diffusive happiness
appears in every part: happiness which is established on
the broadest basis. The wisdom of Lycurgus and Solon
never conferred on man one half of the blessings and
uninterrupted prosperity which the Pennsylvanians now
possess: the name of *Penn,* that simple but illustrious
citizen, does more honour to the English nation than
those of many of their kings.

In order to convince you that I have not bestowed
undeserved praises in my former letters on this celebrated government; and that either nature or the climate seems to be more favourable here to the arts and
sciences, than to any other American province; let us
together, agreeable to your desire, pay a visit to Mr.
John Bertram, the first botanist, in this new hemisphere:
become such by a native impulse of disposition. It is to
this simple man that America is indebted for several
useful discoveries, and the knowledge of many new
plants. I had been greatly prepossessed in his favour by
the extensive correspondence which I knew he held with
the most eminent Scotch and French botanists; I knew
also that he had been honoured with that of Queen
Ulrica of Sweden.

His house is small, but decent; there was something
peculiar in its first appearance, which seemed to distinguish it from those of his neighbours: a small tower

in the middle of it, not only helped to strengthen it but afforded convenient room for a staircase. Every disposition of the fields, fences, and trees, seemed to bear the marks of perfect order and regularity, which in rural affairs, always indicate a prosperous industry.

I was received at the door by a woman dressed extremely neat and simple, who without courtesying, or any other ceremonial, asked me, with an air of benignity, who I wanted? I answered, I should be glad to see Mr. Bertram. If thee wilt step in and take a chair, I will send for him. No, I said, I had rather have the pleasure of walking through his farm, I shall easily find him out, with your directions. After a little time I perceived the Schuylkill, winding through delightful meadows, and soon cast my eyes on a new-made bank, which seemed greatly to confine its stream. After having walked on its top a considerable way I at last reached the place where ten men were at work. I asked, if any of them could tell me where Mr. Bertram was? An elderly looking man, with wide trousers and a large leather apron on, looking at me said, "My name is Bertram, dost thee want me?" Sir, I am come on purpose to converse with you, if you can be spared from your labour. "Very easily," he answered, "I direct and advise more than I work." We walked toward the house, where he made me take a chair while he went to put on clean clothes, after which he returned and sat down by me. The fame of your knowledge, said I, in American botany, and your well-known hospitality, have induced me to pay you a visit, which I hope you will not think troublesome: I should be glad to spend a few hours in your garden. "The greatest advantage," replied he, "which I receive from what thee callest my botanical fame, is the pleasure which it often procureth me in receiving the visits of friends and foreigners: but our jaunt into the garden must be postponed for the present, as the bell is ringing for dinner." We entered into a large hall, where there was a long table full of victuals; at the lowest part sat his negroes, his hired men were next, then the family and myself; and at the head, the venerable father and his wife presided. Each reclined his head and said his prayers, divested of the tedious cant of some, and of the ostentatious style of others. "After the luxuries of our cities," observed he, "this plain fare must appear to thee a severe fast." By no means, Mr. Bertram, this honest country dinner convinces me, that you receive me as a friend and an old acquaintance. "I am glad of it, for thee art heartily welcome. I never knew how to use ceremonies; they are insufficient proofs of sincerity; our society, besides, are utterly strangers to what the world calleth polite expressions. We treat others as we treat ourselves. I received yesterday a letter from Philadelphia, by which I understand thee art a Russian; what motives can possibly have induced thee to quit thy native country and to come so far in quest of knowledge or pleasure? Verily it is a great compliment thee payest to this our young province, to think that anything it exhibiteth may be worthy thy attention." I have been most amply repaid for the trouble of the passage. I view the present Americans as the seed of future nations, which will replenish this boundless continent; the Russians may be in some respects compared to you; we likewise are a new people, new I mean in knowledge, arts, and improvements. Who knows what revolutions Russia and America may one day bring about; we are perhaps nearer neighbours than we imagine. I view with peculiar attention all your towns, I examine their situation and the police, for which many are already famous. Though their foundations are now so recent, and so well remembered, yet their origin will puzzle posterity as much as we are now puzzled to ascertain the beginning of those which time has in some measure destroyed. Your new buildings, your streets, put me in mind of those of the city of *Pompeii,* where I was a few years ago; I attentively examined everything there, particularly the footpath which runs along the houses. They appeared to have been considerably worn by the great number of people which had once travelled over them. But now how distant; neither builders nor proprietors remain; nothing is known! "Why thee hast been a great traveller for a man of thy years." Few years, Sir, will enable anybody to journey over a great tract of country; but it requires a superior degree of knowledge to gather harvests as we go. Pray, Mr. Bertram, what banks are those which you are making: to what purpose is so much expense and so much labour bestowed? "Friend Iwan, no branch of industry was ever more profitable to any country, as well as to the proprietors; the Schuylkill in its many windings once covered a great extent of ground, though its waters were but shallow even in our highest tides: and though some parts were always dry, yet the whole of this great tract presented to the eye nothing but a putrid swampy soil, useless either for the plough or for the scythe. The proprietors of these grounds are now incorporated; we yearly pay to the treasurer of the company a certain sum, which makes an aggregate, superior to the casualties that generally happen either by inundations or the musk squash. It is owing to this happy contrivance that so many thousand acres of meadows have been rescued from the Schuylkill, which now both enricheth and embellisheth so much of the neighbourhood of our city. Our brethren of Salem in New Jersey have carried the art of banking to a still higher degree of perfection." It is really an admirable contrivance, which greatly redounds to the honour of the parties concerned; and shows a spirit of discernment and perseverance which is highly praiseworthy: if the Virginians would imitate your example, the state of their husbandry would greatly improve. I have not heard of any such association in any other parts of the continent; Pennsylvania hitherto seems to reign the unrivalled queen of these fair provinces. Pray, Sir, what expense are you at e'er these grounds be fit for the scythe? "The expenses are very considerable, particularly when we have land, brooks, trees, and brush to clear away. But such is the excellence of these bottoms and the goodness of the grass for fattening of cattle, that the produce of three years pays all advances." Happy the country where nature has bestowed such rich treasures, treasures superior to mines, said I: if all this fair province is thus cultivated, no wonder it has acquired such reputation for the prosperity and the industry of its inhabitants.

By this time the working part of the family had finished their dinner, and had retired with a decency and silence which pleased me much. Soon after I heard, as I thought, a distant concert of instruments.—However simple and pastoral your fare was, Mr. Bertram, this is the dessert of a prince; pray what is this I hear? "Thee must not be alarmed, it is of a piece with the rest of thy treatment, friend Iwan." Anxious I followed the sound, and by ascending the staircase, found that it was the effect of the wind through the strings of an Eolian harp; an instrument which I had never before seen. After dinner we quaffed an honest bottle of Madeira wine, without the irksome labour of toasts, healths, or sentiments; and then retired into his study.

I was no sooner entered, than I observed a coat of arms in a gilt frame with the name of *John Bertram.* The novelty of such a decoration, in such a place, struck me; I could not avoid asking, Does the society of Friends take any pride in those armorial bearings, which sometimes serve as marks of distinction between families, and much oftener as food for pride and ostentation? "Thee must know," said he, "that my father was a Frenchman, he brought this piece of painting over with him; I keep it as a piece of family furniture, and as a memorial of his removal hither." From his study we went into the garden, which contained a great variety of curious plants and shrubs; some grew in a greenhouse, over the door of which were written these lines:

> "Slave to no sect, who takes no private road,
> But looks through nature, up to nature's God!"

He informed me that he had often followed General Bouquet to Pittsburgh, with the view of herbalising; that he had made useful collections in Virginia, and that he had been employed by the king of England to visit the two Floridas.

Our walks and botanical observations engrossed so much of our time, that the sun was almost down ere I thought of returning to Philadelphia; I regretted that the day had been so short, as I had not spent so rational a one for a long time before. I wanted to stay, yet was doubtful whether it would not appear improper, being an utter stranger. Knowing, however, that I was visiting the least ceremonious people in the world, I bluntly informed him of the pleasure I had enjoyed, and with the desire I had of staying a few days with him. "Thee art as welcome as if I was thy father; thee art no stranger; thy desire of knowledge, thy being a foreigner besides, entitleth thee to consider my house as thine own, as long as thee pleaseth: use thy time with the most perfect freedom; I too shall do so myself." I thankfully accepted the kind invitation.

We went to view his favourite bank; he showed me the principles and method on which it was erected; and we walked over the grounds which had been already drained. The whole store of nature's kind luxuriance seemed to have been exhausted on these beautiful meadows; he made me count the amazing number of cattle and horses now feeding on solid bottoms, which but a few years before had been covered with water. Thence we rambled through his fields, where the right-angular fences, the heaps of pitched stones, the flourishing clover, announced the best husbandry, as well as the most assiduous attention. His cows were then returning home, deep bellied, short legged, having udders ready to burst; seeking with seeming toil to be delivered from the great exuberance they contained: he next showed me his orchard, formerly planted on a barren sandy soil, but long since converted into one of the richest spots in that vicinage.

"This," said he, "is altogether the fruit of my own contrivance; I purchased some years ago the privilege of a small spring, about a mile and a half from hence, which at a considerable expense I have brought to this reservoir; therein I throw old lime, ashes, horse-dung, etc., and twice a week I let it run, thus impregnated; I regularly spread on this ground in the fall, old hay, straw, and whatever damaged fodder I have about my barn. By these simple means I mow, one year with another, fifty-three hundreds of excellent hay per acre, from a soil, which scarcely produced *five-fingers* [*a small plant resembling strawberries*] some years before." This is, Sir, a miracle in husbandry; happy the country which is cultivated by a society of men, whose application and taste lead them to prosecute and accomplish useful works. "I am not the only person who does these things," he said, "wherever water can be had it is always turned to that important use; wherever a farmer can water his meadows, the greatest crops of the best hay and excellent after-grass, are the sure rewards of his labours. With the banks of my meadow ditches, I have greatly enriched my upland fields, those which I intend to rest for a few years, I constantly sow with red clover, which is the greatest meliorator of our lands. For three years after, they yield abundant pasture; when I want to break up my clover fields, I give them a good coat of mud, which hath been exposed to the severities of three or four of our winters. This is the reason that I commonly reap from twenty-eight to thirty-six bushels of wheat an acre; my flax, oats, and Indian corn, I raise in the same proportion. Wouldst thee inform me whether the inhabitants of thy country follow the same methods of husbandry?" No, Sir; in the neighbourhood of our towns, there are indeed some intelligent farmers, who prosecute their rural schemes with attention; but we should be too numerous, too happy, too powerful a people, if it were possible for the whole Russian Empire to be cultivated like the province of Pennsylvania. Our lands are so unequally divided, and so few of our farmers are possessors of the soil they till, that they cannot execute plans of husbandry with the same vigour as you do, who hold yours, as it were from the Master of nature, unencumbered and free. Oh, America! exclaimed I, thou knowest not as yet the whole extent of thy happiness: the foundation of thy civil polity must lead thee in a few years to a degree of population and power which Europe little thinks of! "Long before this happens," answered the good man, "we shall rest beneath the turf; it is vain for mortals to be presumptuous in their conjectures: our country, is, no doubt, the cradle of an extensive future population; the old world is growing weary of its inhabitants, they must come here to flee from the tyranny of the great. But doth not thee imagine, that the great will, in the course of years, come over here also; for it is the misfortune of all societies everywhere to hear of great men, great rulers, and of great tyrants." My dear Sir, I replied, tyranny never can take a strong hold in this country, the land is too widely distributed: it is poverty in Europe that makes slaves. "Friend Iwan, as I make no doubt that thee understandest the Latin tongue, read this kind epistle which the good Queen of Sweden, *Ulrica,* sent me a few years ago. Good woman! that she should think in her palace at Stockholm of poor John Bertram, on the banks of the Schuylkill, appeareth to me very strange." Not in the least, dear Sir; you are the first man whose name as a botanist hath done honour to America; it is very natural at the same time to imagine, that so extensive a continent must contain many curious plants and trees: is it then surprising to see a princess, fond of useful knowledge, descend sometimes from the throne, to walk in the gardens of Linnæus? " 'Tis to the directions of that learned man," said Mr. Bertram, "that I am indebted for the method which has led me to the knowledge I now possess; the science of botany is so diffusive, that a proper thread is absolutely wanted to conduct the beginner." Pray, Mr. Bertram, when did you imbibe the first wish to cultivate the science of botany; were you regularly bred to it in Philadelphia? "I have never received any other education than barely reading and writing; this small farm was all the patrimony my father left me, certain debts and the want of meadows kept me rather low in the beginning of my life; my wife brought me nothing in money, all her riches consisted in her good temper and great knowledge of housewifery. I scarcely know how to trace my steps in the botanical career; they appear to me now like unto a dream: but thee mayest rely on what I shall relate, though I know that some of our friends have laughed at it." I am not one of those people, Mr. Bertram, who aim at finding out the ridiculous in what is sincerely and honestly averred. "Well, then, I'll tell thee: One day I was very busy in holding my plough (for thee seest that I am but a ploughman) and being weary I ran under the shade of a tree to repose myself. I cast my eyes on a *daisy,* I plucked it mechanically and viewed it with more curiosity than common country farmers are wont to do; and observed therein very many distinct parts, some perpendicular, some horizontal. *What a shame, said my mind, or something that inspired my mind, that thee shouldst have employed so many years in tilling the earth and destroying so many flowers and plants, without being acquainted with their structures and their uses!* This seeming inspiration suddenly awakened my curiosity, for these were not thoughts to which I had been accustomed. I returned to my team, but this new desire did not quit my mind; I mentioned it to my wife, who greatly discouraged me from prosecuting my new scheme, as she called it; I was not opulent enough, she said, to dedicate much of my time to studies and labours which might rob me of that portion of it which is the only wealth of the American farmer. However her prudent caution did not discourage me; I thought about it continually, at supper, in bed, and wherever I went. At last I could not resist the impulse; for on the fourth day of the following week, I hired a man to plough for me, and went to Philadelphia. Though I knew not what book to call for, I ingeniously told the bookseller my errand, who provided me with such as he thought best, and a Latin grammar beside. Next I applied to a neighbouring schoolmaster, who in three months taught me Latin enough to understand Linnæus, which I purchased afterward. Then I began to botanise all over my farm; in a little time I became acquainted with every vegetable that grew in my neighbourhood; and next ventured into Maryland, living among the Friends: in proportion as I thought myself more learned I proceeded farther, and by a steady application of several years I have acquired a pretty general knowledge of every plant and tree to be found in our continent. In process of time I was applied to from the old countries, whither I every year send many collections. Being now made easy in my circumstances, I have ceased to labour, and am never so happy as when I see and converse with my friends. If among the many plants or shrubs I am acquainted with, there are any thee wantest to send to thy native country, I will cheerfully procure them, and give thee moreover whatever directions thee mayest want."

Thus I passed several days in ease, improvement, and pleasure; I observed in all the operations of his farm, as well as in the mutual correspondence between the master and the inferior members of his family, the greatest ease and decorum; not a word like command seemed to exceed the tone of a simple wish. The very negroes themselves appeared to partake of such a decency of behaviour, and modesty of countenance, as I had never before observed. By what means, said I, Mr. Bertram, do you rule your slaves so well, that they seem to do their work with all the cheerfulness of white men? "Though our erroneous prejudices and opinions once induced us to look upon them as fit only for slavery, though ancient custom had very unfortunately taught us to keep them in bondage; yet of late, in consequence of the remonstrances of several Friends, and of the good books they have published on that subject, our society treats them very differently. With us they are now free. I give those whom thee didst see at my table, eighteen pounds a year, with victuals and clothes, and all other privileges which white men enjoy. Our society treats them now as the companions of our labours; and by this management, as well as by means of the education we have given them, they are in general become a new set of beings. Those whom I admit to my table, I have found to be good, trusty, moral men; when they do not what we think they should do, we dismiss them, which is all the punishment we inflict. Other societies of Christians keep them still as slaves, without teaching them any kind of religious principles: what motive beside fear can they have to behave well? In the first settlement of this province, we employed them as slaves, I acknowledge; but when we found that good example, gentle admonition, and religious principles could lead them to subordination and sobriety, we relinquished a method so contrary to the profession of Christianity. We gave them freedom, and yet few have quitted their ancient masters. The women breed in our families; and we become attached to one another. I taught mine to read and write; they love God, and fear his judgments. The oldest person among them transacts my business in Philadelphia, with a punctuality, from which he has never deviated. They constantly attend our meetings, they participate in health and sickness, infancy and old age, in the advantages our society affords. Such are the means we have made use of, to relieve them from that bondage and ignorance in which they were kept before. Thee perhaps hast been surprised to see them at my table, but by elevating them to the rank of freemen, they necessarily acquire that emulation without which we ourselves should fall into debasement and profligate ways." Mr. Bertram, this is the most philosophical treatment of negroes that I have heard of; happy would it be for America would other denominations of Christians imbibe the same principles, and follow the same admirable rules. A great number of men would be relieved from those cruel shackles, under which they now groan; and under this impression, I cannot endure to spend more time in the southern provinces. The method with which they are treated there, the meanness of their food, the severity of their tasks, are spectacles I have not patience to behold. "I am glad to see that thee hast so much compassion; are there any slaves in thy country?" Yes, unfortunately, but they are more properly civil than domestic slaves; they are attached to the soil on which they live; it is the remains of ancient barbarous customs, established in the days of the greatest ignorance and savageness of manners! and preserved notwithstanding the repeated tears of humanity, the loud calls of policy, and the commands of religion. The pride of great men, with the avarice of landholders, make them look on this class as necessary tools of husbandry; as if freemen could not cultivate the ground. "And is it really so, Friend Iwan? To be poor, to be wretched, to be a slave, are hard indeed; existence is not worth enjoying on those terms. I am afraid thy country can never flourish under such impolitic government." I am very much of your opinion, Mr. Bertram, though I am in hopes that the present reign, illustrious by so many acts of the soundest policy, will not expire without this salutary, this necessary emancipation; which would fill the Russian empire with tears of gratitude. "How long hast thee been in this country?" Four years, Sir. "Why thee speakest English almost like a native; what a toil a traveller must undergo to learn various languages, to divest himself of his native prejudices, and to accommodate himself to the customs of all those among whom he chooseth to reside."

Thus I spent my time with this enlightened botanist —this worthy citizen; who united all the simplicity of rustic manners to the most useful learning. Various and extensive were the conversations that filled the measure of my visit. I accompanied him to his fields, to his barn, to his bank, to his garden, to his study, and at last to the meeting of the society on the Sunday following. It was at the town of Chester, whither the whole family went in two waggons; Mr. Bertram and I on horseback. When I entered the house where the friends were assembled, who might be about two hundred men and women, the involuntary impulse of ancient custom made me pull off my hat; but soon recovering myself, I sat with it on, at the end of a bench. The meeting-house was a square building devoid of any ornament whatever; the whiteness of the walls, the conveniency of seats, that of a large stove, which in cold weather keeps the whole house warm, were the only essential things which I observed. Neither pulpit nor desk, fount nor altar, tabernacle nor organ, were there to be seen; it is merely a spacious room, in which these good people meet every Sunday. A profound silence ensued, which lasted about half an hour; every one had his head reclined, and seemed absorbed in profound meditation, when a female friend arose, and declared with a most engaging modesty, that the spirit moved her to entertain them on the subject she had chosen. She treated it with great propriety, as a moral useful discourse, and delivered it without theological parade or the ostentation of learning. Either she must have been a great adept in public speaking, or had studiously prepared herself; a circumstance that cannot well be supposed, as it is a point, in their profession, to utter nothing but what arises from spontaneous impulse: or else the great spirit of the world, the patronage and influence of which they all came to invoke, must have inspired her with the soundest morality. Her discourse lasted three quarters of an hour. I did not observe one single face turned toward her; never before had I seen a congregation listening with so much attention to a public oration. I observed neither contortions of body, nor any kind of affectation in her face, style, or manner of utterance; everything was natural, and therefore pleasing, and shall I tell you more, she was very handsome, although upward of forty. As soon as she had finished, every one seemed to return to their former meditation for about a quarter of an hour; when they rose up by common consent, and after some general conversation, departed.

How simple their precepts, how unadorned their religious system: how few the ceremonies through which they pass during the course of their lives! At their deaths they are interred by the fraternity, without pomp, without prayers; thinking it then too late to alter the course of God's eternal decrees: and as you well know, without either monument or tombstone. Thus after having lived under the mildest government, after having been guided by the mildest doctrine, they die just as peaceably as those who being educated in more pompous religions, pass through a variety of sacraments, subscribe to complicated creeds, and enjoy the benefits of a church establishment. These good people flatter themselves, with following the doctrines of Jesus Christ, in that simplicity with which they were delivered: an happier system could not have been devised for the use of mankind. It appears to be entirely free from those ornaments and political additions which each country and each government hath fashioned after its own manners.

At the door of this meeting house, I had been invited to spend some days at the houses of some respectable farmers in the neighbourhood. The reception I met with everywhere insensibly led me to spend two months among these good people; and I must say they were the golden days of my riper years. I never shall forget the gratitude I owe them for the innumerable kindnesses they heaped on me; it was to the letter you gave me that I am indebted for the extensive acquaintance I now have throughout Pennsylvania. I must defer thanking you as I ought, until I see you again. Before that time comes, I may perhaps entertain you with more curious anecdotes than this letter affords.—Farewell.   I——N AL——Z.

LETTER XII

I wish for a change of place; the hour is come at last, that I must fly from my house and abandon my farm! But what course shall I steer, inclosed as I am? The climate best adapted to my present situation and humour would be the polar regions, where six months day and six months night divide the dull year: nay, a simple Aurora Borealis would suffice me, and greatly refresh my eyes, fatigued now by so many disagreeable objects. The severity of those climates, that great gloom, where melancholy dwells, would be perfectly analogous to the turn of my mind. Oh, could I remove my plantation to the shores of the Oby, willingly would I dwell in the hut of a Samoyede; with cheerfulness would I go and bury myself in the cavern of a Laplander. Could I but carry my family along with me, I would winter at Pello, or Tobolsky, in order to enjoy the peace and innocence of that country. But let me arrive under the pole, or reach the antipodes, I never can leave behind me the remembrance of the dreadful scenes to which I have been a witness; therefore never can I be happy! Happy, why would I mention that sweet, that enchanting word? Once happiness was our portion; now it is gone from us, and I am afraid not to be enjoyed again by the present generation! Whichever way I look, nothing but the most frightful precipices present themselves to my view, in which hundreds of my friends and acquaintances have already perished: of all animals that live on the surface of this planet, what is man when no longer connected with society; or when he finds himself surrounded by a convulsed and a half dissolved one? He cannot live in solitude, he must belong to some community bound by some ties, however imperfect. Men mutually support and add to the boldness and confidence of each other; the weakness of each is strengthened by the force of the whole. I had never before these calamitous times formed any such ideas; I lived on, laboured and prospered, without having ever studied on what the security of my life and the foundation of my prosperity were established: I perceived them just as they left me. Never was a situation so singularly terrible as mine, in every possible respect, as a member of an extensive society, as a citizen of an inferior division of the same society, as a husband, as a father, as a man who exquisitely feels for the miseries of others as well as for his own! But alas! so much is everything now subverted among us, that the very word misery, with which we were hardly acquainted before, no longer conveys the same ideas; or rather tired with feeling for the miseries of others, every one feels now for himself alone. When I consider myself as connected in all these characters, as bound by so many cords, all uniting in my heart, I am seized with a fever of the mind, I am transported beyond that degree of calmness which is necessary to delineate our thoughts. I feel as if my reason wanted to leave me, as if it would burst its poor weak tenement: again I try to compose myself, I grow cool, and preconceiving the dreadful loss, I endeavour to retain the useful guest.

You know the position of our settlement; I need not therefore describe it. To the west it is inclosed by a chain of mountains, reaching to ——; to the east, the country is as yet but thinly inhabited; we are almost insulated, and the houses are at a considerable distance from each other. From the mountains we have but too much reason to expect our dreadful enemy; the wilderness is a harbour where it is impossible to find them. It is a door through which they can enter our

country whenever they please; and, as they seem determined to destroy the whole chain of frontiers, our fate
cannot be far distant: from Lake Champlain, almost all
has been conflagrated one after another. What renders
these incursions still more terrible is, that they most
commonly take place in the dead of the night; we never
go to our fields but we are seized with an involuntary
fear, which lessens our strength and weakens our labour.
No other subject of conversation intervenes between the
different accounts, which spread through the country,
of successive acts of devastation; and these told in chim-
ney-corners, swell themselves in our affrighted imaginations into the most terrific ideas! We never sit down
either to dinner or supper, but the least noise immediately spreads a general alarm and prevents us from enjoying the comfort of our meals. The very appetite
proceeding from labour and peace of mind is gone; we
eat just enough to keep us alive: our sleep is disturbed
by the most frightful dreams; sometimes I start awake,
as if the great hour of danger was come; at other times
the howling of our dogs seems to announce the arrival
of the enemy: we leap out of bed and run to arms; my
poor wife with panting bosom and silent tears, takes
leave of me, as if we were to see each other no more;
she snatches the youngest children from their beds, who,
suddenly awakened, increase by their innocent questions
the horror of the dreadful moment. She tries to hide
them in the cellar, as if our cellar was inaccessible to
the fire. I place all my servants at the windows, and myself at the door, where I am determined to perish. Fear
industriously increases every sound; we all listen; each
communicates to the other his ideas and conjectures.
We remain thus sometimes for whole hours, our hearts
and our minds racked by the most anxious suspense:
what a dreadful situation, a thousand times worse than
that of a soldier engaged in the midst of the most severe

conflict! Sometimes feeling the spontaneous courage of a man, I seem to wish for the decisive minute; the next instant a message from my wife, sent by one of the children, puzzling me beside with their little questions, unmans me: away goes my courage, and I descend again into the deepest despondency. At last finding that it was a false alarm, we return once more to our beds; but what good can the kind sleep of nature do to us when interrupted by such scenes! Securely placed as you are, you can have no idea of our agitations, but by hear-say; no relation can be equal to what we suffer and to what we feel. Every morning my youngest children are sure to have frightful dreams to relate: in vain I exert my authority to keep them silent, it is not in my power; and these images of their disturbed imagination, instead of being frivolously looked upon as in the days of our happiness, are on the contrary considered as warnings and sure prognostics of our future fate. I am not a superstitious man, but since our misfortunes, I am grown more timid, and less disposed to treat the doctrine of omens with contempt.

Though these evils have been gradual, yet they do not become habitual like other incidental evils. The nearer I view the end of this catastrophe, the more I shudder. But why should I trouble you with such unconnected accounts; men secure and out of danger are soon fatigued with mournful details: can you enter with me into fellowship with all these afflictive sensations; have you a tear ready to shed over the approaching ruin of a once opulent and substantial family? Read this I pray with the eyes of sympathy; with a tender sorrow, pity the lot of those whom you once called your friends; who were once surrounded with plenty, ease, and perfect security; but who now expect every night to be their last, and who are as wretched as criminals under an impending sentence of the law.

As a member of a large society which extends to many parts of the world, my connection with it is too distant to be as strong as that which binds me to the inferior division in the midst of which I live. I am told that the great nation, of which we are a part, is just, wise, and free, beyond any other on earth, within its own insular boundaries; but not always so to its distant conquests: I shall not repeat all I have heard, because I cannot believe half of it. As a citizen of a smaller society, I find that any kind of opposition to its now prevailing sentiments, immediately begets hatred: how easily do men pass from loving, to hating and cursing one another! I am a lover of peace, what must I do? I am divided between the respect I feel for the ancient connection, and the fear of innovations, with the consequence of which I am not well acquainted; as they are embraced by my own countrymen. I am conscious that I was happy before this unfortunate Revolution. I feel that I am no longer so; therefore I regret the change. This is the only mode of reasoning adapted to persons in my situation. If I attach myself to the Mother Country, which is 3000 miles from me, I become what is called an enemy to my own region; if I follow the rest of my countrymen, I become opposed to our ancient masters: both extremes appear equally dangerous to a person of so little weight and consequence as I am, whose energy and example are of no avail. As to the argument on which the dispute is founded, I know little about it. Much has been said and written on both sides, but who has a judgment capacious and clear enough to decide? The great moving principles which actuate both parties are much hid from vulgar eyes, like mine; nothing but the plausible and the probable are offered to our contemplation. The innocent class are always the victim of the few; they are in all countries and at all times the inferior agents, on which the popular phantom is erected; they clamour,

and must toil, and bleed, and are always sure of meeting
with oppression and rebuke. It is for the sake of the
great leaders on both sides, that so much blood must be
spilt; that of the people is counted as nothing. Great
events are not achieved for us, though it is *by* us that
they are principally accomplished; by the arms, the sweat,
the lives of the people. Books tell me so much that they
inform me of nothing. Sophistry, the bane of freemen,
launches forth in all her deceiving attire! After all, most
men reason from passions; and shall such an ignorant
individual as I am decide, and say this side is right, that
side is wrong? Sentiment and feeling are the only guides
I know. Alas, how should I unravel an argument, in
which reason herself hath given way to brutality and
bloodshed! What then must I do? I ask the wisest
lawyers, the ablest casuists, the warmest patriots; for I
mean honestly. Great Source of wisdom! inspire me
with light sufficient to guide my benighted steps out of
this intricate maze! Shall I discard all my ancient principles, shall I renounce that name, that nation which I
held once so respectable? I feel the powerful attraction;
the sentiments they inspired grew with my earliest knowledge, and were grafted upon the first rudiments of my
education. On the other hand, shall I arm myself against
that country where I first drew breath, against the play-
mates of my youth, my bosom friends, my acquaintance?
—the idea makes me shudder! Must I be called a parri-
cide, a traitor, a villain, lose the esteem of all those
whom I love, to preserve my own; be shunned like a
rattlesnake, or be pointed at like a bear? I have neither
heroism nor magnanimity enough to make so great a
sacrifice. Here I am tied, I am fastened by numerous
strings, nor do I repine at the pressure they cause; ignorant as I am, I can pervade the utmost extent of the
calamities which have already overtaken our poor afflicted country. I can see the great and accumulated ruin

yet extending itself as far as the theatre of war has reached; I hear the groans of thousands of families now ruined and desolated by our aggressors. I cannot count the multitude of orphans this war has made; nor ascertain the immensity of blood we have lost. Some have asked, whether it was a crime to resist; to repel some parts of this evil. Others have asserted, that a resistance so general makes pardon unattainable, and repentance useless; and dividing the crime among so many, renders it imperceptible. What one party calls meritorious, the other denominates flagitious. These opinions vary, contract, or expand, like the events of the war on which they are founded. What can an insignificant man do in the midst of these jarring contradictory parties, equally hostile to persons situated as I am? And after all who will be the really guilty?—Those most certainly who fail of success. Our fate, the fate of thousands, is then necessarily involved in the dark wheel of fortune. Why then so many useless reasonings; we are the sport of fate. Farewell education, principles, love of our country, farewell; all are become useless to the generality of us: he who governs himself according to what he calls his principles, may be punished either by one party or the other, for those very principles. He who proceeds without principle, as chance, timidity, or self-preservation directs, will not perhaps fare better; but he will be less blamed. What are *we* in the great scale of events, we poor defenceless frontier inhabitants? What is it to the gazing world, whether we breathe or whether we die? Whatever virtue, whatever merit and disinterestedness we may exhibit in our secluded retreats, of what avail? We are like the pismires destroyed by the plough; whose destruction prevents not the future crop. Self-preservation, therefore, the rule of nature, seems to be the best rule of conduct; what good can we do by vain resistance, by useless efforts? The cool, the distant spectator, placed in safety, may arraign me for ingratitude, may bring forth the principles of Solon or Montesquieu; he may look on me as wilfully guilty; he may call me by the most opprobrious names. Secure from personal danger, his warm imagination, undisturbed by the least agitation of the heart, will expatiate freely on this grand question; and will consider this extended field, but as exhibiting the double scene of attack and defence. To him the object becomes abstracted, the intermediate glares, the perspective distance and a variety of opinions unimpaired by affections, presents to his mind but one set of ideas. Here he proclaims the high guilt of the one, and there the right of the other; but let him come and reside with us one single month, let him pass with us through all the successive hours of necessary toil, terror and affright, let him watch with us, his musket in his hand, through tedious, sleepless nights, his imagination furrowed by the keen chisel of every passion; let his wife and his children become exposed to the most dreadful hazards of death; let the existence of his property depend on a single spark, blown by the breath of an enemy; let him tremble with us in our fields, shudder at the rustling of every leaf; let his heart, the seat of the most affecting passions, be powerfully wrung by hearing the melancholy end of his relations and friends; let him trace on the map the progress of these desolations; let his alarmed imagination predict to him the night, the dreadful night when it may be his turn to perish, as so many have perished before. Observe then, whether the man will not get the better of the citizen, whether his political maxims will not vanish! Yes, he will cease to glow so warmly with the glory of the metropolis; all his wishes will be turned toward the preservation of his family! Oh, were he situated where I am, were his house perpetually filled, as mine is, with miserable victims just escaped from the flames and the scalping knife, telling of barbarities and murders that make human nature tremble; his situation would suspend every political reflection, and expel every abstract idea. My heart is full and involuntarily takes hold of any notion from whence it can receive ideal ease or relief. I am informed that the king has the most numerous, as well as the fairest, progeny of children, of any potentate now in the world: he may be a great king, but he must feel as we common mortals do, in the good wishes he forms for their lives and prosperity. His mind no doubt often springs forward on the wings of anticipation, and contemplates us as happily settled in the world. If a poor frontier inhabitant may be allowed to suppose this great personage the first in our system, to be exposed but for one hour, to the exquisite pangs we so often feel, would not the preservation of so numerous a family engross all his thoughts; would not the ideas of dominion and other felicities attendant on royalty all vanish in the hour of danger? The regal character, however sacred, would be superseded by the stronger, because more natural one of man and father. Oh! did he but know the circumstances of this horrid war, I am sure he would put a stop to that long destruction of parents and children. I am sure that while he turned his ears to state policy, he would attentively listen also to the dictates of nature, that great parent; for, as a good king, he no doubt wishes to create, to spare, and to protect, as she does. Must I then, in order to be called a faithful subject, coolly, and philosophically say, it is necessary for the good of Britain, that my children's brains should be dashed against the walls of the house in which they were reared; that my wife should be stabbed and scalped before my face; that I should be either murdered or captivated; or that for greater expedition we should all be locked up and burnt to ashes as the family of the B———n was? Must I with meekness wait for that last pitch of desolation, and receive with perfect resignation so hard a fate, from ruffians, acting at such a distance from the eyes of any superior; monsters, left to the wild impulses of the wildest nature. Could the lions of Africa be transported here and let loose, they would no doubt kill us in order to prey upon our carcasses! but their appetites would not require so many victims. Shall I wait to be punished with death, or else to be stripped of all food and raiment, reduced to despair without redress and without hope. Shall those who may escape, see everything they hold dear destroyed and gone. Shall those few survivors, lurking in some obscure corner, deplore in vain the fate of their families, mourn over parents either captivated, butchered, or burnt; roam among our wilds, and wait for death at the foot of some tree, without a murmur, or without a sigh, for the good of the cause? No, it is impossible! so astonishing a sacrifice is not to be expected from human nature, it must belong to beings of an inferior or superior order, actuated by less, or by more refined principles. Even those great personages who are so far elevated above the common ranks of men, those, I mean, who wield and direct so many thunders; those who have let loose against us these demons of war, could they be transported here, and metamorphosed into simple planters as we are, they would, from being the arbiters of human destiny, sink into miserable victims; they would feel and exclaim as we do, and be as much at a loss what line of conduct to prosecute. Do you well comprehend the difficulties of our situation? If we stay we are sure to perish at one time or another; no vigilance on our part can save us; if we retire, we know not where to go; every house is filled with refugees as wretched as ourselves; and if we remove we become beggars. The property of farmers is not like that of merchants; and absolute poverty is worse than death. If we take up arms to defend ourselves, we are denominated rebels; should we not be rebels against nature, could we be shamefully passive? Shall we then, like martyrs, glory in an allegiance, now become useless, and voluntarily expose ourselves to a species of desolation which, though it ruin us entirely, yet enriches not our ancient masters. By this inflexible and sullen attachment, we shall be despised by our countrymen, and destroyed by our ancient friends; whatever we may say, whatever merit we may claim, will not shelter us from those indiscriminate blows, given by hired banditti, animated by all those passions which urge men to shed the blood of others; how bitter the thought! On the contrary, blows received by the hands of those from whom we expected protection, extinguish ancient respect, and urge us to self-defence—perhaps to revenge; this is the path which nature herself points out, as well to the civilised as to the uncivilised. The Creator of hearts has himself stamped on them those propensities at their first formation; and must we then daily receive this treatment from a power once so loved? The Fox flies or deceives the hounds that pursue him; the bear, when overtaken, boldly resists and attacks them; the hen, the very timid hen, fights for the preservation of her chickens, nor does she decline to attack, and to meet on the wing even the swift kite. Shall man, then, provided both with instinct and reason, unmoved, unconcerned, and passive, see his subsistence consumed, and his progeny either ravished from him or murdered? Shall fictitious reason extinguish the unerring impulse of instinct? No; my former respect, my former attachment vanishes with my safety; that respect and attachment was purchased by protection, and it has ceased. Could not the great nation we belong to have accomplished her designs by means of her numerous armies, by means of those fleets which cover the ocean? Must those who are masters of two thirds of the trade of the world; who have in their hands the power which almighty gold can give; who possess a species of wealth that increases with their desires; must they establish their conquest with our insignificant innocent blood!

Must I then bid farewell to Britain, to that renowned country? Must I renounce a name so ancient and so venerable? Alas, she herself, that once indulgent parent, forces me to take up arms against her. She herself, first inspired the most unhappy citizens of our remote districts, with the thoughts of shedding the blood of those whom they used to call by the name of friends and brethren. That great nation which now convulses the world; which hardly knows the extent of her Indian kingdoms; which looks toward the universal monarchy of trade, of industry, of riches, of power: why must she strew our poor frontiers with the carcasses of her friends, with the wrecks of our insignificant villages, in which there is no gold? When, oppressed by painful recollection, I revolve all these scattered ideas in my mind, when I contemplate my situation, and the thousand streams of evil with which I am surrounded; when I descend into the particular tendency even of the remedy I have proposed, I am convulsed—convulsed sometimes to that degree, as to be tempted to exclaim—Why has the master of the world permitted so much indiscriminate evil throughout every part of this poor planet, at all times, and among all kinds of people? It ought surely to be the punishment of the wicked only. I bring that cup to my lips, of which I must soon taste, and shudder at its bitterness. What then is life, I ask myself, is it a gracious gift? No, it is too bitter; a gift means something valuable conferred, but life appears to be a mere accident, and of the worst kind: we are born to be victims of diseases and passions, of mischances and death: better not to be than to be miserable.—Thus impiously I roam, I fly from one erratic thought to another, and my mind, irritated by these acrimonious reflections, is ready sometimes to lead me to dangerous extremes of violence. When I recollect that I am a father, and a husband, the return of these endearing ideas strikes deep into my heart. Alas! they once made it to glow with pleasure and with every ravishing exultation; but now they fill it with sorrow. At other times, my wife industriously rouses me out of these dreadful meditations, and soothes me by all the reasoning she is mistress of; but her endeavours only serve to make me more miserable, by reflecting that she must share with all these calamities, the bare apprehensions of which I am afraid will subvert her reason. Nor can I with patience think that a beloved wife, my faithful helpmate, throughout all my rural schemes, the principal hand which has assisted me in rearing the prosperous fabric of ease and independence I lately possessed, as well as my children, those tenants of my heart, should daily and nightly be exposed to such a cruel fate. Self-preservation is above all political precepts and rules, and even superior to the dearest opinions of our minds; a reasonable accommodation of ourselves to the various exigencies of the time in which we live, is the most irresistible precept. To this great evil I must seek some sort of remedy adapted to remove or to palliate it; situated as I am, what steps should I take that will neither injure nor insult any of the parties, and at the same time save my family from that certain destruction which awaits it, if I remain here much longer. Could I insure them bread, safety, and subsistence, not the bread of idleness, but that earned by proper labour as heretofore; could this be accomplished by the sacrifice of my life, I would willingly give it up. I attest before heaven, that it is only for these I would wish to live and to toil: for these whom I have brought into this miserable existence. I resemble, methinks, one of the stones of a ruined arch, still retaining that pristine form that anciently fitted the place I occupied, but the centre is tumbled down; I can be nothing until I am replaced, either in the former circle, or in some stronger one. I see one on a smaller scale, and at a considerable distance, but it is within my power to reach it: and since I have ceased to consider myself as a member of the ancient state now convulsed, I willingly descend into an inferior one. I will revert into a state approaching nearer to that of nature, unencumbered either with voluminous laws, or contradictory codes, often galling the very necks of those whom they protect; and at the same time sufficiently remote from the brutality of unconnected savage nature. Do you, my friend, perceive the path I have found out? it is that which leads to the tenants of the great ———— village of ————, where, far removed from the accursed neighbourhood of Europeans, its inhabitants live with more ease, decency, and peace, than you imagine: where, though governed by no laws, yet find, in uncontaminated simple manners all that laws can afford. Their system is sufficiently complete to answer all the primary wants of man, and to constitute him a social being, such as he ought to be in the great forest of nature. There it is that I have resolved at any rate to transport myself and family: an eccentric thought, you may say, thus to cut asunder all former connections, and to form new ones with a people whom nature has stamped with such different characteristics! But as the happiness of my family is the only object of my wishes, I care very little where we be, or where we go, provided that we are safe, and all united together. Our new calamities being shared equally by all, will become lighter; our mutual affection for each other, will in this great transmutation become the strongest link of our new society, will afford us every joy we can receive on a foreign soil, and preserve us in unity, as the gravity and coherency of matter prevents the world from dissolution. Blame me not, it would be cruel in you, it would besides be entirely useless; for when you receive this we shall be on the wing. When we think all hopes are gone, must we, like poor pusillanimous wretches, despair and die? No; I perceive before me a few resources, though through many dangers, which I will explain to you hereafter. It is not, believe me, a disappointed ambition which leads me to take this step, it is the bitterness of my situation, it is the impossibility of knowing what better measure to adopt: my education fitted me for nothing more than the most simple occupations of life; I am but a feller of trees, a cultivator of land, the most honourable title an American can have. I have no exploits, no discoveries, no inventions to boast of; I have cleared about 370 acres of land, some for the plough, some for the scythe; and this has occupied many years of my life. I have never possessed, or wish to possess anything more than what could be earned or produced by the united industry of my family. I wanted nothing more than to live at home independent and tranquil, and to teach my children how to provide the means of a future ample subsistence, founded on labour, like that of their father. This is the career of life I have pursued, and that which I had marked out for them and for which they seemed to be so well calculated by their inclinations, and by their constitutions. But now these pleasing expectations are gone, we must abandon the accumulated industry of nineteen years, we must fly we hardly know whither, through the most impervious paths, and become members of a new and strange community. Oh, virtue! is this all the reward thou hast to confer on thy votaries? Either thou art only a chimera, or thou art a timid useless being; soon affrighted, when ambition, thy great adversary, dictates, when war re-echoes the dreadful sounds, and poor helpless individuals are mowed down by its cruel reapers like useless grass. I have at all times generously relieved what few distressed people I have met with; I have encouraged the industrious; my house has always been opened to travellers; I have not lost a month in illness since I have been a man; I have caused upwards of an hundred and twenty families to remove hither. Many of them I have led by the hand in the days of their first trial; distant as I am from any places of worship or school of education, I have been the pastor of my family, and the teacher of many of my neighbours. I have taught them as well as I could, the gratitude they owe to God, the father of harvests; and their duties to man: I have been as useful a subject; ever obedient to the laws, ever vigilant to see them respected and observed. My wife hath faithfully followed the same line within her province; no woman was ever a better economist, or spun or wove better linen; yet we must perish, perish like wild beasts, included within a ring of fire!

Yes, I will cheerfully embrace that resource, it is an holy inspiration: by night and by day, it presents itself to my mind: I have carefully revolved the scheme; I have considered in all its future effects and tendencies, the new mode of living we must pursue, without salt, without spices, without linen and with little other clothing; the art of hunting, we must acquire, the new manners we must adopt, the new language we must speak; the dangers attending the education of my children we must endure. These changes may appear more terrific at a distance perhaps than when grown familiar by practice: what is it to us, whether we eat well made pastry, or pounded àlagrichés; well roasted beef, or smoked venison; cabbages, or squashes? Whether we wear neat home-spun or good beaver; whether we sleep on feather-beds, or on bear-skins? The difference is not worth attending to. The difficulty of the language,

fear of some great intoxication among the Indians;
finally, the apprehension lest my younger children
should be caught by that singular charm, so dangerous
at their tender years; are the only considerations that
startle me. By what power does it come to pass, that
children who have been adopted when young among
these people, can never be prevailed on to readopt
European manners? Many an anxious parent I have seen
after the last war, who at the return of the peace, went
to the Indian villages where they knew their children
had been carried in captivity; when to their inexpressible sorrow, they found them so perfectly Indianised,
that many knew them no longer, and those whose more
advanced ages permitted them to recollect their fathers
and mothers, absolutely refused to follow them, and
ran to their adopted parents for protection against the
effusions of love their unhappy real parents lavished on
them! Incredible as this may appear, I have heard it
asserted in a thousand instances, among persons of
credit. In the village of ———, where I purpose to go,
there lived, about fifteen years ago, an Englishman and
a Swede, whose history would appear moving, had I
time to relate it. They were grown to the age of men
when they were taken; they happily escaped the great
punishment of war captives, and were obliged to marry
the *Squaws* who had saved their lives by adoption. By
the force of habit, they became at last thoroughly
naturalised to this wild course of life. While I was there,
their friends sent them a considerable sum of money to
ransom themselves with. The Indians, their old masters,
gave them their choice, and without requiring any
consideration, told them, that they had been long as
free as themselves. They chose to remain; and the
reasons they gave me would greatly surprise you: the
most perfect freedom, the ease of living, the absence of
those cares and corroding solicitudes which so often pre-

vail with us; the peculiar goodness of the soil they cultivated, for they did not trust altogether to hunting; all
these, and many more motives, which I have forgot,
made them prefer that life, of which we entertain such
dreadful opinions. It cannot be, therefore, so bad as we
generally conceive it to be; there must be in their social
bond something singularly captivating, and far superior
to anything to be boasted of among us; for thousands of
Europeans are Indians, and we have no examples of
even one of those Aborigines having from choice become
Europeans! There must be something more congenial to
our native dispositions, than the fictitious society in
which we live; or else why should children, and even
grown persons, become in a short time so invincibly attached to it? There must be something very bewitching
in their manners, something very indelible and marked
by the very hands of nature. For, take a young Indian
lad, give him the best education you possibly can, load
him with your bounty, with presents, nay with riches;
yet he will secretly long for his native woods, which you
would imagine he must have long since forgot; and on
the first opportunity he can possibly find, you will see
him voluntarily leave behind him all you have given
him, and return with inexpressible joy to lie on the mats
of his fathers. Mr. ——, some years ago, received from
a good old Indian, who died in his house, a young lad,
of nine years of age, his grandson. He kindly educated
him with his children, and bestowed on him the same
care and attention in respect to the memory of his
venerable grandfather, who was a worthy man. He intended to give him a genteel trade, but in the spring
season when all the family went to the woods to make
their maple sugar, he suddenly disappeared; and it was
not until seventeen months after, that his benefactor
heard he had reached the village of Bald Eagle, where
he still dwelt. Let us say what we will of them, of their

inferior organs, of their want of bread, etc., they are as stout and well made as the Europeans. Without temples, without priests, without kings, and without laws, they are in many instances superior to us; and the proofs of what I advance, are, that they live without care, sleep without inquietude, take life as it comes, bearing all its asperities with unparalleled patience, and die without any kind of apprehension for what they have done, or for what they expect to meet with hereafter. What system of philosophy can give us so many necessary qualifications for happiness? They most certainly are much more closely connected with nature than we are; they are her immediate children, the inhabitants of the woods are her undefiled off-spring: those of the plains are her degenerated breed, far, very far removed from her primitive laws, from her original design. It is therefore resolved on. I will either die in the attempt or succeed; better perish all together in one fatal hour, than to suffer what we daily endure. I do not expect to enjoy in the village of ———— an uninterrupted happiness; it cannot be our lot, let us live where we will; I am not founding my future prosperity on golden dreams. Place mankind where you will, they must always have adverse circumstances to struggle with; from nature, accidents, constitution; from seasons, from that great combination of mischances which perpetually lead us to new diseases, to poverty, etc. Who knows but I may meet in this new situation, some accident from whence may spring up new sources of unexpected prosperity? Who can be presumptuous enough to predict all the good? Who can foresee all the evils, which strew the paths of our lives? But after all, I cannot but recollect what sacrifice I am going to make, what amputation I am going to suffer, what transition I am going to experience. Pardon my repetitions, my wild, my trifling reflections, they proceed from the agitations of my mind.

and the fulness of my heart; the action of thus retracing them seems to lighten the burden, and to exhilarate my spirits; this is besides the last letter you will receive from me; I would fain tell you all, though I hardly know how. Oh! in the hours, in the moments of my greatest anguish, could I intuitively represent to you that variety of thought which crowds on my mind, you would have reason to be surprised, and to doubt of their possibility. Shall we ever meet again? If we should, where will it be? On the wild shores of ——. If it be my doom to end my days there, I will greatly improve them; and perhaps make room for a few more families, who will choose to retire from the fury of a storm, the agitated billows of which will yet roar for many years on our extended shores. Perhaps I may repossess my house, if it be not burnt down; but how will my improvements look? why, half defaced, bearing the strong marks of abandonment, and of the ravages of war. However, at present I give everything over for lost; I will bid a long farewell to what I leave behind. If ever I repossess it, I shall receive it as a gift, as a reward for my conduct and fortitude. Do not imagine, however, that I am a stoic—by no means: I must, on the contrary, confess to you, that I feel the keenest regret, at abandoning an house which I have in some measure reared with my own hands. Yes, perhaps I may never revisit those fields which I have cleared, those trees which I have planted, those meadows which, in my youth, were a hideous wilderness, now converted by my industry into rich pastures and pleasant lawns. If in Europe it is praiseworthy to be attached to paternal inheritances, how much more natural, how much more powerful must the tie be with us, who, if I may be permitted the expression, are the founders, the creators of our own farms! When I see my table surrounded with my blooming offspring, all united in the bonds of the strongest affection, it kindles in my paternal heart a variety of tumultuous sentiments, which none but a father and a husband in my situation can feel or describe. Perhaps I may see my wife, my children, often distressed, involuntarily recalling to their minds the ease and abundance which they enjoyed under the paternal roof. Perhaps I may see them want that bread which I now leave behind; overtaken by diseases and penury, rendered more bitter by the recollection of former days of opulence and plenty. Perhaps I may be assailed on every side by unforeseen accidents, which I shall not be able to prevent or to alleviate. Can I contemplate such images without the most unutterable emotions? My fate is determined; but I have not determined it, you may assure yourself, without having undergone the most painful conflicts of a variety of passions;—interest, love of ease, disappointed views, and pleasing expectations frustrated;—I shuddered at the review! Would to God I was master of the stoical tranquillity of that magnanimous sect; oh, that I were possessed of those sublime lessons which Appollonius of Chalcis gave to the Emperor Antoninus! I could then with much more propriety guide the helm of my little bark, which is soon to be freighted with all that I possess most dear on earth, through this stormy passage to a safe harbour; and when there, become to my fellow passengers, a surer guide, a brighter example, a pattern more worthy of imitation, throughout all the new scenes they must pass, and the new career they must traverse. I have observed notwithstanding, the means hitherto made use of, to arm the principal nations against our frontiers. Yet they have not, they will not take up the hatchet against a people who have done them no harm. The passions necessary to urge these people to war, cannot be roused, they cannot feel the stings of vengeance, the thirst of which alone can compel them to shed blood: far superior in their motives of action to the Europeans, who for sixpence per day, may be engaged to shed that of any people on earth. They know nothing of the nature of our disputes, they have no ideas of such revolutions as this; a civil division of a village or tribe, are events which have never been recorded in their traditions: many of them know very well that they have too long been the dupes and the victims of both parties; foolishly arming for our sakes, sometimes against each other, sometimes against our white enemies. They consider us as born on the same land, and, though they have no reasons to love us, yet they seem carefully to avoid entering into this quarrel, from whatever motives. I am speaking of those nations with which I am best acquainted, a few hundreds of the worst kind mixed with whites, worse than themselves, are now hired by Great Britain, to perpetuate those dreadful incursions. In my youth I traded with the ——, under the conduct of my uncle, and always traded justly and equitably; some of them remember it to this day. Happily their village is far removed from the dangerous neighbourhood of the whites; I sent a man last spring to it, who understands the woods extremely well, and who speaks their language; he is just returned, after several weeks absence, and has brought me, as I had flattered myself, a string of thirty purple wampum, as a token that their honest chief will spare us half of his wigwam until we have time to erect one. He has sent me word that they have land in plenty, of which they are not so covetous as the whites; that we may plant for ourselves, and that in the meantime he will procure for us some corn and some meat; that fish is plenty in the waters of ——, and that the village to which he had laid open my proposals, have no objection to our becoming dwellers with them. I have not yet communicated these glad tidings to my wife, nor do I know how to do it; I tremble lest she should refuse to follow me; lest the sudden idea of this removal rushing on her mind, might be too powerful. I flatter myself I shall be able to accomplish it, and to prevail on her; I fear nothing but the effects of her strong attachment to her relations. I will willingly let you know how I purpose to remove my family to so great a distance, but it would become unintelligible to you, because you are not acquainted with the geographical situation of this part of the country. Suffice it for you to know, that with about twenty-three miles land carriage, I am enabled to perform the rest by water; and when once afloat, I care not whether it be two or three hundred miles. I propose to send all our provisions, furniture, and clothes to my wife's father, who approves of the scheme, and to reserve nothing but a few necessary articles of covering; trusting to the furs of the chase for our future apparel. Were we imprudently to encumber ourselves too much with baggage, we should never reach to the waters of ——, which is the most dangerous as well as the most difficult part of our journey; and yet but a trifle in point of distance. I intend to say to my negroes—In the name of God, be free, my honest lads, I thank you for your past services; go, from henceforth, and work for yourselves; look on me as your friend, and fellow labourer; be sober, frugal, and industrious, and you need not fear earning a comfortable subsistence.—Lest my countrymen should think that I am gone to join the incendiaries of our frontiers, I intend to write a letter to Mr. ——, to inform him of our retreat, and of the reasons that have urged me to it. The man whom I sent to —— village, is to accompany us also, and a very useful companion he will be on every account.

You may therefore, by means of anticipation, behold me under the Wigwam; I am so well acquainted with the principal manners of these people, that I entertain not the least apprehension from them. I rely more securely on their strong hospitality, than on the witnessed compacts of many Europeans. As soon as possible after my arrival, I design to build myself a wigwam, after the same manner and size with the rest, in order to avoid being thought singular, or giving occasion for any railleries; though these people are seldom guilty of such European follies. I shall erect it hard by the lands which they propose to allot me, and will endeavour that my wife, my children, and myself may be adopted soon after our arrival. Thus becoming truly inhabitants of their village, we shall immediately occupy that rank within the pale of their society, which will afford us all the amends we can possibly expect for the loss we have met with by the convulsions of our own. According to their customs we shall likewise receive names from them, by which we shall always be known. My youngest children shall learn to swim, and to shoot with the bow, that they may acquire such talents as will necessarily raise them into some degree of esteem among the Indian lads of their own age; the rest of us must hunt with the hunters. I have been for several years an expert marksman; but I dread lest the imperceptible charm of Indian education, may seize my younger children, and give them such a propensity to that mode of life, as may preclude their returning to the manners and customs of their parents. I have but one remedy to prevent this great evil; and that is, to employ them in the labour of the fields, as much as I can; I am even resolved to make their daily subsistence depend altogether on it. As long as we keep ourselves busy in tilling the earth, there is no fear of any of us becoming wild; it is the chase and the food it procures, that have this strange effect. Excuse a simile—those hogs which range in the woods, and to whom grain is given once a week, preserve their former degree of tameness; but if, on the contrary, they are reduced to live on ground nuts, and on what they can get, they soon become wild and fierce. For my part, I can plough, sow, and hunt, as occasion may require; but my wife, deprived of wool and flax, will have no room for industry; what is she then to do? like the other squaws, she must cook for us the nasaump, the ninchickè, and such other preparations of corn as are customary among these people. She must learn to bake squashes and pumpkins under the ashes; to slice and smoke the meat of our own killing, in order to preserve it; she must cheerfully adopt the manners and customs of her neighbours, in their dress, deportment, conduct, and internal economy, in all respects. Surely if we can have fortitude enough to quit all we have, to remove so far, and to associate with people so different from us; these necessary compliances are but part of the scheme. The change of garments, when those they carry with them are worn out, will not be the least of my wife's and daughter's concerns: though I am in hopes that self-love will invent some sort of reparation. Perhaps you would not believe that there are in the woods looking-glasses, and paint of every colour; and that the inhabitants take as much pains to adorn their faces and their bodies, to fix their bracelets of silver, and plait their hair, as our forefathers the Picts used to do in the time of the Romans. Not that I would wish to see either my wife or daughter adopt those savage customs; we can live in great peace and harmony with them without descending to every article; the interruption of trade hath, I hope, suspended this mode of dress. My wife understands inoculation perfectly well, she inoculated all our children one after another, and has successfully performed the operation on several scores of people, who, scattered here and there through our woods, were too far removed from all medical assistance. If we can persuade but one family to submit to it, and it succeeds, we shall then be as happy as our situation will admit of; it will raise her into some degree of consideration, for whoever is useful in any society will always be respected. If we are so fortunate as to carry one family through a disorder, which is the plague among these people, I trust to the force of example, we shall then become truly necessary, valued, and beloved; we indeed owe every kind office to a society of men who so readily offer to assist us into their social partnership, and to extend to my family the shelter of their village, the strength of their adoption, and even the dignity of their names. God grant us a prosperous beginning, we may then hope to be of more service to them than even missionaries who have been sent to preach to them a Gospel they cannot understand.

As to religion, our mode of worship will not suffer much by this removal from a cultivated country, into the bosom of the woods; for it cannot be much simpler than that which we have followed here these many years: and I will with as much care as I can, redouble my attention, and twice a week, retrace to them the great outlines of their duty to God and to man. I will read and expound to them some part of the decalogue, which is the method I have pursued ever since I married.

Half a dozen of acres on the shores of ——, the soil of which I know well, will yield us a great abundance of all we want; I will make it a point to give the overplus to such Indians as shall be most unfortunate in their huntings; I will persuade them, if I can, to till a little more land than they do, and not to trust so much to the produce of the chase. To encourage them still farther, I will give a quirn to every six families; I have built many for our poor back-settlers, it being often the want of mills which prevents them from raising grain. As I am a carpenter, I can build my own plough, and can be of great service to many of them; my example alone, may rouse the industry of some, and serve to direct others in their labours. The difficulties of the language will soon be removed; in my evening conversations, I will endeavour to make them regulate the trade of their village in such a manner as that those pests of the continent, those Indian traders, may not come within a certain distance; and there they shall be obliged to transact their business before the old people. I am in hopes that the constant respect which is paid to the elders, and shame, may prevent the young hunters from infringing this regulation. The son of —— will soon be made acquainted with our schemes, and I trust that the power of love, and the strong attachment he professes for my daughter, may bring him along with us: he will make an excellent hunter; young and vigorous, he will equal in dexterity the stoutest man in the village. Had it not been for this fortunate circumstance, there would have been the greatest danger; for however I respect the simple, the inoffensive society of these people in their villages, the strongest prejudices would make me abhor any alliance with them in blood: disagreeable no doubt, to nature's intentions which have strongly divided us by so many indelible characters. In the days of our sickness, we shall have recourse to their medical knowledge, which is well calculated for the simple diseases to which they are subject. Thus shall we metamorphose ourselves, from neat, decent, opulent planters, surrounded with every conveniency which our external labour and internal industry could give, into a still simpler people divested of everything beside hope, food, and the raiment of the woods: abandoning the large framed house, to dwell under the wigwam; and the featherbed, to lie on the mat, or bear's skin. There shall we sleep undisturbed by fruitful dreams and apprehensions; rest and peace of mind will make us the most ample amends for what we shall leave behind.

These blessings cannot be purchased too dear; too long have we been deprived of them. I would cheerfully go even to the Mississippi, to find that repose to which we have been so long strangers. My heart sometimes seems tired with beating, it wants rest like my eyelids, which feel oppressed with so many watchings.

These are the component parts of my scheme, the success of each of which appears feasible; from whence I flatter myself with the probable success of the whole. Still the danger of Indian education returns to my mind, and alarms me much; then again I contrast it with the education of the times; both appear to be equally pregnant with evils. Reason points out the necessity of choosing the least dangerous, which I must consider as the only good within my reach; I persuade myself that industry and labour will be a sovereign preservative against the dangers of the former; but I consider, at the same time, that the share of labour and industry which is intended to procure but a simple subsistence, with hardly any superfluity, cannot have the same restrictive effects on our minds as when we tilled the earth on a more extensive scale. The surplus could be then realised into solid wealth, and at the same time that this realisation rewarded our past labours, it engrossed and fixed the attention of the labourer, and cherished in his mind the hope of future riches. In order to supply this great deficiency of industrious motives, and to hold out to them a real object to prevent the fatal consequences of this sort of apathy; I will keep an exact account of all that shall be gathered, and give each of them a regular credit for the amount of it to be paid them in real property at the return of peace. Thus, though seemingly toiling for bare subsistence on a foreign land, they shall entertain the pleasing prospect of seeing the sum of their labours one day realised either in legacies or gifts, equal if not superior to it. The yearly expense of the clothes which they would have received at home, and of which they will then be deprived, shall likewise be added to their credit; thus I flatter myself that they will more cheerfully wear the blanket, the matchcoat, and the Moccasins. Whatever success they may meet with in hunting or fishing, shall only be considered as recreation and pastime; I shall thereby prevent them from estimating their skill in the chase as an important and necessary accomplishment. I mean to say to them: "You shall hunt and fish merely to show your new companions that you are not inferior to them in point of sagacity and dexterity." Were I to send them to such schools as the interior parts of our settlements afford at present, what can they learn there? How could I support them there? What must become of me; am I to proceed on my voyage, and leave them? That I never could submit to. Instead of the perpetual discordant noise of disputes so common among us, instead of those scolding scenes, frequent in every house, they will observe nothing but silence at home and abroad: a singular appearance of peace and concord are the first characteristics which strike you in the villages of these people. Nothing can be more pleasing, nothing surprises an European so much as the silence and harmony which prevails among them, and in each family; except when disturbed by that accursed spirit given them by the wood rangers in exchange for their furs. If my children learn nothing of geometrical rules, the use of the compass, or of the Latin tongue, they will learn and practise sobriety, for rum can no longer be sent to these people; they will learn that modesty and diffidence for which the young Indians are so remarkable; they will consider labour as the most essential qualification; hunting as the second. They will prepare themselves in the prosecution of our small rural schemes, carried on for the benefit of our little community, to extend them further when each shall receive his inheritance. Their tender minds will cease to be agitated by perpetual alarms; to be made cowards by continual terrors: if they acquire in the village of ——, such an awkwardness of deportment and appearance as would render them ridiculous in our gay capitals, they will imbibe, I hope, a confirmed taste for that simplicity, which so well becomes the cultivators of the land. If I cannot teach them any of those professions which sometimes embellish and support our society, I will show them how to hew wood, how to construct their own ploughs; and with a few tools how to supply themselves with every necessary implement, both in the house and in the field. If they are hereafter obliged to confess, that they belong to no one particular church, I shall have the consolation of teaching them that great, that primary worship which is the foundation of all others. If they do not fear God according to the tenets of any one seminary, they shall learn to worship him upon the broad scale of nature. The Supreme Being does not reside in peculiar churches or communities; he is equally the great Manitou of the woods and of the plains; and even in the gloom, the obscurity of those very woods, his justice may be as well understood and felt as in the most sumptuous temples. Each worship with us, hath, you know, its peculiar political tendency; there it has none but to inspire gratitude and truth: their tender minds shall receive no other idea of the Supreme Being, than that of the father of all men, who requires nothing more of us than what tends to make each other happy. We shall say with them, Soungwanèha, èsa caurounkyawga, nughwonshauza neattèwek, nèsalanga.—*Our father, be thy will done in earth as it is in great heaven.*

Perhaps my imagination gilds too strongly this distant prospect; yet it appears founded on so few, and simple principles, that there is not the same probability of adverse incidents as in more complex schemes. These vague rambling contemplations which I here faithfully retrace, carry me sometimes to a great distance; I am lost in the anticipation of the various circumstances attending this proposed metamorphosis! Many unforeseen accidents may doubtless arise. Alas! it is easier for me in all the glow of paternal anxiety, reclined on my bed, to form the theory of my future conduct, than to reduce my schemes into practice. But when once secluded from the great society to which we now belong, we shall unite closer together; and there will be less room for jealousies or contentions. As I intend my children neither for the law nor the church, but for the cultivation of the land, I wish them no literary accomplishments; I pray heaven that they may be one day nothing more than expert scholars in husbandry: this is the science which made our continent to flourish more rapidly than any other. Were they to grow up where I am now situated, even admitting that we were in safety; two of them are verging toward that period in their lives, when they must necessarily take up the musket, and learn, in that new school, all the vices which are so common in armies. Great God! close my eyes for ever, rather than I should live to see this calamity! May they rather become inhabitants of the woods.

Thus then in the village of ——, in the bosom of that peace it has enjoyed ever since I have known it, connected with mild hospitable people, strangers to *our* political disputes, and having none among themselves; on the shores of a fine river, surrounded with woods, abounding with game; our little society united in perfect harmony with the new adoptive one, in which we shall be incorporated, shall rest I hope from all fatigues, from all apprehensions, from our perfect terrors, and from our long watchings. Not a word of politics shall cloud our simple conversation; tired either with the chase or the labour of the field, we shall sleep on our mats without distressing want, having learnt to retrench every superfluous one: we shall have but two prayers to make to the Supreme Being, that he may shed his fertilising dew on our little crops, and that he will be pleased to restore peace to our unhappy country. These shall be the only subject of our nightly prayers, and of our daily ejaculations: and if the labour, the industry, the frugality, the union of men, can be an agreeable offering to him, we shall not fail to receive his paternal blessings. There I shall contemplate nature in her most wild and ample extent; I shall carefully study a species of society, of which I have at present but very imperfect ideas; I will endeavour to occupy with propriety that place which will enable me to enjoy the few and sufficient benefits it confers. The solitary and unconnected mode of life I have lived in my youth must fit me for this trial, I am not the first who has attempted it; Europeans did not, it is true, carry to the wilderness numerous families; they went there as mere speculators; I, as a man seeking a refuge from the desolation of war. They went there to study the manner of the aborigines; I to conform to them, whatever they are; some went as visitors, as travellers; I as a sojourner, as a fellow hunter and labourer, go determined industriously to work up among them such a system of happiness as may be adequate to my future situation, and may be a sufficient compensation for all my fatigues and for the misfortunes I have borne: I have always found it at home, I may hope likewise to find it under the humble roof of my wigwam.

O Supreme Being! if among the immense variety of planets, inhabited by thy creative power, thy paternal and omnipotent care deigns to extend to all the individuals they contain; if it be not beneath thy infinite dignity to cast thy eye on us wretched mortals; if my future felicity is not contrary to the necessary effects of those secret causes which thou hast appointed, receive the supplications of a man, to whom in thy kindness thou hast given a wife and an offspring: View us all with benignity, sanctify this strong conflict of regrets, wishes, and other natural passions; guide our steps through these unknown paths, and bless our future mode of life. If it is good and well meant, it must proceed from thee; thou knowest, O Lord, our enterprise contains neither fraud, nor malice, nor revenge. Bestow on me that energy of conduct now become so necessary, that it may be in my power to carry the young family thou hast given me through this great trial with safety and in thy peace. Inspire me with such intentions and such rules of conduct as may be most acceptable to thee. Preserve, O God, preserve the companion of my bosom, the best gift thou hast given me: endue her with courage and strength sufficient to accomplish this perilous journey. Bless the children of our love, those portions of our hearts; I implore thy divine assistance, speak to their tender minds, and inspire them with the love of that virtue which alone can serve as the basis of their conduct in this world, and of their happiness with thee. Restore peace and concord to our poor afflicted country; assuage the fierce storm which has so long ravaged it. Permit, I beseech thee, O Father of nature, that our ancient virtues, and our industry, may not be totally lost: and that as a reward for the great toils we have made on this new land, we may be restored to our ancient tranquillity, and enabled to fill it with successive generations, that will constantly thank thee for the ample subsistence thou hast given them.

The unreserved manner in which I have written must give you a convincing proof of that friendship and esteem, of which I am sure you never yet doubted. As members of the same society, as mutually bound by the ties of affection and old acquaintance, you certainly cannot avoid feeling for my distresses; you cannot avoid mourning with me over that load of physical and moral evil with which we are all oppressed. My own share of it I often overlook when I minutely contemplate all that hath befallen our native country.

NOTES

Note I. *The Title-page, Advertisements, and Dedication.*—
The author's use of the name "J. Hector St. John" is dis-
cussed in our Introduction and in Note III. The title-page
of the first French edition (two volumes) is as follows:
LETTRES *d'un* CULTIVATEUR *Américain*, ECRITES
A. W. S. ECUYER, *Depuis l'Année* 1770, *jusqu'à* 1781.
Traduites de l'Anglois par * * * *A Paris*, chez *Cuchet*,
Libraire, rue & hôtel Serpente. MDCCLXXXIV. The second
edition of this French paraphrase runs to three volumes, with
maps and engravings, and is dated 1787. There is an English
motto—*Keen feelings inspire resistless thoughts*—as well as
a Latin one; the *Lettres* are not *écrites* but *addresées* to
"W. S. Ecuyer"—who now appears as "Wm. S. . .on, Esqr."
Crèvecœur's loyalist friend at New York, William Seaton, is
thus indicated.

The "advertisements" which appear in the English edition
of the *Letters* are omitted in the French. The dedication to
the Abbé Raynal (1713-1796) is replaced by a dedication to
the Marquis de Lafayette—the generous young friend of
Washington, whose fame in America was never dimmed by
the failures of his later years. Raynal was an indefatigable
hack-writer of liberal sentiments; he had talent, but scarcely
deserved Crèvecœur's eulogy. His *Histoire Philosophique et
politique des établissemens et du commerce des Européens
dans les deux Indes* (1770), referred to (page 5), and his subsequent *Tableau de la Révolution des colonies Anglaises de
l'Amérique Septentrionale*, have little value as history (*see*
Note V).

Note II. *Hazlitt and Grimm on Crèvecœur.*—William Haz-
litt's remarks on the American Farmer, referred to in the
Introduction, are found in his essay on "American Literature:
Dr. Channing," in the *Edinburgh Review* of October 1829.
They are reproduced in the tenth volume of his *Collected
Works,* ed. Waller and Glover (J. M. Dent & Co., 1904). A

French translation of this essay was published in the *Revue Britannique* of January 1832, and the essay is quoted by Philarète Chasles in his *Etudes sur la Littérature et les Mœurs des Anglo-Américains* (Paris, 1851).

It would be easy to collect such French criticism as the book received, but Grimm's remarks (*Correspondance,* éd. Tourneaux, xiv. 88), made in January 1785, must suffice:

"This book, written without method and without art, but with a high degree of interest and sensibility, perfectly fulfils the object that the author seems to have proposed: that of making America loved. There are to be found in it minute details, very common truths, repetitions, and lengthy passages; but it attracts by its simple and true pictures, and by its expression of an honest soul."

NOTE III. *Crèvecœur's Name, Faith, and Offspring.*—In a letter to Franklin (*see* Note IX.) Crèvecœur explains how he came to call himself St. John. The life of the American Farmer by his great-grandson, Robert de Crèvecœur (*Saint-Jean de Crèvecœur: Sa Vie et ses Ouvrages,* Paris, 1883) informs us that his descendants possess his marriage certificate, dated September 30, 1769. Herein our author is named Michel-Guillaume Saint-Jean; in the act of baptism, one of his children is "Michel-Guillaume Saint-John de Crèvecœur, otherwise named Saint-John." "If," writes Robert de Crèvecœur, "the name of Saint-John was to him but a kind of pseudonym, it became the legal name of his children—all three of them born in America." Crèvecœur's marriage to Mehetable (Mahetable) Tippet, daughter of Isaac Tippet, high sheriff of Westchester County, New York, said to have sprung of Huguenot stock,[1] was performed by Rev. J. P. Têtard, a clergyman of the French Reformed Church, formerly of Charleston, S.C., later of New York City. Crèvecœur had been brought up by the Jesuits, but his Catholicism was lukewarm, as might be suspected from the fact that he established such cordial relations with Madame d'Houdetot, who was, besides, a friend of his father before him (*see* Notes IX. and X.). Prof. Moses Coit Taylor, in his *Literary History of*

[1] *Pennsylvania Magazine of History and Biography,* xxx., p. 257.

the American Revolution (New York, 1897; ii. 348), regards it
as probable that Crèvecœur became a member of the Society
of Friends, as does Professor Trent in the work already cited.
There is no evidence of this, unless we accept his high regard
for Quakers and Quakerism as such. Crèvecœur's two sons
seem to have been brought up as Catholics; his daughter
alone, to whom was given the high-sounding name *Frances-
America* (1770-1823), was educated as a Protestant, and married a Protestant—Count Louis Otto, born in Baden in 1754,
and christened Ludwig Wilhelm Otto. This gentleman was
a member of the French Legation in the United States from
1779. Of the sons, the elder, William Alexander—"Ally"—
died without issue;[1] the younger, Philippe-Louis, had one
son, Guillaume-Alexandre Saint-John de Crèvecœur, whose
son, Robert Saint-John de Crèvecœur, was born in 1833, was
an auditor of the French Council of State, and wrote the
biography of his great-grandfather cited in these notes. A son
of M. Robert de Crèvecœur is still living at Paris.

NOTE IV. *On the Situation, etc., of an American Farmer.*—
One drawback of this situation, suggested by an English
traveller—see *Travels in America 100 Years Ago,* by Thomas
Twining, in the reprint (New York, 1894; pp. 65, 98)—was
the scarcity of such labour as the blacksmith's or baker's.

[1] From Paris, in 1791, Crèvecœur addressed to "Monsieur Short,
chargé d'Affaires of ye Congress" (*see* Note IX.), a letter dated
December 17, much too long to be reproduced, though it shows a
touching interest in advancing "Ally's" fortunes. Crèvecœur desires
Short to apply to the French Minister of the Interior, M. Cahier de
Gerville, petitioning for the boy's admission to the *Ecole des Ponts
et Chaussées* at Paris, "for many years past one of the best in
Europe." There are but two ways of being admitted, Crèvecœur
writes, "the first is that of Elèves Intended to serve in that usefull
corps; ye Second is that of young Foreigners recommended by their
Ministers." His son is, he adds, "tho' the son of a Frenchman, yet
in true and legal sense of ye word a native of the State of New
York; and subject therefore of ye United States of America."
Crèvecœur encloses a form to be followed by Short in making the
application: it was given to him by the Administrator of the
School, M. de la Millière. These documents are found at the Library of Congress, in Washington.

Neither trade was represented in the stretch of country—one day's ride—between Baltimore and Georgtown: this in 1796. "And as for medical assistance in case of sickness or accident amongst the scattered inhabitants, there was apparently none whatever." Twining comments:

"The few farm-houses visible were also formed by bars or logs of wood, covered with laths and plaster. The situation of the inhabitants of these sequestered dwellings did not appear very enviable, though it doubtless had its charms, or its recompenses at least. Every first settler in a new country labours less for the present than for the future, for himself than for his posterity, and it is this honourable consciousness that invigorates his toil, cheers his solitude, and alleviates his privations."

This is so fair a statement that it deserves extended quotation. Professor W. P. Trent of Columbia University, in his *History of American Literature* (New York, 1903), suggests that Crèvecœur may have been responsible for the evil fortunes of 500 Norman families that emigrated to Ohio and founded the town of Gallipolis. This familiar charge may be traced to Volney in his *Tableau des Etats-Unis* (Paris, 1803). As early as 1783 an Englishman, Rev. Samuel Ayscough, attacked Crèvecœur in a pamphlet which expressed alarm lest his book should encourage emigration from England. The pamphlet bears the impressive title: *Remarks on the Letters from an American Farmer; or a Detection of the Errors of Mr. J. Hector Saint John; Pointing out the Pernicious Tendency of These Letters to Great Britain* (London: John Fielding).

True, Crèvecœur boasts in the last of his *Letters* that he has "caused upwards of an hundred and twenty families to remove thither;" true, he writes that American laws are

"Simple and just, we are a race of cultivators, our cultivation is unrestrained, and therefore everything is prosperous and flourishing."

Crèvecœur makes notable reservations, none the less, and in his later book, *Voyage dans la Haute Pensylvanie* (sic), he adds:

"They are mistaken, who believe that they will enrich themselves by agriculture; they will not enrich themselves in these northern states. The seasons are too rapid, the winters too long, and labour still too costly; it procures to those who are industrious ease and abundance. . . . It is indispensable to know the nature and quality of the soils." (I. 62-63; *see also* II. 197.)

Benjamin Franklin, in a sprightly pamphlet, probably written in September 1782, sought to correct "Ambitious Ideas or Expectations of what was to be found in America."

"He finds it is imagined by Numbers that the inhabitants of North America are rich, capable of rewarding and disposed to reward all sorts of Ingenuity; that they are at the same time ignorant of all the sciences and, consequently, that Strangers, possessing Talents in the Belles-lettres, fine arts, &c., must be highly esteemed, and so well paid, as to be easily rich themselves. . . . That the Governments too, to encourage Emigration from Europe, not only pay the Expence of personal Transportation but give Land gratis to Strangers with Negroes to work for them, Utensils of Husbandry and Stocks of Cattle. These are all Imaginations."

Instead, happy mediocrity prevails, rather than extreme poverty or wealth. The only "gentlemen" in America are those described in the following "Observation of a Negro":

"Boccarorra (meaning the white men) make de black man workee, make de Horse workee, make de Ox workee, make eberyting workee: only de Hog. He, de hog, no workee; he eat, he drink, he walk about, he go to sleep when he pleases, he libb like a gentleman."

In short, America is the land of labour, and by no means, according to Franklin, "the French *Pays de Cocagne,* where the streets are said to be paved with half-baked loaves, the houses til'd with Pancakes, and where the Fowls fly about, ready roasted, crying, *Come, eat me!*"

The author of this satire on the would-be lotus-eaters of the West wrote to Crèvecœur in 1788 that the

"favourable Light in which you have so kindly plac'd our country will I am persuaded have the good Effect of inducing many worthy European characters to remove and settle among us, the Acquisition of whom will be greatly advantageous to us."

To a "prospective emigrant" Franklin wrote in recommendation of the *Letters from an American Farmer:*

"As I know the author to be an observing, intelligent man I suppose the information to be good so far as it goes."

But the book was not a guide or piece of propaganda, and it would be a mistake so to consider it. It doubtless had more to do with the Pantisocracy scheme of Southey and Coleridge than with European emigration. Southey's letters to Grosvenor C. Bedford (Bath, December 14, 1793, and August 1, 1794) are worth reading in this connection *(Life and Correspondence,* London, 1849; i. 196, 216); so too Coleridge's letter to Southey, written from London, September 6, 1794:

"£2000 will do . . . twelve men may *easily* clear 300 acres in 4 or 5 mos . . . every possible assistance will be given us; we may get credit for the land for 10 yrs. or more, as we settle upon."

This is the letter in which Coleridge writes that a schoolboy-friend who had spent five years in America "never saw a *bison* in his life, but had heard of them; they are quite backwards. The mosquitoes are not so bad as our gnats."

NOTE V. *What is an American.*—It would be diverting to contrast Crèvecœur's remarks on the religious sects of America with Voltaire's on the English sects, in his *Lettres philosophiques;* but perhaps it is more profitable to refer to the *Mémoire sur les rélations commerciales des Etats-unis avec l'Angleterre,* drawn up by Talleyrand, and quoted by Mr. Bernard de Lacombe in *Talleyrand the Man* (London, 1911; pp. 83-84). Talleyrand's American exile occurred in 1794. He exclaimed at the "perfect calm" in which the sects existed side by side: "In the same house, father, mother, and children peacefully follow without opposition the form of worship which each one prefers!" The ex-Archbishop-Duke of Rheims, the future Cardinal-Archbishop of Paris, concludes:

"The liberty, and above all the equality—of all forms of worship, is one of the strongest guarantees of social tranquillity; for where consciences are respected, other rights cannot fail to be respected likewise."

Crèvecœur writes, in this chapter "What is an American" (p. 43), that in Nova Scotia the population is very thin, though

"some parts of it flourished once, and it contained a mild harmless set of people. But for the fault of a few leaders, the whole were banished. The greatest political error committed in America was to cut off men from a country which wanted nothing but men!"

The story of the "French Neutrals" of Nova Scotia has been often told: generally from a prejudiced standpoint. Some of the materials for the historian of their misfortunes are found in Galerm's *Relation of the Misfortunes of the French Neutrals as laid before the Assembly of the Province of Pennsylvania* (Philadelphia, 1756). The author was one of the Acadian exiles, and describes the plight of those sent to Philadelphia. Francis Parkman's *Pioneers of France in the New World*, part one (Boston, 1899), gives some of the facts as to their deportation. Judge Haliburton's *History of Nova Scotia* (1829) states the British side of the case. Crèvecœur's friend, the unfrocked Jesuit Raynal, sentimentalises the political issues and hardships involved in volume five of his *History of Settlements and Trade in the East and West Indies* (London, 1798), a mere compilation. *See* Archibald MacMechan's instructive essay, "Evangeline and the Real Acadians," in the *Atlantic Monthly* (Boston), February 1907.

Note VI. *The Island of Nantucket, etc.*—In the eighteenth-century editions of the *Letters*, maps of Nantucket and Martha's Vineyard, Massachusetts, are included. In this edition, since the maps are omitted, we omit also the following sentence: "A table of references to the map is added below" —and the table itself (page 102 of the London, 1782, edition; corresponding to page 92 of the present volume). One other change we have made in our text: we have amended the indications of the position of Nantucket, which Crèvecœur would have his readers believe to lie north of Boston! Though certain changes are made in the second edition of the *Letters* (London, 1783), Crèvecœur failed to correct these curious errors.

Crèvecœur's statements about the opium eating of Nantucket Islanders are curious indeed. There is no evidence to substantiate them. In the "Proceedings of the Nantucket Historical Association," Eleventh Annual Meeting, July 18, 1905; page 43, there is an article entitled "An American Farmer's Letters from Nantucket." The anonymous contributor of this article says that a copy of the first edition of Crèvecœur's book is found in the Nantucket Library, and that there are annotations by various hands, among them, and principally, that of the late F. C. Sanford, who protests against the opium statement. "He believes it to have grown out of a magnified story of a man well known as a gossip and who was an opium eater by his own admission, the only one so known on the island." "A lie without a shade of foundation" is the strong statement of another annotator. A third, thought to be Mr. Sanford again, says: "Dr. Tucker or Tupper had told the author Crèvecœur that the custom prevailed," while it is unmistakably Mr. Sanford who writes: "It was only an old man's whim, and none other on the island."

NOTE VII. *On snakes,* etc.—Crèvecœur, the amateur naturalist, deserves a book all to himself. It is noteworthy that in expanding his *Letters* for French readers (to no good purpose otherwise) he added pages of natural description and anecdote. It is scarcely necessary to examine into the absolute accuracy of all his observations; both in the present volume and in his three-volume *Voyage dans la Haute Pensylvanie* (sic) *et dans l'Etat de New York* (Paris, 1801), he is at least far less preposterous than such an arrant "nature-faker" as the English traveller, John Josselyn, whose *New England's Rareties Discovered* (London, 1672) is one of the jests of colonial literature.

Crèvecœur credits his *Voyage,* on the title-page, to "an adopted member of the Oneida Nation." He professes to translate this book from a manuscript written in English, found in the custom-house at Copenhagen. He tells us that the manuscript was saved from the wreck of the *Morning Star* outbound from Philadelphia. This *Voyage* is a work of slight worth; although translated into German and Dutch, it does not seem to have been reprinted. The book describes travels in America more extensive than any we positively know Crèvecœur to have made: here he set an example for Chateaubriand to follow! And that Chateaubriand was familiar with Crèvecœur's *Letters* there is sufficient evidence in the letter which he addressed to Fontanes, October 2, 1801, shortly before publishing his *Genius of Christianity:* "You see, my dear friend, my eagerness to serve you. I send you my rimes of the Ohio and I give them a title, which presents them *as a simple extract from the work of M. de Crèvecœur*" (*Correspondance Générale,* Paris, 1812; i. 57).

Since Chateaubriand is, from a literary point of view, the most noteworthy of European travellers in America during the eighteenth century, it is interesting to compare with his highly imaginative descriptions of the bison and the Mississippi Basin Crèvecœur's practical thoughts on the same subjects. In the first volume of Crèvecœur's *Voyage* (pp. 529 ff.) is supplied a note on the "Buffaloes and the Savannas":

"Before the whites crossed the Alleghanys and founded the colonies of Tennessee, Kentucky, etc., considerable troops of buffaloes or bisons appeared in the natural prairies of these vast regions; and multiplied prodigiously; but for several years no more of them has been seen: a great part has been destroyed and the others, fleeing so redoubtable an enemy, have crossed the Mississippi and rejoined their kind in the great grassy plains which stretch from the west bank of this river to unknown distances."

Instead of indulging in picturesque descriptions of the buffaloes, Crèvecœur exclaims at the stupidity of the "American nations" in not having tried to domesticate the animal. The Indians' failure to seize upon this idea suggests to him "that their intellectual organisation is inferior to that of the European and Asiatic nations."

Some of the natural history recorded in Crèvecœur's *Voyage* deserves perpetuation. Thus a note to the second volume (pp. 396-397) gives astonishing information as to the *mouches luisantes,* or fireflies:

"They much resemble bees in color and size: like scarabs, they have two pairs of wings . . . when they fly, they develop a third set whence issue rays of light, which give to the lower and posterior part of their bodies the appearance of a lighted coal. . . . They do no harm and never rise to more than four or six feet above the ground. One can catch them easily and make use of them as a reading light."

NOTE VIII. *John Bertram, Botanist* (1699-1777).—Crève-cœur uses the orthography of the Scottish branch of the Bartram family, which none of the Pennsylvanians ever used. The house of the sturdy Quaker naturalist still stands, in West Philadelphia; part of his Botanic Garden[1] is preserved as a city park: for no longer do farms surround it. Though Crèvecœur's account of Bartram is, in general, accurate enough, he was mistaken in making him say, "My father was a Frenchman." A remote ancestor is said to have "come with William the Conqueror" into England, "and settled in the north;" but that was as near as Bartram came to owning French allegiance. Crèvecœur represents a Russian gentleman, Mr. Iwan Al . . . z (Alexiowitz), as having paid the visit described; but one suspects that he himself was the "Russian gentleman." Certainly Bartram fulfils in many ways the requirements of an ideal portrait of the American Cultivator. Bartram's *Observations on the Inhabitants, Climate, Soil, Rivers, Productions, Animals, etc., in his Travels from Pennsilvania* (sic) *to Onondago, Oswego, and the Lake Ontario in Canada,* was published at London in 1751. The travels of his son William Bartram were a source for Coleridge in England and for Chateaubriand in France.

NOTE IX. *Crèvecœur's Correspondents.*—The author of *Letters from an American Farmer* was not brilliant in private correspondence. He was none the less favoured in his friendships. Some of his letters—those, for example, to Ethan Allen, the Vermont patriot—have not yet been discovered by students of his life. There is, however, in the Library of Congress, at Washington, a formidable budget of letters

[1] ". . . He was, perhaps, the first Anglo-American who conceived the idea of establishing a BOTANIC GARDEN for the reception and cultivation of the various vegetables, native of the country, as well as of exotics; and of travelling for the discovery and acquisition of them."—William Bartram (his son, likewise a distinguished naturalist and traveller); see *Memorials of John Bartram,* etc., by William Darlington (Philadelphia, 1849).

addressed to Allen's fellow-countrymen. Crèvecœur's three epistles to George Washington are purely formal and congratulatory—rather too much so. More interesting is the correspondence with Thomas Jefferson and Benjamin Franklin.

Crèvecœur's acquaintance with Franklin he owed to the kindly Madame d'Houdetot (*see* Note X.). In the summer of 1781 this lady sent to Franklin a letter, preserved in the Library of the Pennsylvania Historical Society at Philadelphia, an English translation of a portion of which follows:

"I was given to hope in the Spring, my dear Doctor, that I should see you some day at Sanois. . . . May I, my dear Doctor, make use of it [your good opinion] in regard to a young American who has just arrived and who should have been presented and recommended to you before? He is a Frenchman by birth, but for a long time has been established in your country, under the protection of your laws, to which he is faithful. His name is Crèvecœur, and he is the son of a friend, of more than twenty years' standing, of my husband and myself. . . ."

This letter was written from Paris, August 10, 1781. With it is preserved a letter from Crèvecœur himself, indited a fortnight later:

"CAEN, *28th August*, 1781.

"SIR,—Chance Enabled me the other day to take 5 Americans by ye hand who had fortunately escaped from ye English prisons & Crossed the Channell,—Luckily for me as well as for them I was Just arrived from N. America, where I have resided 27 years—I brought them to my father's Seat, who Tells me that he had Several Times the pleasure of dining with you at the Count de Houdetot's —the Capt. of ye boat readily brought them here, and presented them to ye Count de Blanchy the Commandant of this Province, who received them with Kindness and left them under my care— they gave their declarations before the admiralty, & were duly acknowledg'd to be Americans—as they are genteel discreet men from the Massachusetts I have placed them in a good House and procured them the Hospitality of the City—all went on well when I heard that their boat belonged of right to the Duke of Penthièvre —In consequence of this Information I visited the Intendent's, who Told me that if I wrote a petition in their name to the admiral, he would Inclose it in a Letter of his & recommend the contents; this I have done & thought it my duty to send you a Copy of ye

Same, that you may if necessary unite your good Endeavours in order to procure to the 5 brave men the Slender Plank on which they have reached this shore—however, as it is uncertain, whether or no the Ravens of office will not Swallow all—I have procured them all they want—one of the Company Luckily heard Yesterday that his brother was the Second in Command on board the black Princess—him I have sent off by the Post with a Sufficient Passeport—the other intend for L'orient as soon as they have heard from you—that space of Time they shall pass at my Father's house—

The adventure of these Men as well as that of many more who have Landed here, hath Suggested me an Idea which I beg to Communicate—Policy as well as humanity points out the Necessity of appointing in these Ports some Persons who should have proper authority to claim protect and befriend all such Americans as should Land on this Coast—by those simple Means those people would find protection everywhere & not be exposed as many of them are to be treated as English prisoners, which Treatment Tends to Nourish prejudices, that ought to be extinguished—if from the Information you might receive of me from the Count de Houdetot you thought me capable of discharging this office I'd readily accept of it without either fee or Reward, glad on the contrary as a good Frenchman and as a good American to contribute my Mite towards the Success of this grand this useful revolution—Excuse this Letter it is zeal and the purest zeal which hath dictated it; with so much the more confidence that tho' I have not the pleasure of being acquainted with you, yet I well know Mr. John Jay now in Spaign, Mr. Governor Morris, Mr. Duwane &c. & all the New York delegates—I hope the representations these 5 Americans have made you will be Successfull, for they are worthy of your patronage. I hope also that you will approve my conduct and Intentions.

> "I Remain with the most unfeigned Respect
> "Your very Humble Servant
> "St. John.

"At Mr. Le Mozier Merch$_d$, Rue St. Jean."

Acknowledgment of this long letter was promptly made by the learned Doctor (Passy, September 2, 1781). A draft of the letter, filed away at Washington, is addressed to "M. St. John, chez M. Le Mozier, Marchand, Rue St. Jean, Caën, Normandie," and offers thanks for the other's kindness. There is, says Franklin, "no doubt of the Success of their Petition relating to their Boat, the same case having happened several

Times, and such Requests always readily comply'd with by
the Goodness of the Duc de Penthièvre." Franklin offers
to reimburse Crèvecœur if he has disbursed any money on
account of the Americans, and adds:

"I am much oblig'd by your offer of continuing your kind
Offices towards our People who may hereafter arrive in your Parts.
The Congress lately sent out a Consul General for France, with
Power of Appointing Sub-Consuls in the different Ports.[1] The
Vessel was unfortunately lost with all on board: But it is probable
his Place will soon be Supply'd. On his Arrival I shall acquaint
him with your generous Proposition. With great Regard,
                    "I have the honour to be, etc."

Crèvecœur's answer to this letter seems not to have been
preserved; but in the same collection at Washington is found
the draft of a second letter from Franklin, written at Passy,
September 21, 1781. This letter is printed in A. H. Smythe's
monumental *Life and Writings of Benjamin Franklin* (New
York, 1905-1907), viii. 308. In the course of it, Franklin
says:

"Made. la Comtesse d'Houdetot has warmly recommended to
me a M. Crèvecœur who had lived long in America. Please to
informe me if you are the same Person."

Both Madame d'Houdetot and Crèvecœur himself hastened
to assure Dr. Franklin that St. John and Crèvecœur were one
and the same individual. As he had been so long absent from
France, the former had "no personal knowledge of him" at
this date, but had "always heard him well spoken of by his
father, and it is for his sake, my dear Doctor, that I claim
your kindness for his son. I know that he is very much attached to the United States, and that no one has felt more
than he the calamities attendant upon the present war."
Crèvecœur's letter may well be reproduced at length:

                    "CAEN, *September* 26, 1781.
"SIR,—Yes Sir I am the Same Person whom Madame La Comtesse de Houdetot has been so kind as to mention to you,—the

[1] As Franklin informed Crèvecœur in his next letter, the person
thus appointed was Colonel William Palfrey (1741-1780), a former
aide to General Washington, and Paymaster-General.

Reason of this mistake proceeds from the Singularity of ye french Customs, which renders their Names, allmost arbitrary, & often leads them to forget their Family ones; it is in Consequence of *this,* that there are more alias dictios in this than in any other Country in Europe. The name of our Family is St. Jean, in English St. John, a name as Antient as the Conquest of England by Wm. the Bastard.

"I am so great a Stranger to the manners of this, tho' my native Country (having quitted it very young) that I Never dreamt I had any other, than the old family name—I was greatly astonished when at my late return, I saw myself under the Necessity of being Called by that of Crèvecœur.—Excuse this Tedious explanation, which I hope you will not think Improper, as I have run the risk of either remaining unknown to you, or of Losing the good effects which were Intended by Madame la Comtesse de Houdetot in mentioning me to you—I don't mean to be Troublesome, very far from it, I am much more ambitious of ye Honor of your Esteem than of any thing else; I flatter myself with being able to Cultivate that of your acquaintance this Winter—being invited to spend [letter torn] Le Marquis de Turgot's house brother to ye Late Comptrolleur general—the Intendant of the City has thought proper to write to ye Insignificant admiralty of Bayeux, in consequence of which I have been put in possession of ye wherry in which the 5 americans Came over; this has prevented the Intendant from Sending to ye admiral the Memorial, a copy of which I had taken the Liberty to send you. No sooner had I received the wherry than I offered it to ye Intendant who accepted of it—as soon as he make me some pecuniary Present, which I expect, I have informed my friends at Lorient to draw on me for the Sum granted whatever it will be—I have not Seen the Intendant yet.

"Poor Colol. Palfry I am Sincerely sorry for him; after having served his Country in the field, he wou'd have greatly have Served her here also, where such an Establishment is so Necessary—I earnestly wish them another equally capable may succeed him—the English Language being Common to both the Americans as well as to the Inhabitants of Great Britain the former become often Exposed to be Treated as Ennemies Instead of being taken by the hand & received as Friends—

"I thank you very kindly for your recommendations, I make no doubt of their Weight

"I have the honor to be with unfeigned Respect Sir

"Your Very Humble Servant

"St. John de Crevecœur.

"Chez Mr. Le Mozier Marchd. Rue St. Jean, Caen."

Again addressing Dr. Franklin from Caen, December 5, 1781, Crèvecœur expresses joy at the successes of the Americans under General Washington, and in a postscript adds:

"The Americans who escaped from England last summer are happily embark'd at Nantes for Newberry in the State of Massachusetts."

A letter of Madame d'Houdetot, addressed to Franklin from Sanois, October 18, 1782, refers to a presentation copy of these *American Letters,* about whose receipt Crèvecœur had expressed concern. A letter of Franklin's, dated February 16, 1788, extends cordial thanks to Crèvecœur for a copy of this "excellent work" (evidently the French edition of 1787), as well as for "the honourable mention you have been so good as to make of me in it."

Franklin was not, however, Crèvecœur's only friend among great Americans. Thomas Jefferson, political philosopher, educator, freethinker, and second President of the United States, was by the nature of things one of his chief correspondents. Perhaps the first letter which Crèvecœur addressed to Jefferson was the following:[1]

"NEW YORK, 23d *January,* 1784.

"SIR,—Encourag'd by Mr. le Chevr. de Chastelux whom I saw lately in Paris, as well as by several others, French officers, who had the Honor of your acquaintance while on this Continent, I have been led to hope you'd not refuse giving an answer to the Question I take the Liberty of sending you.—Give me leave to add that I am commissioned to do so by the Minister who is at the head of the Nurseries established throughout the Kingdom.—It has been said in France that in some of the remotest settlements of Virginia or Carolina, Brandy has been distilled from Potatoes.

"That this Root Contains a Spirit as strong as that which is obtained from grain is beyond a Doubt; but the Method of bringing it, in a State of Fermentation, is What Puzzles the Learned Chymists, Spite of the Many Tryals they have Made. I shou'd be most Sincerely thankfull, If I cou'd be Informed of the American Method, through your kind assistance.—From the Respect with which I have heard your name mentioned as well as from your extensive knowledge & Taste for the Arts & Sciences, I can't but

[1] Library of Congress.

hope you'll be Generous enough to communicate [to] me your thoughts on the subject, which is More a Matter of Curiosity than of real or usefull Import. I am likewise commanded to ask you whether the Map of Virginia undertaken by subscription before the Revolution has ever been engrav'd & where it may be had? Least [sic] this shou'd Miscarry through the Imperfection of American Posts, it will be forwarded to you by his excellency the Chevr. de la Luserne. I have the Honor to be with the Most Sincere Respect and Esteem Your very Humble Servt

"St. John.
"French Consul for ye States of N.Y., N.J. & Connecticut."

When Jefferson projected a voyage from Boston to a French port, Crèvecœur—in New York—thus expressed himself (July 15, 1784):

"I . . . am glad for your sake that you shou'd have found a convenient Vessel, the Capt. of which has engaged to Land you on ye Coast of France, but I am afraid you'll set your feet on some barbarous coast [?] where you'll find neither Horses nor Carriages. . . .

"I intended to have given you Letters of Introduction to several Persons in Paris worthy of your acquaintance & Esteem.

"I hope you have given orders in Virginia for ye gathering of those Seeds which you yourself want and part of which you have promised me—you'll find them very acceptable in Paris.

"I beg you'd put Mr. Franklin in Mind of Introducing you to ye good duke of La rochefoucauld. He is the pearl of all ye Dukes a Good Man & an most able chymist. his House is ye center . . . [illegible] where Men of Genius & abilities often meet. You have therefore a great right to share his Friendship—he honours me with his Esteem and Friendship. I write to him by this Packet & announce you to him. . . .

"Maiden Lane No. 20: next door where you boarded."

The last of the Crèvecœur-Jefferson letters which we will quote is that written from Lorient, July 10, 1790. Crèvecœur refers in this to

"the rising which is to take place in Paris on the 14th Instant. I tremble lest the Good Marquis [the Marquis de Lafayette] shou'd not be able to maintain Peace & Good Order among so great a concourse of People as will Flock there from every Part of ye Kingdom."

And Crèvecœur does not fail to inform his correspondent that in Brittany (whence he is writing) "the sparks of the old Fanaticism have been kindled by the Priests."

Other letters of Crèvecœur's were addressed to William Short—a long-lived Virginian (1759-1849), who in 1784 went to France as Jefferson's Secretary of Legation. Subsequently Short held a number of other posts; but he liked Paris so well, and was so little inclined to "mend his fences" at home, that when, in 1808, President Jefferson nominated him to be Minister to Russia, the United States Senate refused to confirm his nomination.

Mr. Short wrote to Crèvecœur from Paris on August 6, 1787 (Crèvecœur then acting as French Consul-General at New York):

"Things now appear to approach an important crisis in several parts of Europe & particularly in France." [1]

Some of Crèvecœur's letters to Short[2] are written half in English, half in French. As American chargé d'affaires at Paris, Short seems to have held a high opinion of Crèvecœur's value as a correspondent. On July 4, 1790, the diplomatist wrote to him to learn something of his impressions of home affairs—for Crèvecœur had recently returned from New York:

"If you were here in Person I should put you to the question ordinary and extraordinary—I know your turn for observation & am sure you have a vast fund of new ideas relative to the United States. I wish your countrymen legislators here would take lessons from you on the business of making a revolution & forming a constitution—for they are two things that should be treated very differently—experience has taught us this before—I wish this country to learn it without a dear-bought experience."

Note X. *La Comtesse d'Houdetot.*—Several letters from this lady to Benjamin Franklin have been quoted or summarised in Note IX. Franklin met her in 1782, when he paid a visit at her country estate at Sanois. She felt herself greatly honoured by this attention from one who was "all the cry;" she prepared verses which were recited on his arrival—verses

[1] Pennsylvania Historical Society.
[2] Library of Congress.

that one of Franklin's American biographers describes as "none the less fulsome because they were true." But these stanzas interest us chiefly because of their self-revelation:

> "Jeune, j'aimai; le temps de mon bel âge,
> Ce temps si court, l'amour seul le remplit.
> Quand j'atteignis la saison d'être sage,
> Toujours j'aimai; la raison me le dit.
> Mais l'âge vient, et le plaisir s'envole;
> Mais mon bonheur ne s'envole aujourd'hui;
> Car j'aime toujours, et l'amour me console,
> Rien n'aurait pu me consoler de lui."

To quote the chronicler: "The venerable sage (Franklin), with his gray hair flowing down upon his shoulders, his staff in hand, the spectacles of wisdom on his nose, was the perfect picture of true philosophy and wisdom." But Mr. P. E. More, an American critic, holds that "the 'sage' must have found his virtue a burden on that day." The ceremony closed with the planting of a Virginia locust by the "true philosopher."

It was as an old lady that Franklin knew the Comtesse d'Houdetot. Born in 1730, Elisabeth-Françoise-Sophie, Comtesse d'Houdetot, was of the family of the Live de Belle-garde, and a daughter of a farmer-general. Though the men of letters who thronged her salon in the days of her greatness praised her beauty no less than her wit, she is said to have been cross-eyed and marked by the smallpox. These defects did not keep her from marrying the Captain (later Lieutenant-General) the Count d'Houdetot: this in 1748. The sister-in-law of Madame d'Epinay, she was the intimate friend of Rousseau (who has something to say of her in his *Confessions!*) and the Encyclopædists, as well as of Benjamin Franklin. Franklin's own copies of some of his letters to her are preserved at Washington in the Congressional Library:

"PHILA., *April* 17, 1787.
"I received in their time my dear Friend's kind Letters of the last year. An infinity of Affairs public and private have so devour'd my time, that I am become necessarily a bad correspondent. I can however never forget the many Instances of your Benevolence and Friendship while I resided in France: They have made indeh-ble Impression on my Mind of Gratitude and Affection.

"I wish it had been in my Power to have render'd some Service to the Person you recommended to me. But he landed far from me in New England, and I have never yet seen him. I recommended him to the Governor of that State (Massachusetts) and have not since heard of him.

"My Health continues good, my old Malady excepted; and that, thanks to God, does not grow worse; so that I am capable of going thro' the Business of the Station to which I was chosen for the second year in November last, by the unanimous Vote of my Country in the General Assembly of their Representatives. And I am happy in my Family, having an affectionate Daughter to take care of me, and a Number of her young Children to amuse me, with whose pretty Actions & Prattle, and promising Tempers and Qualities of Body & Mind, I am extreamly pleased & entertained.

"Adieu, my dear & much respected Friend, and believe me ever, with sincere & great Esteem and Affection,

"Your most obedt. humle. Servt.

"B. FRANKLIN."

The following letter is undated:

"I have received several kind Letters from my beloved Friend, all of which gave me great Pleasure as they inform'd me of your Welfare. The Memory of your Friendship & of the happy Hours I pass'd in your Genial Society at Sanois has often made me regret the Distance, that makes our ever meeting again impossible. I wrote a few lines to you last year, and sent them under Cover to M. St. Jean de Crèvecœur, believing him then in France, but he arrived here soon after. I hope however that my letter may have reach'd you; for as I grow older, I find writing more painful; and I never have been more burthen'd with Business than since my Return. This however will cease in a great degree with the third & last year of my Presidentship, of which near four Months are now spent. The Accounts I have heard of the Misunderstandings and Troubles that have arisen in the Government of that dear Country in which I pass'd nine of the happiest years of my life, gave me a great deal of Pain; but I hope all will tend to its Good in the End. We have been labouring here to establish a new form of Federal Government for all the United States, and there is a Probability of its being adopted and carried into Execution, tho' it meets with a good deal of Opposition, it being difficult to reconcile and accomodate so many different & jarring Interests. If the Project succeeds our Government will be more energetic, and we shall be in a better condition of being serviceable to our Friends on many future Occasions. Adieu ma chère et toujours aimable Amie; and believe me ever

> "Yours most affectionately,
> "B. FRANKLIN."

The sprightly bluestocking to whom the philosopher wrote these letters was herself the author of a few *Pensées*. She survived until 1813. Chateaubriand, in his *Mémoires*, describes meeting Saint-Lambert, author of the *Saisons*, etc., and Madame d'Houdetot in the Marais, ten years before the end came:

"Both represented the opinions and the freedom of days gone by, carefully packed up and preserved; it was the 18th century dying and married after its own fashion. One need but hold on to life for unlawfulness to become lawful. Men feel an infinite esteem for immorality because it has not ceased to exist, and because time has adorned it with wrinkles. . . .

"It became difficult to understand certain pages of the *Confessions* when one had seen the object of Rousseau's transports. Had Madame d'Houdetot kept the letters which Jean-Jacques wrote to her, and which he says were more brilliant than those of the *Nouvelle Héloïse?* It is believed that she made a sacrifice of them to Saint-Lambert. . . .

"She never went to bed without striking the floor three times with her slipper and saying, 'Good-night, dear,' to the late author of the *Saisons*. That was what the philosophy of the 18th century amounted to in 1803."

A letter of Madame de Rémusat to her husband, written from Sanois, May 12, 1805, says of Madame d'Houdetot:

". . . I am convinced that her society would be dangerous to a woman of weak character, or to one whose life was not happy. Any woman who was hesitating between love and virtue would do well to shun her; she is a hundred times more dangerous than an utterly corrupt person. She is so peaceful, so happy, so free from anxiety as to the next life. It would seem that she trusts to the words of the Gospel: 'Her sins, which are many, are forgiven: for she loved much.'"

Another letter from the same correspondent, written toward the end of January 1813, reports the death of the octogenarian relict of the eighteenth-century philosophy, and remarks on the peacefulness of her old age in spite of political storms. "No one could possess more—I will not say goodness, but kindness—than Madame d'Houdetot. Goodness implies the choice of good as against evil; it perceives the evil and forgives it. Madame d'Houdetot never perceived evil in any one. . . ." Happy are those who die in their illusions! To the end Madame d'Houdetot enjoyed beautiful landscapes and the song of birds; she loved flowers as well as verse, and during the Reign of Terror she lived, as Madame de Rémusat writes, "in the country; her place of retreat was respected, her kinsfolk surrounded her with attentions. It is quite possible that her only recollections of this time were those of the family affection and intimacy, to which danger and anxiety gave an unexpected value."

The better side of Madame d'Houdetot's nature found its expression in her relations with the American Farmer, whose friend and protector she became, advancing his interests at court, and showing for his sons (in the words of Robert de Crèvecœur) "a truly maternal tenderness." There seems to have been some sort of coolness between Madame d'Houdetot and Saint-John de Crèvecœur before the end came; when she died, however, her old protégé drew up a set of "recollections."